AF413964

ART BY CARL LAVOIE

Vastarien

A Literary Journal

Volume Six, Issue One

Jon Padgett, Editor-in-Chief

Paula D. Ashe, Associate Editor

Daniel Braum, Associate Editor

Alex Jennings, Associate Editor

New Orleans, Louisiana

ACKNOWLEDGMENTS

Thanks to all our benefactors, particularly James Michael Baker, Samuel Cottrill, Matthew Henshaw, and Tyson Sereda.

ART BY BRIAN THUMMLER

Tenebrous Ramblings

by Romana Lockwood

After my dance of penitence met with the approval of my watchers, the fact of which I discovered in a dream in which I struggled to divest my body of fat-legged red spiders, meeting with eventual success and rapidly fading bruises that sang elegiacally as they melted away, I knew the time had come to audition carers.

I did so by posting an advertisement on an index card and tacking it onto the supermarket community bulletin board.

I shall tell you about some of the candidates. Interesting to me: these types seem universal, timeless, ageless. I feel I have met them all before, some I may have shared time with, others perhaps I've passed in the street—but any one of them could have leapt living and breathing from 1930, from 1950, from 1970 or 80. The only differences are the vocabulary and the wristwatches.

I know this is not a unique observation and that it's one that can be applied to people in general, but in my defense, I necessarily limit direct contact with people, and seeing this many in so short a time—less than a fortnight—is something of a novelty.

My first caller was a young woman obviously very impressed with herself. She was tiny, insectile without being buggish, possessed of an angular jaw, an abrupt nudge of a nose, and cruel gray eyes. She was all acute angles and sharp points. I find smugness unappealing, and it often belies the air of confidence affected by its bearers. No, people very assured of themselves are too often careless and therefore haphazard in the commission of their duties.

Still, I proceeded with the interview to see whether my initial judgment was misbegotten. She spoke exceedingly well, obviously by rote, scripted, as though she'd undergone rigorous training in how to be the subject of an interview. She was not prepared for unexpected questions, and my query regarding the goblin problem threw her into a baffled, stuttering tizzy from which she did not recover.

A kink in the smugness: good.

But. Her blouse was misbuttoned. Any doubts I had as to my own objections were cast away when I noticed that.

The next was a boy with feathered hair, encased in a too-tight sweater vest and ironed shirt. He was unsure of himself in an appealing way. He often paused in apparent thought before answering a question, and the length of the pauses I found uncomfortable, but I begrudgingly admit that his answers were cogent, intelligent, and honest. On instinct, offering him tea, I brushed the back of his hand with mine and saw bloody murder in his heart. This could be positive or negative—he may well have been fated to spill blood on my behalf or in my defense—but I chose not to chance it.

After this was another young woman who dressed rather like a carpenter. Optimistic, idealistic, she possessed a singular desire to be of service. She seemed to live for praise, and she tittered and blushed when I tested her with superficial compliments. She was quite agreeable, if a little cloying, but not prohibitively so, or so I thought, until she began—and did not stop— referencing and at times directly quoting popular entertainments of which I am deliberately, if not pointedly, ignorant. Young women, I can smile falsely for only so long.

The next, a woman in her fifties affecting the look and manner of the typical midwestern suburban housewife, had clearly done her research, as she referenced some of my secret bents and tried to assert her occult bona fides by confessing in colorful detail to the ritualistic sacrifice of a Damascus goat kid. Goats are sensitive, intelligent creatures who evince a playfulness and even a hint of a sense of humor, and her actions, if true, smacked of the wannabe, the dilletante, the callow and stupidly cruel. I told her as much and cast a twenty-six-hour nausea spell on her in the guise of suggesting some reading material.

Another who I shall not describe thinks he is a vampire—one needn't put up with that sort of silliness.

The last, about which I must be somewhat circumspect, was a young fellow as cute as a donkey foal. He dressed like a child, in a colorful shirt with horizontal stripes and over-large shorts—everything but a propeller hat. He was bouncy, exuberant, and, I determined after a mere two minutes in his company, extraordinarily dangerous. I encouraged him, made noises that would lead him to think he was my most favored candidate. The moment he was off of my property, I locked the door, spread salt across all entrances, and made one phone call and one invocation (as backup). The boy was to be dismembered in a very strict order and in a very specific manner. I provided a list of coordinates at which his body parts must be buried, and precise measurements for how deep. That was the phone call. The invocation, should the recipient of the phone call fail in his endeavors, which would necessarily be a fatal failure, was fiercer and would come at a terrible cost to me, and possibly to the other candidates, but one I must indeed be prepared to pay.

In the meantime, I settled on one Myrna George. She's a retired schoolteacher—maths—as plump and as tiny as a wren, pudgy cheeked and easy to smile, and it's a cute smile too, shy and girlish without being precocious. She gathers her wiry gray hair in a careless bun. She favors cotton muumuus with intricate, playful patterns of blue and white, which reminds me of my mother's wallpaper growing up. She is brusque, precise in her use of language, and already protective of me; when I misplaced my balance, nearly dropping my teacup, she put a steadying hand on my right wrist and a reassuring one on my left shoulder.

We are in the process of making arrangements for her to move in on a trial basis. I have conveyed to her the importance of privacy and balancing that with necessary care.

This morning I am to meet her son. She showed me a picture. He is muscled, unshaven, was clad in a leather vest and a tacky black straw cowboy hat with a concho and leather chin strap. About this meeting I have trepidations.

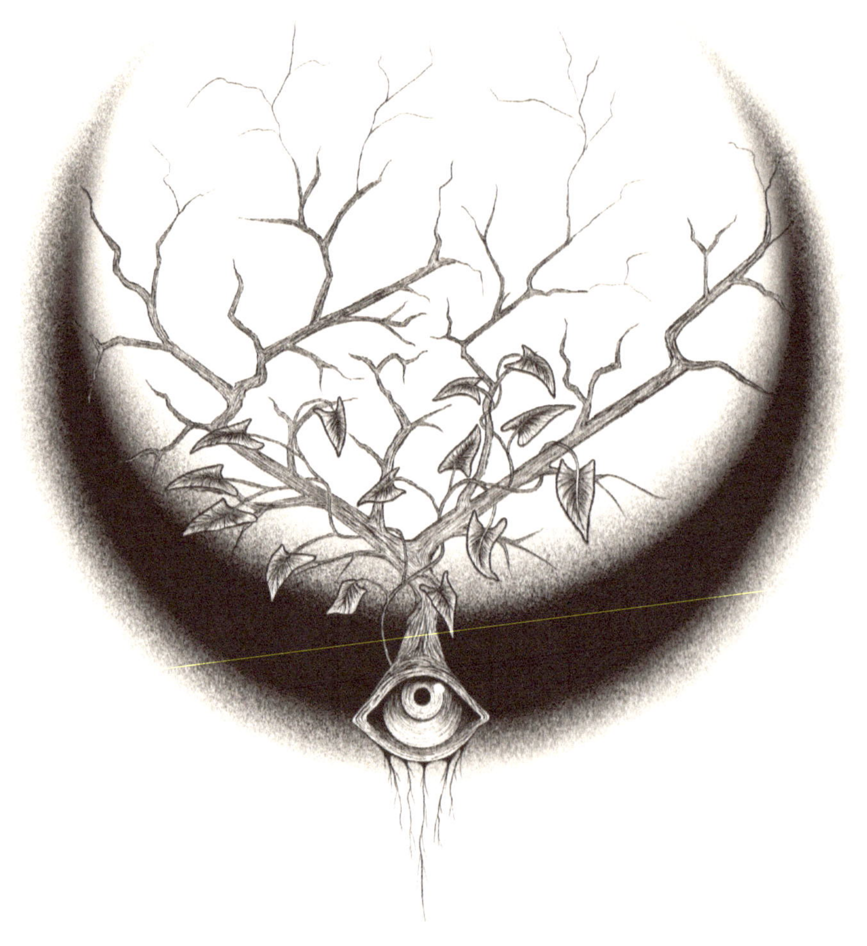

Significant Dreamers of the Twenty-first Century: An Introduction

Christi Nogle

A s you'll know if you have read anything, spoken to anyone, or watched a program in the past five to ten years, dreaming has changed. Big time.

When my wife Colleen and I set out to write about the most illustrious dreamers of our times, we hoped to tour the world interviewing our subjects, describing their lives and environments, even living alongside them when that hospitality was extended. We hoped this book would be the start to long and fulfilling careers, leading to documentary films, additional books, television appearances, and so on. Maybe we'd be immortalized in a bio picture and then fictionalizations.

This idea did not withstand much scrutiny. To give credence to our work, didn't we need to get degrees, or failing that, hire people with degrees? (and in what? Journalism I guessed, but, no, my wife thought anthropology). We were only lowly craftspeople, she a cobbler and me an old-fashioned potter specializing in stoneware jugs with goofy faces on them. We did not know how to do right by our initial plan. And how would we raise funds, anyway? And who would publish our book? No idea.

For most people, that would have been the end of that, but we were not most people. We too were dreamers—not of the sort you will meet in these pages, of course, but idealists, optimists.

One day as we dusted the living room together, Colleen said, "Maybe it would be all right to just do some good old fashioned documentary work."

I didn't know what she meant, but her pupils had dilated; she radiated energy. It made me take the feather duster from her and kiss her sweaty neck.

"Just plain old documentary work, you know, like in the WPA days. It's progressive, it's humanistic in the most extreme sense. This kind of work says *You, little guy, you matter. Let's see what we can learn from your life.*" I loved seeing her inspired.

She said, "And it passes that same respect onto the documentarian, who need only be one of those marvels, a curious human being." It was true. We didn't need to bring anything but our passion for the project.

"You'll do the actual writing, though," she said. "I don't mind helping with all the rest, but I just find that kind of distasteful."

I said, "Anything you say, dear," and we made it so.

Here we have created something humbler, smaller, and more intimate than we'd ever intended, and yet the results have pleased us beyond our wildest hopes. It is the greatest gift we could have given each other, an absolute love letter.

While we have emails and transcripts from video calls from across the world, in many cases these are initial interviews only, as the Internet ended for good a few weeks into our preparations.

We sold and gave away most of our possessions and loaded all that remained into a small solar-powered campervan. In-person interviews are confined to a few stops in the Mountain West and Pacific Northwest regions of the United States. We were quite limited once our "love-bus" kicked the bucket on us.

The journey continued by other means.

Chapter One, Beginnings, focuses on our preparations, and Chapter Two: Theories of the Dream-Change explores the academic and journalistic literature. We are but amateur scholars but have kept up as much as we could, employing a messenger service to deliver articles to our campsites along the way. We have missed much, to be sure.

The dominant theory maintains that, through the heavy use of and then gradual withdrawal from the Internet, humanity has brought about accelerated change in our being. We developed something akin to an organ that helped us process the overwhelming visual and verbal stimuli of the web, and now that the original use for that organ is gone, we use it in dreaming. More and less generous interpretations of this core theory abound. Some say that people are accustomed to a certain level of manipulation from advertising and the like, and when it is reduced, they are compelled to manufacture their own manipulations. Though evidence of telepathic connection is inconclusive, some believe that the link between minds that occurred with the web has been carried on biologically.

Fringe theories also abound. Some maintain that the dream-change is a sign that we are living in a simulation, that we have all passed over into the afterlife, that waking life is the dream and dreamlife the reality.

"And other such hooey," as Colleen would often say when we encountered these ideas.

Some readers may wish to skip ahead to chapter three, where begins the main focus of our project, the dreamers. Here we provide a small sample of the fascinating dreamers you will meet in those chapters.

Section Two: Dream Inventions will document the experiences of some of the very first creative dreamers. Honey Whitcomb from Chapter Four: The Ingenious Whitcomb Family of Southern Idaho:

> In my dream, I am standing at the vet looking at an X-ray of my dog Wilbur, only in the dream he's not mine; he belongs to my neighbor, Curtis. And it's not an X-ray; it's more like a psychedelic painting with all the dog's anatomy as well as his chakras and the vet's notes about his personality and traumas and memories. Really beautiful.
>
> It reminds me of a cave painting like in Lascaux caves, come to think of it.
>
> The vet is telling us of a small tumor they are going to remove from the shoulder, and I just get this overwhelming rush of gratitude because back in the old days, we would have had to traumatize and medicate the dog, but now he can just go into stasis. I think how grateful I am that I will be able to go into stasis instead of ever lingering through any suffering, and I swell with pride in human technology, and I wake up still feeling just in awe of the dream, and certain that it's real.
>
> I took Wilbur in to have his shoulder looked at, and sure enough. . .
>
> He didn't go into stasis, he did get traumatized and medicated, but he came out the other end of it. The bill paid and everything, I gave Wilbur to my neighbor, Curtis. Or I guess you could say I let Curtis adopt Wilbur. I walked him over there and said I thought he ought to live with Curtis from now on. Curtis asked why and I tried not to say. I tried

getting away with, "Look, you're all alone, and he needs attention," which was part of the truth, but I don't know. Something just broke. I told my dream and I said, "I looked at the X-ray this certain way, and that was the way you looked at Wilbur, and I knew you ought to have Wilbur and I ought to go back to college and major in computer programming or something." I laughed—I'd never taken so much as one class in it, but I knew it was where I was meant to go. "And maybe not just computer science, maybe I need to take veterinary science too," and then I said, "Wait, does this sound too far out there?"

Curtis was down at eye level with Wilbur, scratching his ruff. You could see how happy they were. He said no, it sounded like a plan. I asked if he'd dreamed it too—I wasn't used to that kind of immediate trust—and he said he hadn't but that he'd been having strange dreams too and thought they were trying to tell him something.

From the moment I took that dog over, it was like a genius and a giddy mania fell over me and did not come off of me either, not until I had seen that device into reality.

The trust I'd seen in Curtis I did not see for another year or two from others, but then it started to come, and by then I'd taken some introductory courses so that I had an idea of how to explain what I meant to do. I marched into the university and told them what courses I'd need instead of the other way around. I marched straight into the bank and made my case, not for a loan but for a meeting with people in town looking to invest. It should have been impossible, but it happened.

The AI-assisted Animal Imaginer Honey invented has led to a range of medical breakthroughs serving people as well as pets—and hers is only one of dozens of inventions brought to life by the Whitcomb family, previously ranchers and schoolteachers demonstrating little sign of innovation before the dream-change began.

"I wish we could have imaged Jerry Poodle," Colleen said as we looked over Honey's stunning portfolio of animal diagrams. I kissed the top of her head, and we shared a moment thinking of our big, long-gone goof. He was a Labradoodle, really, but we'd always called him Jerry Poodle.

Section Three, The Social Good will explore dreamers' effects on their communities. We traveled to a new intentional community in an undisclosed rural location to meet Wallace Glee from Chapter Nine: Dream Villages:

> I dreamed my wife and I had moved out to a place in the country, not so remote you couldn't see houses, but they were just specks far away. Regardless, the neighbors were friendly, and some drove out to welcome us. The house was about fifteen thousand square feet. We were going to live on the upper level because the lower was just a big open space but fancy with arches, lots of woodwork, and a "grand staircase."
>
> We went exploring the outbuildings and found a bouncy castle in one of them. Mentioned it to the neighbor who said, "Oh yeah, we like to put things like that out on Fridays for the neighborhood kids to play on over the weekends."
>
> We went to sleep upstairs and woke in the night. There were birds in the bedroom! We saw several different species of owls. My wife was upset because she said that owls mean

death, and we went out to see what was up. We descended the grand staircase and found that the lower level was filled with all manner of animals as in The Peaceable Kingdom—lions, giraffes, bears, ferrets, everything. And *all* the neighbors were happily seated at some picnic tables that had been brought in. We were both very happy and full of wonder. We said, "What is this?"

"Oh, didn't we say?" a neighbor said. "We always hold the annual Animal Show right here."

And the warm place they built—with friends, with family—was just as the dream foretold. Colleen and I missed the Animal Show, but we happened to pull up on a Friday just as the bus was dropping off the community's children. Indeed, a bouncy castle stood at the lip of the Glee driveway. Other driveways held water slides, concession stands, puppet shows, and more. The children and adults rushed around as at a carnival, but it wasn't a special event at all; it was just what happened every Friday.

"I'd love to come retire here sometime," said Colleen as the children ran squealing all around, and we squeezed each other's hands.

To create happiness such as we have seen at the compound, well, if that is all the new dreaming does, it is enough.

Section Four: The Dream Architects and Cartographers focuses on dream spaces. In Chapter Eleven: Maps of Other Lives, Iris Mont of Tacoma Washington shows us an intricately detailed eight by ten-foot three-dimensional map of all the places she visits in dreams. Many of these cities and homes exist in the world but in different relationships than on her "dream island."

Iris maintains that each of us has a unique dream island, certain spaces within it shared with other dreamers. To map each dreamer's Island and then map the routes these islands take in order for their shared places to touch and overlap, she says we will finally have our map of the afterlife.

"Imagine how your own map would map onto mine," Iris said, leaving us there to commune with the image for long hours. We swayed from lack of sleep.

"It's like that time we went to the Rothko Chapel," said Colleen finally.

"Spiritual," I said.

"No," she said. "That's not what I mean at all."

Section Five: Physical Transformation documents physical changes experienced as the result of dreams, as well as physical objects created or "brought over" from dreams. In Chapter Twelve: Organs, Limbs, Flesh, and Teeth, Mo Wendover of Seattle, Washington shares a passage from their dream journal:

> I dreamed that I had woken up, only to realize I had these horrible black metal dentures that I did not remember going into surgery for. My jaw was paralyzed, and I was in a really fucked up, half-finished house. It was horrible. There were stairs in the bathroom, and everything was patched together with garbage. Along come my (dead) mother and her ex-roommate. The roommate was trying to suck up to me. She gave me a gift of candles and I threw it back and pitched a fit. I kept trying to scream "I don't remember any of this" but my jaw wouldn't open. I worked myself into such a state that I passed out, and when I woke up, I was just about to go into dental surgery—sad now to realize that my mom was dead and also that time seemed to be moving backward and forward at the same time.

"I wrote that all out, and only after that did I think to look in a mirror," Mo said.

We were not entirely rapt after Mo's recital of the dream entry, but when they followed up with a broad smile, we noticed how flat and chalky white their teeth were.

"This is just paint; it'll peel right off," they said, taking a fingernail to the front teeth, and it was so.

Mo pulled up their upper lip and showed the ridged black material of the dentures, invited us to touch. It was something like plastic, something like metal, cooler than it ought to have been.

"Can you take them out?" Colleen said.

"They don't come out. They're all tied up in my gums. Sometimes I think I feel them growing up into my sinuses, going for my brain." I felt a chill go through my entire spine and into my own sinuses, and Mo's expression was pained.

"What are you thinking right now?" Colleen asked.

"I'm thinking how I'm carrying around something from a nightmare and everyone wants to marvel over how cool it is."

Section Six: Persons and Creatures details the people, animals, monsters, and gods that people have met since the dream-change. In Chapter Fourteen: Animal Children, Melody Happness shares the experience of giving birth to and raising a fox-baby and claims the ghost of the child still visits her from the forest. She thinks it is an omen of her death. Rachelle Swin shows us a hundred-gallon aquarium of fascinating creatures much like the once-debunked Sea Monkeys and tells us that these are her children originating from an accidental parthenogenic experience in a dream.

"Are you afraid of them in any way?" Colleen asked. It wasn't clear.

"Only in the sense that they might decide to grow one of these days," said

Rachelle. "There are thousands of them."

"I'm so glad we never had any children," Colleen said that night as we bundled in our blankets and turned off the lights.

"Yes," I said with a little pang, thinking of the bouncy castles.

"If we could have kept them in a tank like that, then maybe. . ." she said but was asleep before she finished the thought.

Further along in Section Six, in Chapter Eighteen: Dream Selves, Louis Mimd describes coming over from a dream himself:

> There wasn't much to it. I just went to sleep and woke up here. It took me a day or two to realize what had happened because I just figured my phone was broken.
>
> The Internet isn't down where I come from. It never even started to go down—and where I come from, that wouldn't be possible. If it went down, someone would build it back up. You wouldn't have electricity and all of that but no Internet. You wouldn't lose the knowledge of how to do something like that.
>
> It's why I say this is the dream and that was the real life. People say, "Oh, you're one of the ones who came over," and I say, "No, more likely you all are figments of my imagination."
>
> Don't worry—you're being unreal to me doesn't mean I'm going to do anything against you. Just not my way.
>
> It feels like I got brought to a different country against my will. I don't speak the language.
>
> There wasn't any "dream-change" there either. Everything that has come from the dream-change—the

touchy-feely way people have and all the "trust" and "there are no limits" and all of that bullshit—it never happened. Not where I come from.

Going to bed in my apartment and then waking up here—still in my apartment but here, in this world—it feels like an endless nightmare. Nothing exactly threatening about it. I mean, I feel "safe" as far as that goes. There's nothing here out to get me that I can tell, but to know that the world can just shift on you like that, it's pretty terrifying.

The next time I go to sleep I could wake up somewhere worse. Even if that never happens, I won't ever get home again.

Shortly after the interview with Mr. Mimd, our van broke down. I had seen it coming.

"Don't you think it's funny how everything went so smoothly," Colleen said as we drove away from that interview. "We sold the house, just like that. We bought the love-bus and it had everything we wanted. Solar power, ample storage, excellent visibility. And everyone we have called has said yes. . . and nothing has gone wrong at all, has it?"

"You're not letting that guy get to you," I said.

"And I have not dreamed once, not since this whole thing started. Have you?"

"You forget them, is all."

"What if he's right?" she said. "What if we and everything here is something he's dreamed?"

We were silent listening to the tires on wet highway. We began to laugh uncomfortably, and then came real strong laughter. I wanted to stop for the night and show her how much I loved her, how real we were, but it was too early for such thoughts. We stopped for lunch, and when we returned to the love-bus, it would not turn on.

We used the diner payphone to call repair shops, and they all refused to come see. They said this model of van did not exist, could not exist.

"I'm looking at it right now," I said to the last one we called, finally frustrated, turning back to look at the van, but I was not sure it *was* there. It was as though one eye saw it and the other did not.

Colleen stood staring at me. "I shouldn't look, should I?" she said.

I slammed down the receiver. "We'll walk to the next interview; it isn't far," I said, "and then we'll deal with this mess."

Colleen came with me. She would not look back where the van was—or had been. "I'm scared," she said. "It's dream logic, isn't it? Remember all those interviewees who said they'd be dreaming of someone who was dead, only in the dream they hadn't died, or the people who dreamed of living in a house they'd already sold. You forget things."

I pinched my arm, hard. "There, see?"

"See what?

"We're not dreaming."

"I never said that. I said we were. . ."

"What?"

"We were being dreamed."

We walked what felt a lifetime that day, finally arriving at a charming farmhouse set far back from the road in a crescent of shade trees. Just inland from the Oregon Coast, it was *a lovely place to spend some time*, I thought on first sight, though I had no idea how long we would stay. Fascinating sculptures were strewn over the yard and porch and mobiles hung from the trees. This was the home of the twin dream-artisans Harry and Henry Monroe. It was the place where we would finally learn to dream, and in so doing, continue our interviews with significant dreamers from around the world.

We would, as well, write this book in our dreams, just as Harry and Henry crafted their spinning "amusements" and their towering "entities." Section Seven: An Education chronicles our oneiric lessons and Section Eight: The Grandest Tour our astral projections into the homes of a score of worldwide dreamers we'd never have been able to access by the usual means.

We live at the Monroe's still, dreaming and crafting, writing for word on how advance copies of this book have been received by reviewers.

No word has come to us.

"We didn't ever write it," Colleen says sometimes. She has returned to her cobbling and does not think of documentary work anymore. I think she is happy, but I long to feel her old energy and see those eyes of hers brighten and pulse with inspiration again.

*Of course we wrote the thing—of course we are real—*I long to say, but instead I kiss her forehead, tuck her into bed so she can get some work done. She wants me to get back to my stoneware jugs in earnest, and perhaps one day soon that's what I'll do.

But of course, we wrote the book. It's all here, just after this page. You see it, don't you?

ART BY JESSE PEPER

TILBERI

Brian Evenson

D URING COMMUNION, EVA took the wine into her mouth and held it there unswallowed, a puddle slipping over her tongue and making it tingle. She kept her head bowed and her eyes lowered—not out of reverence, no: only so as not to have to speak to anyone. The moment the service concluded, she made for the door. When she was lucky and was seated on the aisle in the back row—as indeed she was the first two times—she was the first out. She would hurry through the too-large chapel doors and turn left, and then left again, and then left yet again, until she was directly behind the church. There she would stop and tug the curved bone from where she'd hidden it between her breasts. The whole time, throughout the entire service, she had felt it there, burning, the bone unhappy to be in God's house. But now the bone was out, and in her hand, a strand of twisted gray wool wound around it like a collar. She held onto this strand and brought the bone close to her lips, and then, all at once, spat out the communion wine, blowing the spatter all over the bone.

She did this twice with ease. The third time, because of difficulties with her mother, Eva arrived too late to take her place on the aisle of the back pew. The congregation was already singing the hymn, the service having begun. She could, it was true, have sat a few pews forward, but she would have been in the row's middle. It would have been impossible to leave the pew at the end of the service without someone talking to her, without her either having to answer back or be thought to be deliberately slighting the person.

There were no free aisle seats. Not any. For a moment, she contemplated turning on her heel and striding back out, leaving the service entirely, abandoning the bone she was grooming, taking the rib and breaking it and discarding its broken bits instead of making it a living, breathing thing. Or, well, not breathing exactly—a bone would never breathe, at least she didn't think so. And not living either, not exactly. But not exactly dead either. A thing that, alive or no, could move and be bent to her will. But it had been hard enough to steal the first rib, and now that the defiled grave had been discovered, it would be all but impossible to steal another bone without being caught.

She considered her options. They were not good ones.

She carefully started up the aisle just as the hymn drew to a close and the priest rose to approach the pulpit. She scurried forward, head bowed, the words of the sermon already beginning, the bone against her breast beginning to itch, grow hot. She kept moving. She heard the priest's voice catch, briefly, as he noticed her—unless it caught for some other reason. She looked up and there he was, lips moving, taking about the Lord God casting *a deep sleep upon the man*, and while this man was asleep the Lord God took something from the man *and closed up its place with flesh*, and then shaped what he had taken into woman. The priest was staring right at her. She quickly looked down and slid into a place in the front pew. There wasn't a place on the aisle, but that didn't matter since there were no pews before her. Once the service was over, she could simply stand and leave.

But, she began to worry as the service progressed, could she really? By the time she started down the central aisle churchgoers would be pouring out, blocking her way. Someone would speak to her, and when she didn't answer they would know that something was wrong. They might be offended, might ask what they had done to upset her, might even insist she answer them. Some might even suspect that she was in the process of turning away from the Lord God, of becoming a lesser version of God. No, it just wouldn't do.

The bone was hotter than it had been the first two times, hot enough to blister her skin. She shifted uncomfortably, stretched, trying to reposition the bone just a little, to give it new flesh to sear. The priest was staring at her again, and for a moment everything seemed so absurd that it was all she could do not to laugh. What must her face look like, contorted, trying to hold her laughter in? She could smell something burning, probably her skin. Or perhaps she was having a stroke. Finally the priest looked away. *He knows*, she thought. She was sure he knew.

A blessing uttered in a language that not a single person within the walls of the church knew. Even the priest, Eva thought, did not know the language: he had just memorized the sounds. A curve of pain exactly the shape of the rib tucked there spread around the curve of one breast. She answered the call, stood, and came forward, queued behind the others. She kneeled. A wafer was deposited into her mouth and with her tongue she pressed it up against her mouth's roof, until it stuck. Wine was given to her to sip, and she held it unswallowed on her tongue. Her whole body was aflame now. She stood and started back toward her pew, but at the last minute turned, hurried down the central aisle toward the doors. She could feel the eyes of the priest following her, burning into her back. Whether they really were or not did not matter: what mattered was that she felt them. She pushed the doors ajar and slid out. She was already moving widdershins around the church when she heard the doors bang shut.

Left, then left—until she was directly behind the church, in exactly the place where God was blind. She clawed the bone out, the wool thread dyed red now with her blood. She lifted the bone and brought it close and blew consecrated spatter all over it.

The bone moved. It hinged open at one end, split to reveal its tiny mouth. It gave a little shriek, and then began to wriggle in her hands.

Somehow, she managed to get it home unseen. By the time she had gotten to her front door the bone had begun to sprout appendages of a sort, its side growing jiggly nubs that she imagined would eventually become arms, its base splitting into what she was sure would eventually become legs. Or something like legs anyway.

What did it look like? Not like anything, not like a rib bone and not like a baby either. The ritual had brought it into a place where it was both of this world and not.

What precisely was it her mother had said, years ago, as she had knitted in front of the fire? *Both bone and body and yet neither too. A thing that should not be and yet is.* Her mother had rocked and knitted, and the flames had danced, and Eva had watched her, watched.

"Have you ever made one?" Eva had asked.

"Hmmm?" her mother said, half distracted. "Made what?" She held up the half-knitted sweater, examined it critically.

"You know," said Eva. "The bone baby."

"A tilberi?" Her mother's hands stopped, and she looked up from her knitting, fixed her eyes on Eva, gaze steady. "What do you think?"

"I don't know what to think," Eva said, confused. "You seem to know so much about how to go about it."

"Are you saying that you believe I would defy God?"

Eva started to shake her head and then stopped. She wasn't sure. "Would you?" she asked.

"Well, would I?"

"Why do you answer me only with questions?"

"Why do you think?" answered her mother, then gave a smile that showed the sharp tips of her canines. What Eva thought was that her mother took a certain pleasure in torturing her. Eva watched her mother turn back to her knitting, her fingers beginning to move again, forcing the long strand of yarn into a new form, an unnatural shape.

"Perhaps I did," said her mother. "Perhaps I made a tilberi and perhaps it became something else. Perhaps that something is the room with me right now."

Startled, Eva looked left, then right, and, seeing nothing, suddenly realized her mother must mean her.

That was all years ago. Her mother was no longer the same, wasn't capable of communicating verbally anymore. Or, really, in any other way. She lay in her bed and stared at the ceiling and groaned. Her hair was mostly gone, the little that was left a greyish-white nimbus aswirl around her head. Sometimes, above the covers or beneath them, her hands moved, that gentle, not imprecise movement that made Eva believe her mother still thought herself to be knitting a sweater, when all she was knitting was air.

Back from church, Eva placed the tilberi on its back, to the degree that it could be said to have a back. She left it on the floor in the kitchen and went to check on her mother.

Her mother was there as always, in the bed, staring at the ceiling, hands pursuing that useless motion. The bag attached to her catheter was mostly full.

"How are we today, mother?" asked Eva in a cheery voice.

Her mother groaned, but her eyes didn't flick over, stayed fixed to the ceiling. Eva took the cream jar off the bedside table, smeared some onto her mother's eyes to keep them from drying out. Even when her eyes were touched, her mother didn't even blink. It was impossible to be sure how much she understood, if anything at all.

She clamped off the catheter line. She unhooked the bag, walked it to the en suite bathroom, and emptied it into the sink. She tried to ignore the bitter, pungent odor until the bag was empty and she could turn on the faucet and wash the last of it down.

She returned to the bedroom, reattached the bag, unclamped the line. "All done," she said briskly, clutching herself in her own arms. Then left the room.

This was, she thought, her own private hell. First a mother who, for years, had kept her thumb tightly pressed against her back, holding her down to the ground so that it was impossible for her to move on with her life. And now, now that she was older, the ghost of that same mother, rattling around in her ravaged body, refusing to leave. Was it any wonder that she had wanted to make her own tilberi?

She clucked with her tongue, calling the tilberi as if it were a cat. Or a bird perhaps. She entered the kitchen, still clucking, but it was not there where she had left it. Where was it?

She looked under the table, but it was not there. The pantry door was slightly ajar, but it did not seem to be in there either. She crouched low and peered under the stove and there, deep and far under, there it was, the light reflecting off its eyes making it just visible.

"There you are," she said, and began to reach for it.

It hissed and shuffled further back.

She dropped to her knees and, groaning, spread herself flat on the floor. She slid forward until her shoulder was tight in the gap between stove and floor and began to grope around. She touched the tilberi, felt it writhe. She tried, carefully, to work her hand around it. It didn't resist at first, but when she began to tighten her grip it hissed again, and she felt a stabbing pain in her thumb. She cried out and whipped her hand back and wriggled out and sat up. She stared at her thumb. A drop of blood shivered there at the tip of it, where the tilberi had bitten her, then slid away and splashed to the floor, another drop already beginning to form.

A moment later, she heard the sound of scuffling, a low swish-swish, and there it was, lifting what passed for a head and snuffling at the air. She watched it come, drawn forward, a few scuttling movements forward, then a brief recoil, hunched, as if expecting to be struck, waiting cowering to see what Eva would do. When Eva did nothing, it came the rest of the way forward and sniffed at the spilled blood on the floor and then began, slowly, deliberately, to lap it up.

When it had finished, its color had changed, had flushed a delicate pink. It looked up at her with pinhead black eyes and slowly rose on its hind leg-nubs, reaching for her thumb.

She held her hand steady, watching it come until its tiny, jagged mouth touched the beading blood and began to tremble. The tilberi was gentle now, bound to her by this gift of blood.

What was it her mother used to say, sitting before the fire, telling Eva what she called *the old stories*? "Just stories," her mother used to say. "Nothing true about them. Except for the ones that are true."

Of the tilberi, she had said, "You must feed it and make it your own child, just as I did with you."

"I'm not really a tilberi, am I?"

"If you're a real child, tell me: who's your father?"

She had, it was true, never known a father, had never heard her mother talk about one. "What do I feed it?" she asked.

Her mother made a scoffing noise. "Why would you think you'd be able to make one? You're not clever enough."

"I am," said Eva. "I am clever enough!"

Her mother shook her head.

"What do you feed it?" asked Eva, after a moment.

"Blood, of course," said her mother. "Fresh blood, warm from the body. You must let it nuzzle you and worm about until it finds the place on your thigh where it can suckle."

"My thigh?"

Her mother nodded. "It's not milk it wants, but blood."

"Blood?"

"It will fetch milk for you, from the sheep, from the cattle, steal it, if that's what you want. It will make itself large and flat like a sheet and then drape itself over the animal and suck the milk from its udders. It will come home sloshing and then spit it all into a jug for you. But you must feed it your blood if it is to do anything for you at all."

For a long moment her mother rocked in silence, the fire crackling before her.

"You must take a knife," she finally said, "and cut into your thigh. But be careful, not too big a cut, just enough to draw it to you. It will suckle, and in a day or two you will grow a blood nipple there. You must feed it every day or it will set about finding blood on its own. And you must not show anyone the nipple on your thigh or they will know exactly what you are."

"And what is that?"

"Why, a witch of course," said her mother.

The blood had stopped dripping from her thumb. The tilberi must have had an analgesic in its saliva, for very quickly the pain had stopped. It prodded her thumb for a moment and then dropped back down, and then, like a tiny but strangely elongated dog, circled around itself and settled onto the floor, sated, and fell asleep.

She got up. Maybe she got up too quickly or maybe the creature had taken more blood from her than she had realized: as she stood her vision started to darken and she nearly blacked out. She steadied herself on the lip of the stove until she felt all right again, and then made for her mother's room.

How much time had passed? She wasn't sure. A few minutes, it felt like, but the light was wrong, was too far gone. She felt like she was residing in a dream. There she was at the doorway, and there was her mother, what was left of her mother, dying in her bed, staring upwards. She moved forward until she stood over her mother and then bent down until she was hanging just above her, looming over her. There, positioned like that, her mother had to look at her—she didn't have any choice. Eva looked deep into her mother's eyes, and even though her mother didn't look back, Eva still felt she could see the fear in her eyes.

She took a deep breath and drew herself up. And then she folded back the blanket and pushed up her mother's gown until her mother's legs were exposed. For the dozenth time, she stared at her mother's left thigh, the place on it where there was a blemish, a lump, a wart.

Unless, perhaps, it was a nipple.

She brought her face down closer, until her mother's dying smell was all around her, and then she reached out and squeezed it between her fingers. Could she have suckled on that, back before she was human? Her mother moaned, but it was no different than the moans she always made. It meant nothing.

Back in the kitchen, she picked up the tilberi, carefully cradling it in one arm. It grumbled but slept on. She murmured to it, stroked it, and carried it into her mother's bedroom.

She settled it there, against her mother's leg, its mouth nearly touching what might be a wart or might be a nipple. Then she pulled the chair closer to the bed so she could watch, see what it would do.

The tilberi was growing pale again, almost white. Soon it would awaken, hungry. Perhaps it would find the thigh nipple, if it was a nipple, and latch on. Or perhaps it wouldn't. Either way, she would know what her mother was or wasn't, and know too by extension what she herself was.

If what happened was what she thought was going to happen, she would wait until the tilberi was suckling, until she saw her mother's blood begin to surge through it, and then, quietly, she would stand, creep to the door, and slip out, locking the door behind her. And then she would go about her life. For how long? For as long as it took for her mother to be drained of blood for good. When she was sure, when she no longer heard the moans, when she heard the tilberi scratching at the door, then and only then would she open it.

And then, according to *the old stories*, one of two things would happen. Either she would open the door and her mother would be lying there dead in the bed, white as a bone while, near the door, something now resembling her mother, but which was anything but, waited, ready to embrace her. Or her mother would be dead in the bed and the tilberi would still be as it was, small and deformed, limbs underdeveloped. If she moved quickly enough, perhaps she could crush it underfoot, kill it.

She did not know which of the two she wanted. But anything would be better than what she had now.

She leaned forward and stared at the sleeping tilberi, at her mother's blemished thigh. She held her breath, waiting for her life to change.

Saúde

Laura Cranehill

My mother said he could shoot himself
and it wouldn't be any different.
He'd still get up and pace the hall
Stinking of bourbon. Halting sometimes
to look past the walls
while we slept.

He was a whiner and a curser
an artist with no art to practice
an alcoholic, a werewolf.
There is only one kind of sadness
and it connects us all.

We woke with rain and the birds
the body full of electricity
disconnected. The old church
buried in the hill
beneath the new church.
The lemon women, emollient,
plunging their hands in the sea.
The turtle eggs white and round.

The water swirling,
dark and confused.
They were tan and beautiful,
had obviously come
from somewhere else.
In Ireland, we burn before we tan.

Afterwards, my brother left
mysteriously for three months.
When he came through the door, sunburned,
my mother asked *Where did you go*
He blinked, *I don't know*
You don't know?
He stared past her,
expecting something. *I*
don't know
Now he spoke a few words
in Portuguese. Spoke them in his sleep
Peixe, caranguejo.
Peixe, caranguejo.
Fish, crab.
And when he poured brandy, *Saúde, pai.*
Saúde, meu amigo.

My father trails down the hallway,
hitting his head against the wall. Crying, I think.
See? It's the same, my mother says.
I watch him.
No it's not.

One sadness, but
so many kinds of happiness.
Just choose one, my mother says. If you can,
just choose one.

We're All in This Together

S. P. Miskowski

for Joe Pulver

Prom A

Private Group   **38 members**

About

This page was created for the benefit of our fellow tenants at The Promenade (limited to Building A). Please let other tenants know about it. Requests to join will be screened by the page administrators on a weekly basis.

Why create this page? In recent email exchanges a number of tenants have expressed feelings of apprehension and confusion over recent events. This is natural. We share your concerns. We know how hard it can be to follow protocols established by a faceless authority in another part of the country. It doesn't help to lose our site managers at the exact moment when calm leadership is needed. Nevertheless.

1. We're all in this together, which is comforting, don't you think?
2. Serious issues are best dealt with through reasonable dialogue.

We all know how a legitimate fear can escalate to frustration, but petty acts of vandalism are not helpful. Since we have this advanced technology, let's use it to develop new and better channels of communication.

Most of us have individual accounts here on Facebook, so we expect members to be able to mingle and share thoughts, or simply chat about life and general concerns, without close monitoring. Feel free to discuss anything related to Prom A. The one rule here is civility.

Jenny Franzen

March 10, 2021

Hello to whoever's on board. Since there was zero formal introduction. I know who started the page, but the newer tenants might not.

I'm not sure how to tell if anybody's tuning in. Are you? Is it the statistics thing at the bottom? That's just a nuisance.

Anyway, if you live here, you probably know me, so hi. If you're brand new to Building A, my name is Jenny Franzen. I'm on the second floor. 214. And I'd like to address the elephant on the screen, or the page, or whatever this is called.

The way the former managers left was shameful. To me, it seemed shameful. Seven years of hard work, and they're let go and they have to take off in the middle of the night? And nobody says a word to the tenants? Like we had no connection to the managers, or like they were robots or something and nobody would care if they disappeared overnight. Why won't the owners or the development company tell us what's going on?

I guess Jim and Heloise never informed the company I have a spare key to their place. Well, I did a little walkthrough this morning. The kitchen was a mess. The clothes were gone except for a pair of winter gloves on the living room floor.

But listen to this. Heloise has this gigantic rhododendron she dotes on like a baby, always spritzing it with this special water. That plant is on the living room shelf just like always. Which tells me maybe Jim and Heloise didn't want to leave.

Also, nobody knows what happened to Pinky.

Here's the real reason I don't believe they threw all their clothes in a trunk and left: They CARED. I keep remembering all the stuff they did for us, every day. Whether it was checking out the reports about a prowler in the garage, or clearing leaves and twigs from the gutters, or turning off the gas fireplaces in the summer to save us all some cash.

Jim did those things. In case you didn't know. Thanks, Jim. Well, I guess he can't read this, can he, since he doesn't live here now? If they come back for the rest of their stuff, and you see them and I don't, tell them I said THANKS and CALL ME. Don't text. I never check those.

I'd at least like to know if they dropped Pinky at a shelter or whatever. I'd be glad to foster until they come back for the rest of their stuff. I think Heloise would want to know that. She loves Pinky so much.

Aside from the admin and the paperwork, Heloise did a lot of babysitting, pet-sitting, plant-sitting, you name it. She was good with kids, but she was best with dogs. She said she always loved dogs, but she never had one of her own, growing up. Isn't that sad?

Well, four months ago she found this stray sitting outside the gym in the pouring rain. No collar. Poor scrawny thing, soaked to the bone. Had a funny kind of roly-poly body, like an otter or a sea lion as much as a dog. Heloise said it was some breed from Iceland or Finland or something. She named it Pinky for its mashed-in nose, all pink like a pig snout, with a white scar across the middle. Must've been in a fight somewhere. Cutest thing, if you looked at it in the right way.

The point is: Heloise LOVED DOGS. So, the complaint lodged against her last month was WAY OFF BASE. Way off. In my opinion. It was a misunderstanding, but it got the ball rolling to where we are now, with no managers.

The tenant was NEW, so he didn't know Pinky, and Pinky didn't know him. Well, tell you what, GET TO KNOW YOUR NEIGHBORS and their habits and pets before you go make a formal complaint that blindsides two hard-working people and their dog! He's gone now too, so he can't read this either.

The official report to the development company was dead wrong. The new tenant was not "bitten" and not "pinned to the wall by a vicious animal" in the lobby. He overreacted to seeing a dog loose, and he embarrassed himself, and then he claimed Pinky was "big and aggressive." When I saw the dog, with my own eyes, a week before the supposed incident, Pinky was about the size of a chubby Labrador. With shorter legs. No threat at all.

Some people, right? If you ask me, the guy just wanted to break his lease, and this was his way out. He crashed into the doggy-poop-clean-up station Heloise had set up in the lobby. He said his suit was ruined by Pinky and the dog poop. He acted like the station was some kind of trap.

It was a CONVENIENCE, for crying out loud, an AMENITY for dog owners. And what was the alternative? Letting dogs poop in the elevator and the halls, and making Heloise clean it up? I guess that's what some people expect a manager to do. Heloise cleaned it up, for the longest time, but then she had the idea for the clean-up station, and people were happy to clean up after their own dogs. It was an INNOVATION.

That Heloise. She really was a gem. I miss talking with her.

Okay, I got distracted by the poop thing.

What I want to say is: Jim and Heloise know this building inside and out. Every hall, closet, vent, and roof tile. They know the upkeep it needs every season, and how far in advance to schedule maintenance and repairs. Broken lamps in the hallway, old appliances, and worn-out fixtures don't get replaced by themselves. Who's going to take care of these things, now? That's all I'm asking.

3 Likes   0 Comments   Seen by 26

Gin Beckwith

March 10, 2021

I moved in a week and a half ago. Hi.

Can someone explain what's going on with the signs in the lobby? The signs with broken frames? Yesterday I noticed another one beside the elevator, and the button panel is scratched and dented. The lobby wasn't in this condition when I viewed the building and signed the lease.

Is this the vandalism the page administrators mentioned? It's inconsiderate to damage things we all have to share. Besides, vandalism makes the place look rundown.

Sorry, this is a long post. You can keep scrolling if you want.

Main topic: Today I met an elderly man sitting on the wooden bench in front of the building. He had a walking stick and an obese dog with tiny legs. I think it had mange—you know, bald patches? The guy was wearing a cloth mask, a bandanna, and it was filthy. I tried to walk around him, but he started talking directly to me, right into my face, and he wouldn't leave me alone. He kept talking at me, all the way to the security door, until I closed it.

Based on what this man said, I have to ask:
1. Who is in charge of the building? Is it the development company? Are there new managers, and why haven't they introduced themselves?

2. The old couple, who rented to me, who I guess got fired right after I moved in, are they really gone? The man on the bench said the old managers were fired and replaced but he also said, "They're with us," and he didn't explain what he meant.

3. What's going on?

4. Should I call the police?

1 Like   5 Comments   Seen by 17

Jenny Franzen

Hi, Gin, so glad to "meet" you. I'm Jenny Franzen. I think you're two doors down from me, on the second floor, in 218. Right? I saw you taking your recycling down to the basement, on Tuesday night. I opened my door and waved but you didn't see me.

Yes. Jim and Heloise were in charge for a LONG TIME, doing a GREAT JOB, until someone decided to make a change WITHOUT TELLING any of us. Now they're GONE.

Are you on this page's email list? You might want to join, to keep up with what's going on via my newsletter which is older than this page, with more detailed information. Some of the gals in the building—Jo and Natalie and Britt—jumped on the idea of a Facebook page for the building because they're already in crochet and puff pastry groups together.

If you were on the EMAIL list, which I manage, you would get the NEWS-LETTER and you would know the thing with the SIGNS happened OVER-NIGHT and the VANDALS haven't been identified. Some legal threats have been hinted at, and some riled-up tenants want everyone to sign a petition. A lot of good that's going to do. I wouldn't bother signing, if I were you.

The man you saw sitting on the bench doesn't sound like any of the tenants. Was his dog on a leash? If you see him again, contact the development company.

Dan Perrault

Last week my wife spotted what looked like a professional photographer taking pictures of the townhome gardens, on the park side. Creeping through the hedges, close to the ground. This is how it starts. Vandalism just "happens" and then everything in the lobby has to be re-done. Next, they'll order renovations every time a tenant moves out—marble countertops, hardwood floors, all the superficial junk. They won't fix the electrical problem in the garage. They won't stop that hooty sound that blows through the vents on a windy night. Wait and see. They'll renovate and if we want to move back in, it will cost twice as much.

Gin Beckwith

Hi, Jenny Franzen. Thanks for the information. Good to know!

Dan Perrault

Of the two, Jim was a lot friendlier to me, at least if I ran into him and it was just us. Heloise wouldn't give me or my wife the time of day. And that potbellied pig she adopted was an ugly nuisance. Are those things even legal here? I think she only took it in so she could scare the tenants she didn't like. I bet she trained it to go after people. That would be just like her, if you ask me. Well, she sure scared somebody. Now she's out of a job.

Jenny Franzen

You're welcome, Gin Beckwith. Good night!

Mitch Poole

March 11, 2021

I have one question. One.

Who the hell is leaving the outside door to the gym propped open?

I've had to close it and lock up twice on my way home, after work. I have to pass the gym to get to my unit. It's the late shift. I'm beat. I don't have time for this.

If you're trying to air out the gym, it's off limits indefinitely, so you can stop. The only people allowed inside, to clean, are professionals under contract. I don't know who that is right now, but it isn't you.

Maintenance used to be Jim. You had a problem—vents blocked, flooding, weird smells—you could just call Jim. Now I don't know who to call.

No one is authorized to use the gym until further notice. This means you. Just because Jim isn't here, it doesn't change the basic rules.

I found sweat stains on the rowing machine. And a puddle of liquid around it. I had to clean up that mess, too, purely as a good neighbor. I'm not getting paid for this.

To review:

Stop using the equipment, and the outside door is only to be used in case of fire. Fire. Got it? No entrance. No exit. Stop propping the door open with a mat. I'm not sure why the open door isn't setting off the alarm. Has somebody messed with the alarm?

0 Likes   0 Comments   Seen by 28

Ashley Gaff

March 11, 2021

This morning my dishwasher died. Is this where we go for tips, now that there's no management? Well, the dishwasher is broken. No warning, just sputtered like the water couldn't get through the pipes and then it died. No leaking, but it won't drain. It's like the pipes are clogged with something solid. And the control panel isn't working. I can't press any of the buttons.

4 Likes   8 Comments   Seen by 10

Clem Dawson

Don't call a repair person. They'll charge too much. Did you contact the managers?

Ashley Gaff

No, I thought they quit. I wanted to compare notes with people. Maybe you have tips based on your experience? Isn't this what the page is for?

Clem Dawson

Sounds like a problem for the managers. Jim can fix anything. Heating, gas fireplace, those tiny 'puck lights' in the kitchen, the ones that blow out when they get too hot, and fly across the room? I'd call Jim.

Jenny Franzen

Ha! Good luck!

Henry Grisham

The dishwashers installed in Prom One were purchased pre-owned. They were refurbished, and some of them are twelve years old. Try to power cycle it. Go to the panel box. Turn the button to off. Wait. Turn back on. See what happens.

Ashley Gaff

Are you talking to me? Because the buttons don't work. I was asking if there were any alternatives, because I can't use the buttons.

Henry Grisham

If it doesn't come back on, let me know.

Ashley Gaff

Are you really telling me to turn it off and then on? Because the thing is, the buttons don't work at all.

Sid R

March 11, 2021

Did anyone else receive an unsigned, no-reply email from prom1bst@promenadeltd.net saying, "One of your neighbors has complained" about cigarette smoke? If so, did the anonymous sender warn about possible fines?

4 Likes   17 Comments   Seen by 8

Aidan Ballard

Tenants are not allowed to smoke on the balconies.

Sid R

I know.

Aidan Ballard

The smoke drifts into the other units, even if the windows are closed.

Sid R

I know. I'm a non-smoker. But it was addressed to me. I was just curious to see if anyone else got the same message, or if it was only me.

Aidan Ballard

Did you write back to the managers?

Sid R

No. I just wanted to see if anyone else received the same email. Has anyone received it? Has anyone reading this thread received the same message?

Aidan Ballard

I thought we were supposed to use our real names on this page. They said I had to use my real name and unit number, to join.

Sid R

I'm using my real name.

Aidan Ballard

Sid R?

Sid R

Yeah. It's my name.

Aidan Ballard

R?

Sid R

Yes!

Aidan Ballard

Okay. Okay. Relax.

Sid R

Seriously?

Aidan Ballard

The point is, if we don't give our actual names and unit numbers, we could be anybody. I could be anybody, just make up the name 'Aidan' or whatever and submit it and get on the list.

Aidan Ballard

Does that make sense?

Aidan Ballard

I could be a stranger. Or a tenant pretending to be someone staying with myself, under a different name. Does that make sense?

Jenny Franzen

March 11, 2021

Just stopping by to remind everyone: Jim and Heloise are GONE. Nobody seems to know if they're officially fired, or if there will be new managers. But you can stop telling each other to call Jim. He's not going to help any of us anymore. I don't know what we'll do when things break, but there you go. I guess somebody who owns this place didn't think ahead. Okay, you're welcome.

2 Likes   0 Comments   Seen by 18

Stacy Marrs

March 11, 2021

My subject might not be appropriate for this page. I don't know. You tell me.

This week—and this seems out of season, I think, so it could be climate change related—maybe we're all speeding up some natural process we're not aware of, by staying in the building full-time instead of going to work at a different location—who knows. Anyway, there's this mind-boggling infestation of flies. Little flies. Not fruit flies, but they're small, with black and gray stripes, and big, red eyes. Btw, not exaggerating by using the word "infestation." It's surreal. Epic. Disgusting.

Every morning the sink is full of flies. I have to run hot water with the sprayer on and flip the switch on the garbage disposal to clear them out. I'm sorry that's gross, but it's really gross. I mean the flies are sickening.

Does anyone know where they might be coming from?

Is this happening because Prom One is next to the river? Is it unavoidable? Why is this going on in the middle of March? What do you recommend?

8 Likes   8 Comments   Seen by 10

Jenny Franzen

There's a carpenter in Prom Two and he used to build window screens to order. He used to post his number on the BULLETIN BOARD in the lobby, the one Jim and Heloise provided as a COURTESY so tenants could swap services and recommendations the old-fashioned way, like neighbors. The bulletin board is GONE, thanks to the VANDALISM. The dog poop station's GONE, thanks to the FALSE COMPLAINT against Heloise. (Has anybody heard from her? If you do, ask her about Pinky.) All of the business cards and takeout menus and coupons are GONE, too. Nobody's going to replace those.

There should be a table in the lobby with MASKS and a bottle of hand sanitizer, but who's going to set that up? Not Heloise. Because she's GONE.

Stacy Marrs

I don't think the flies come in through the windows. Do they? I only see them in the sink.

Henry Grisham

Place a slice of lunch meat in the bottom of a jar. Leave the jar open on your kitchen counter, overnight.

Stacy Marrs

Me? A slice of lunch meat? Like roasted chicken or ham?

Henry Grisham

Try it overnight and see what happens. Anyone with this problem should leave a piece of meat in a jar on their kitchen counter.

Stacy Marrs

Okay, I'll try anything. Thanks!

Henry Grisham

Let me know what happens.

Stacy Marrs

Okay.

Ashley Gaff

March 12, 2021

Is anyone else having trouble with the elevator, after buzzing someone in? Delivery people have been telling me they can't get to the second floor. They call. I hit star-nine. They can enter the front door, but the elevator won't bring them up. I need delivery to drop off my groceries.

2 Likes   8 Comments   Seen by 4

Dan Perrault

The same thing happens to me a couple times a week. I assumed the delivery person was lying and wanted me to come downstairs, so they don't have to come up! LOL

Clem Dawson

Hi, **Ashley Gaff**. I think I know what you mean. From our unit on the ground floor, I can hear a signal whenever someone tries to use the elevator and it won't work because they don't have a fob, and it makes this 'ding' noise. I hear it a few times a day. My partner and I laugh, and we always say, "Someone's drunk and can't remember which floor they live on!" It's pretty funny, especially when we hear it late at night. I mean, who could it be? Btw, we think the elevator's malfunctioning, not the buzzer. Just a guess.

Aidan Ballard

I saw a box of groceries on the counter in the lobby, about ten minutes ago.

Ashley Gaff

Oh no! I'm sure that's for me.

Aidan Ballard

I can bring it up.

Ashley Gaff

I don't want to be a bother. Which floor do you live on?

Aidan Ballard

I'm staying with Henry. I have a mask and gloves. I'll go pick up the box and I'll be right up. No worries.

Ashley Gaff

Thank you!

Mitch Poole

March 13, 2021

Whoever thinks my first post was a joke, trust me, I'm not joking. I found the outside door to the gym propped open again. I had to lock up. Again.

If you're working out, stop working out. Stop leaving your sweat on the rowing machine. It's a safety hazard.

The wet footprints out the side door and down the walk, toward the pier? That's not even funny. The gym is off-limits to ALL of us. Knock it off!

0 Likes 0 Comments Seen by 19

Clem Dawson

March 15, 2021

This is for everybody especially **Ashley** who (I think) brought up the subject first. The elevator signal is now driving us crazy. My partner and I woke up at 2 a.m. because it was making that 'ding' noise over and over. I tried the development company's number and got voicemail. I tried Jim and Heloise's number and it wasn't disconnected but the message was garbled, and I couldn't understand it.

We got dressed and walked down to the elevator. All of the lights at that end of the hall were out. The elevator doors were open and the signal, the 'ding,' had stopped. It was completely quiet. Did anyone else hear it this morning? **Ashley**?

2 Likes 9 Comments Seen by 12

Jenny Franzen

Mitch Poole. **Mitch Poole** might be able to help. Right, **Mitch**? (He's an engineer.)

Clem Dawson

Is he the guy who posted about the gym?

Dan Perrault

I wouldn't count on him. He's imagining things.

Clem Dawson

Well, the elevator has to be operational. It's the law.

Henry Grisham

Take the stairs.

Clem Dawson

Are you talking to me?

Henry Grisham

Take the stairs. It's good exercise.

Clem Dawson

Some people need access to an elevator. I'm thinking of **Ashley**, for one.

Henry Grisham

Taking the stairs saves energy. In the long run, it helps all of us.

Mitch Poole

March 17, 2021

If this is a St. Patrick's Day prank somebody is in deep, serious shit. I don't care what the rules are on this page. I said serious shit, and I mean it.

It's two a.m. and I'm standing in the middle of the gym. All of the towels are on the floor, soaking wet. There's a puddle on the floor at the base of every piece of equipment. Any idea how much this stuff costs? Because the development company's going to calculate the value of anything broken and add it to our rent next year. Just like the dented signs in the lobby. And I don't appreciate that.

The door's propped wide open again! Wide open.

Okay. I see the footprints. This is still not funny. Not. Funny.

You know what? I'm walking right down to the pier. Right now. You're not fooling anybody. I'm coming down there right this minute, and you better have an explanation.

0 Likes   0 Comments   Seen by 12

Clem Dawson

March 19, 2021

Has anyone heard from **Ashley**? My partner and I haven't seen any grocery boxes in the lobby for a while. Most of us just go to the lobby and pick up what we ordered. But the elevator isn't working, so I wonder how she's getting her deliveries. Maybe it's none of our business, but people are struggling these days. Just thought we should ask.

2 Likes   1 Comment   Seen by 7

Henry Grisham

Maybe she's on vacation.

Gin Beckwith

March 19, 2021

Did **Jenny** Franzen ever report the old guy with the Corgi? Because a strange thing just happened.

I was in the kitchen, watching the evening news, and starting to cook dinner. I heard the doorbell ring. I came out to the living room to answer it and I heard someone else's doorbell ring, down the hall. I looked out the peephole.

You know how dark it is in the hall. The sconces are only mounted next to our doors. Between apartments there's hardly any light.

I could just make out this guy with an animal, kind of shuffling to the door across the hall. He moved into the light, and the dog or whatever it was—this big, mangy thing—snorted and slobbered at the threshold like it was starving and searching for food.

Somebody, tell me the guy moved in and he's a neighbor and I'm being stupid and it's not creepy at all, okay?

0 Likes   0 Comments   Seen by 2

Clem Dawson

March 19, 2021

PSA. The elevator's fine. We came back from a walk and there was a maintenance guy in a van pulling out of the parking lot. The elevator lights are on. The buttons work. Seems okay.

0 Likes   0 Comments   Seen by 29

Gin Beckwith

March 20, 2021

I guess nobody saw my previous post. The guy and his "dog" went away. But I have another question.

Is someone moving in? Does anyone know why the side door is open? The one that leads around the building and down to the pier. It's locked in an open position. I couldn't close it. Can somebody else go down there and check it?

0 Likes   7 Comments   Seen by 8

Henry Grisham

Contact the managers.

Gin Beckwith

I thought we didn't have any managers right now.

Henry Grisham

If it's a maintenance issue, tell Mitch Poole.

Gin Beckwith

Is that the guy who keeps yelling at everybody?

Henry Grisham

Mitch is Jim, now. Call Mitch. Then tell us what he says.

Gin Beckwith

About the door?

Henry Grisham

Tell me what he says.

Stacy Marrs

March 21, 2021

Okay, I tried leaving a jar of meat—so gross—on the kitchen counter over-night. A few times. Six times.

In the morning, just like before, the sink is full of flies. Only they're bigger than before. They're the same flies, I mean the same species. Red eyes, etc. Not as many of them now, but they're huge. I mean, as big as bumblebees.

I killed fifteen of them with a fly swatter. Then I had to use bleach to clean the counter. It was so, so gross. This has to stop.

I called the development company, and I was put on automatic hold. Some piece of insipid piano music played over and over. I gave up after thirty minutes. I never even had the option to leave a voice message.

This is a health and safety issue, isn't it? I don't know, I've never seen any-thing like this in any building where I've lived. But it seems like animal con-trol, or a health inspector should examine the plumbing.

Can anyone check this out for me? At least take a look to confirm what's go-ing on?

8 Likes   13 Comments   Seen by 10

Henry Grisham

I can take a look.

Stacy Marrs

You told me to leave lunch meat in a jar, right?

Henry Grisham

You were supposed to close the jar.

Stacy Marrs

What good does that do?

Henry Grisham

You have to put the lid on the jar.

Stacy Marrs

When? In the morning? Because there are too many of these things. By the time I get to the kitchen, they've eaten all the lunch meat and they're buzzing in a circle over the stove. All I can do is smash them with a fly swatter, and it's awful. They *spatter* on the countertop and the linoleum.

Henry Grisham

My nephew is an entomologist.

Stacy Marrs

Can your nephew stop by?

Henry Grisham

I have time.

Stacy Marrs

Will you tell your nephew what they look like, and ask him what to do?

Henry Grisham

See you in a few minutes.

Stacy Marrs

Do you want me to DM the unit number?

Henry Grisham

I know where everyone lives. See you in a few minutes.

Clem Dawson

March 21, 2021

Has anyone spoken with **Mitch Poole** lately? My partner left for a business trip this afternoon and she sent me a text to say the gym door and the outside door were wide open. She tried to close them, but they're stuck.

0 Likes   17 Comments   Seen by 5

Aidan Ballard

I'm in the gym right now.

Clem Dawson

Do I know you?

Aidan Ballard

I'm staying with Henry. I read your post on my phone. I'm documenting the damages.

Clem Dawson

What kind of damages?

Aidan Ballard

Water all over the floor. Footprints. Piles of wet towels. Clumps of fur. Broken equipment.

Clem Dawson

Are you serious?

Aidan Ballard

Come down and see for yourself.

Clem Dawson

See the gym?

Aidan Ballard

Better if we both witness this. Right?

Clem Dawson

Did you call Mitch Poole?

Aidan Ballard

I knocked on his door.

Clem Dawson

What did he say?

Aidan Ballard

No answer.

Aidan Ballard

Two people should see this.

Aidan Ballard

To confirm the damages.

Aidan Ballard

For insurance purposes.

Clem Dawson

Okay, okay. Let me put my shoes on.

Jenny Franzen

March 22, 2021

Hello to whoever's still on board. Which is hardly anybody, I guess, since not one person answered their door this morning when I went around to ask about the water puddles in the hall. Which turned out to be urine.

That's right. Someone's PEEING in the halls. Or letting their dog PEE in the halls.

This is exactly what I was talking about when I said nobody's going to take over all of the responsibilities for Prom One now that Jim and Heloise are GONE.

You take this stuff for granted, for years. Somebody makes a mess, and somebody else cleans it up. You never stop and ask how this happens, do you? What is the NAME of the person cleaning up the mess? Where do they COME FROM? What's their STORY? Why would they get up and leave in the middle of the night without any warning? Where did they go? And what's happened to their dog, Pinky?

If you find out, LET ME KNOW.

1 Like   0 Comments   Seen by 1

[end]

Faithful Friend and Companion

Tim Waggoner

"DO YOU THINK I'm doing the right thing?"

There are tears in Lydia's eyes as she asks this question. She's sitting on a hard plastic chair in a sterile exam room, chilly air heavy with the smell of chemicals. You're sitting next to her, leaning forward to avoid putting any pressure on your back. Your spine feels like it's on fire, and you're shivering, more from the pain than the cold. You've always hated this place. Bad things happen here.

You turn to your wife. "Can we go home? Please?"

She doesn't acknowledge your words. Her attention is fixed on the woman standing before the two of you: petite, late thirties, brown hair, white lab coat.

"No one can answer that for you, Lydia," the vet says. "But Jim's not a young man anymore, and he has intervertebral disc disease. He's had three back operations within the last two years. His spine is basically made of glass."

"But he got better after those operations. He could walk normally and had no pain!" Lydia glances at you. "Well, *almost.*"

"I'll understand if you change your mind and decide to do a fourth operation. But I urge you to think about what that would be like for Jim. Putting him through all that for a fourth time – the pain of surgery, the hard recovery, the physical therapy . . . And for what? A couple months of mobility before another disc ruptures and we're right back where we started? It's a quality-of-life issue. Plus – and I hope this doesn't sound too insensitive – but can you afford another operation? The last three must've put quite a strain on your finances."

"They did," Lydia admits.

Tears begin to run down her cheeks. The vet lifts a box of tissues from the exam table and holds it out to her. She smiles gratefully, takes one.

"Keep them," the vet says, and Lydia takes the box and places it on the floor by her feet.

You're not sure what's happening. You understand the women's words, but you sense an underlying meaning that escapes you. Maybe you could think more clearly if your back didn't hurt so goddamned much. You were mowing the yard last week, being careful, going slow, but something bad happened in your back anyway. Pain flared bright and hot as fire at the base of your spine, so bad you fell to the ground, whimpering.

Sitting hurts but standing is worse. You try to keep as still as possible to minimize the pain, but you're shivering even more now, and your breath is coming in fast, sharp pants, and even these small motions send ripples of agony up and down your spine. You wish you had a blanket. You wish Lydia would hold you and help keep you warm. You wish you were home in your cozy round bed which rests on the floor next to Lydia's. You'd still hurt, but at least you'd be somewhere you know, somewhere *safe*. Not in this place, which smells of pain and fear and death.

"Before you decide on another round of surgery," the vet says, "ask yourself this: Would you be doing it for him or for you?"

Lydia looks at you. Tears stream from her eyes, chest heaves as she sobs. She reaches a trembling hand toward your head and strokes your hair. You don't understand why she's so upset, but you've always been empathetic – it's a trait of your kind – and you start crying as well.

"All right," Lydia says. "Let's do it."

The vet smiles sympathetically. "I'll leave you alone for a few minutes so you can say goodbye."

She steps out of the office and closes the door behind her. It's just you and your wife now, both of you crying hard. Lydia hugs you then. Your back screams in protest, but you don't cry out. You'd endure any amount of pain for her.

The vet returns, an assistant in tow, and Lydia releases you. The assistant's a big man – thick arms and legs, large hands. He carries a tray with two hypodermic needles and two vials of clear liquid. He places the tray on the exam table, then stands quietly, his expression one of sympathy and sorrow.

"Are you ready?" the vet asks.

"No," Lydia grabs a fresh tissue and blows her nose. "But let's do this."

The assistant fills a hypo from one of the vials, then hands it to the vet.

"This will put him to sleep. Once he's out, we'll give him the other one."

The woman walks toward you, and you instinctively sense what's coming. You jump from your chair, run to the door, reach for the handle . . . But the assistant grabs you before you can open it, and you feel a sharp sting in your ass as the vet delivers the sedative. You struggle, but the drug soon begins to take effect, and you feel drowsy. The assistant helps you to the table, lifts you onto it, and you lie there, looking at Lydia, eyes half-lidded. Your back still hurts, but not as much now, and you're grateful for that at least.

"It's okay, Lydia. I understand. I hope you can love again someday."

The vet speaks. "You might think about stopping by the shelter in a few days and picking out a new one – if you're feeling up to it."

Your vision blurs, fades. Just before you fall asleep for the final time, Lydia speaks.

"That's not a bad idea. Maybe I'll get another boy and call him Jim. It'll be almost like this one never left."

These words hurt worse than your back ever did, and you take that pain with you down into the dark.

Creed of the Autophage

Baph Tripp

Meatflesh is merely the larval stage of rot. Growth: a seed for the final flowering of decay. Mountains evolve through erosion to culminate in their ultimate nonexistence. A life-giving star becomes a melanoma machine... and later collapses entirely to purest black. The purpose of existence is to be extinguished, to provide a theatre for its own obliteration – a paean to the essential nothingness that cannot be named. The progress of deterioration. Annihilation as apotheosis.

A knife inserted into the body at the right spot slides in perfectly, like a key fitting its intended lock. The prison gate opens, innards are let out, blood runs free. Liberation, as the lights fade.

So many emancipated in this way by my hand and always in secret. Society does not look kindly upon agents of such transcendence, afraid of the clarifying contrast to its own deficient definitions of freedom.

But who saves the savior? My time is come. When I listen for that still, small voice it is everywhere silent: the clear clarion call of the void. My deliverance, however, is not so simple a matter as those I have commended. As prophet, I require consecration, that I might not only escape but *ascend.*

If you eat only yourself and then defecate thereafter, what does this elucidate? Excrement is that which the body cannot use, does not need: that which is execrate. And if the body rejects parts of itself, finds its own constituents superfluous? The process of autosarcophagy is one of refinement, of purification. The pathway to becoming one's best self. Only what is necessary is retained.

To reduce the likelihood of complications, the skinning is done at first in small sections. Stainless steel grade implements, cleaning and bandaging of the affected areas. This stage does not last long – a trifling amuse-bouche.

Then begin the amputations.

Between meals, work continues on construction and completion of the helper machine, golem verger. Ferric beast of syringes and snipping blades, cauterizing implements and collection plates, rubber tubing and respiration pumps. Apparatus of communion, to both cleave and feed once every limb has been removed and sanctified, leaving me unable to proceed without assistance. The bestowal of a simulacrum of life to inert metal is also simultaneously an offering: new territory for negation to claim, beyond the everyday mineral metamorphosis of corrosion – the immobile made to move so that it will, over time, stop.

Devices shall force blood and oxygen through what is left of my body after the heart and lungs and brain have all been absorbed and what is inessential has been discarded as defecated debris. Eventually, all that will be left is the digestive tract. Then the anus will be stretched around and fed into the mouth, that miniature abyss in all of us – a gaping hole which once took such prominent position in the face and, indeed, led through the very center of the human organism to its excretory partner on the other end. The hollowness at our center, now joined in an unbroken orifical ouroboros.

As this looped circle grows tighter, consuming its way along its own circumference, the lips will eventually swallow the pharynx, then abrade themselves away to nihility. And in that moment the body will suddenly slip corporeal restriction entirely, utterly loose its bonds, and become undifferentiated from the air in the room, the atmosphere, the full emptiness of the whole hole of reality – at one with the universe.

What can be said of the source of all that exists? It must by definition have contained, even consisted of, the potential for all things, including the antitheses of those things, as these also exist. Clearly, this source cannot be said to be one thing or another to the exception of anything else. It can have no characteristics, as all definitions are exclusionary. It must be no thing in particular as segregated from any other thing: no thing. Nothing. An empyrean orifice of elimination – which means to expel, to shit out into the world... but also to *eradicate*, to expunge entirely from creation.

Any physicist will tell you that we are more empty space than not. And I? I am going home to god.

FLESH, PORCELAIN, STEEL

Paula D. Ashe

OUR PARENTS AND grandparents live with them like it's normal. As if the rotten metal beasts that follow them around are just pesky, over-attentive dogs. Two hundred or so years ago, a factory exploded. It had once been a massive brick structure, a place of cogs and engines, a grey sheen surrounding it in a fuliginous halo. The ruins burned for days, turned the sky sulfur yellow, rained ash and shrapnel, bled searing propene into the soil. Months later these dull machines self-sutured from broken parts came into town, stood in the streets, and waited for someone to take them home. I wasn't born yet but I can imagine them; sentinel-still in the toxic dark, coated in cinders, the houses glowing peacefully in the reflections of their blown-bulb eyes.

My first full memory of my mother; we are sick, feverish, she holds me against her and smells of lilacs and sweet ethylene. I think she's humming. My ears are thick with fluid, but the thrum of her desperate music lives in my bones. Her hair tickles my ear. Behind us, the machine watches, its surfaces glistening from our radiating heat in the cool of the evening. Her machine has no face, just a series of panels of metal and glass, blank gauges, and sprockets with nothing to link to. It looms over both of us, sullen in a corner.

My mother's machine hates me.

Growing up, no doorway was free from its bloodied iron shadow. Its hulking gait encouraged me to walk, after too many 'accidents' between its mechanical tread and my grasping fingers. Nothing so terrible as amputation or a break – somehow, the machine knew never to cause any lasting damage. Blood blisters a plenty, welts, carefully crafted strategies to damage the tissues beneath the skin. My mother would look at it with sharp disapproval, sometimes rage. But what could she do to such a behemoth? It had never hurt her, but it could have taken her in its massive grasp and crushed her like a sheaf of flimsy tin. They were locked in each other's enmitying gravity.

As such, I hate it too.

One time I heard mother and her friend Veera laughing in the kitchen because Veera had just said that since everybody had a machine, nobody could sneak around anymore. Veera laughed loudly and mother did not. "Sorry," Veera said. Mother drank her tea. Father took his machine and his city woman and left before I was born. There are no framed pictures of him on the walls or surfaces of our home, but he exists in hazy images pressed behind crinkling skins of cellophane. He and mother laughing, arms around each other, their machines just outside the frame. When mother is at work, I look into these still windows and imagine the automatons don't exist.

Father left.

The machine stayed.

There are no quiet days. Their noise is constant. Thumping, throbbing, whirring, grinding, shuffling, squeaking, creaking, clanging. I don't think I ever realized what quiet could be until we took a school field trip into the city to visit some museum. All of us kids crackling with excitement on the school bus, and as soon as we exited town our attention all snapped to the strange noise around us: the absence of their hum. No wonder people from outside of town rarely came in. Mother said that was probably for the best.

They weren't terribly helpful. Some had conveyor systems, but half the rollers had melted and the belt itself was shredded so badly it just looked like hair. Others had flat platforms you could set things on, but you couldn't leave a room because they'd just follow you and whatever sat on their surfaces would slide off and break.

It would follow my mother to work, God only knows how it hindered her there in the hospital, with all the other nurses and their dumb machines, the patients, and their machines, and then the actual functioning equipment, properly calibrated and useful. I wondered often if envy is why they rose after the explosion, cursed as they were with productive yet inert intentions.

Whatever shocks the slagheap brutes into sentience is coming for me. I am a weird beacon, calling in the dark, steadily assembling my own mechanical god. Because that's what they are. Stupid, wrathful, ready to control and clot up my life with its unasked-for presence. Something about adulthood beckons them and they always come; eager to lurk, to crowd us in, to keep us anchored to this blasted place. I sometimes wonder if maybe father left because he couldn't stand all the noise, the acrid air, the gouges in the floor, the broken furniture. I can't remember a day free from the sound of something precious breaking. I always asked mother why she wouldn't just use cups of wood or metal, but she insisted on porcelain. Perhaps our home was too small for so much flesh and steel.

I can't kill it. People have tried. The only way to stop them is to stop yourself. Early on, a lot of families died that way. People didn't understand. To be honest, we still don't understand. After every funeral, another grave is filled with a body and is guarded by the rusting corpse of a devoted machine. Late at night there are no wailing ghosts; only the sounds of metal clanging against stone, the high-pitched howl of wind whistling through dry pipes, the shearing shriek of mad hinges.

It doesn't take long for me to gather my things; I don't have much. When I was younger, mother would brag about my selflessness, "That child never asks for anything." But the things I wanted were things she couldn't give. I don't hold that against her. The tea will do its job; soft toxins are so easy to come by out here. She'll fall asleep and won't wake up. Her machine will stop then, hopefully choked by the anguish of its emptiness.

I leave our house, quiet as a flesh god's grace.

STILL THERE

Corey Farrenkopf

"I'M SURPRISED YOU hired her," Gifford said when he saw Remy's newest assistant. "You've seen that movie, right?"

"You know I don't watch things like that," Remy replied. "She's quite good in the darkroom. That's what I care about."

Gifford looked over Remy's shoulder, deeper into the gallery, to where Gale stood at the framing table. She was cutting white mat, centering a print of a faceless man walking into the sea.

"You really should," Gifford said before walking out, merging with the Provincetown summer crowd, winding his way back to his own gallery a few doors down.

Remy's gallery, BLUNT, stood at the beginning of Commercial street. Shops and restaurants crowded close, the bay lying quiet over their shoulders. The building had been a church, then a bank, then the gallery. The white steeple pricked the salt-warn sky. The bulletproof vault had been converted into a darkroom. The building suited Remy's aesthetic: Surreal photography, images of men and women descending into landscapes, merging flora and fauna, human no longer separate from nature.

"This looks right, right?" Gale asked, holding up the framed print.

"Perfect. If the wire's set, feel free to hang it," Remy replied.

There were several blank spaces on the wall between the warped windows that had been in place since banking days. Nothing lingered long after a price tag was fixed.

"Thanks for what you said."

"What?" Remy asked.

"To that guy. I appreciate it. It's rough getting a job with my background," Gale replied, eyes trained on the print, the man and the ocean, water lapping over his suit jacket, neon tie half-submerged.

Remy chuckled. "People who put weight on things like that are unprofessional."

"You really haven't seen the movie?"

"No. I'm an analog guy. Anything in the digital world is profane, and YouTube is the pope of that forsaken church."

Gale laughed, pushing a strand of dark hair out of her face, adjusting her glasses.

"I wouldn't hold it against you if you did," Gale said.

"You can't hold anything against me. I'm the guy who cuts your paychecks," Remy said with a smile. "Once you get that hung, feel free to take the rest of the day off."

"You sure?"

"Definitely. Take your girlfriend for an early dinner. Beat the crowds."

"There's no such thing as beating the crowds around here."

"I know."

Remy hadn't watched Gale's student film, *STILL THERE*, but he had read several synopses, and a dozen reviews. Curiosity got the better of him.

Gale made it her senior year at NYU and had been attempting to get it taken down from YouTube ever since. It was on the school's account, gathering millions of views, and had become a reason why a certain type of student applied to the program. It brought in money, so it stayed up. Gale signed the rights away, so there was little she could do to get it removed. Hence the flight from the city, the death of her past life, and the difficulty finding work. Remy was sympathetic. People looked for any reason to write someone off. A poorly received and/or scandalous student film shouldn't be one of the reasons on that list.

The movie was an attempt at found footage, shot at the abandoned air force base in Truro, the next town over from Provincetown. The base had been operational until the early 90s but had been let go since. At the time of filming, the officer housing resembled a small neighborhood from the 50s, twenty houses, white clapboard falling to rot, windows broken, garage doors spray painted with clown faces. Trees grew in living rooms, pushed out of sinks and shower drains amid cascades of black mold.

Remy had shot several photo series there, but never at night.

It was perfect post-human scenery.

The plot followed a man and a woman, Gale the female lead, a man named Shaun the male. His character had been one of the radio operators stationed at the base. After the shutdown, he refused to leave. Something held him there, attempting to stave off the rot and ruin creeping through the grounds, maintaining the buildings even though they'd been condemned, asbestos in the walls, chemicals poisoning the grounds. It was his home. Gale shot the entire thing through a handheld camera as if it were the darkest home movie imaginable.

There were long, drawn-out shots of Shaun hammering boards, sanding and painting walls, attempting to pull encroaching bittersweet from front stoops and back decking. As the film progressed, Shaun's character's already deteriorating mental health declined, his work becoming shoddy, attempting to fix completely rotten flooring, vacuuming rugs that had succumbed to mold.

Gale played the role of caring wife, always trying to edge Shaun away from their current life, attempting to get him help, to make suggestions for where their lives should go.

Each offer was swiftly torpedoed.

Shaun continued to work, but at night, moving between buildings in near darkness. Gale woke to hammer blows and heavy sawing, picking up the camera to find Shaun four houses down, repairing a deck detached from a house, boards crumbling into the leaf litter.

At some point, she tried to remove the hammer from his hand, struggling against his workman's strength.

She fell back into long grass.

He darted into the nearby woods.

Gale tracked him, running through the pine forest, damp foliage sticking in her hair, searching, until she stumbled on the old coal plant at the property's edge. The camera panned to a figure standing at the top of the building, five stories up. She screamed to him, pleading, backlit by the moon.

Then he jumped.

Reviews claimed he wasn't supposed to jump. He was supposed to step back from the ledge, disappear into shadow, into some other world. The movie would fade to black, leaving the audience on an ambiguous note, only Gale's scream reverberating through theater speakers. But he didn't. He leapt, no harness, no cushion.

Shaun ended up in a coma, spinal column snapped, most bones broken. Only life support kept blood thrumming in his veins.

Because he hadn't died, it wasn't snuff. Not technically. Simply an accident. Gale submitted her script to the police, all the storyboards scribbled in notebooks. She showed them the unedited footage. The writing backed up her claim. Charges were never pressed, but that did nothing for her name, for her face plastered across seventeen million YouTube views. She regretted turning in the project, but failure would result in lost time, all those student loans piling up even higher.

The degree hadn't saved her in the end. Shaun had been on life support for years. One tragedy played against the other, life metaphorically and literally snuffed out.

Remy walked against the crowd, returning to the gallery from his lunch break. The surrounding people reeked of sunscreen and vodka, artificially colored ice-cream bars and floral perfume. The brick sidewalk was uneven. He had to be careful, dodging women walking tiny poodles and children escaped from SUV-sized strollers. He couldn't wait until fall arrived and the vacationers left. Yes, he made most of his money during the busy season, but he craved the silence of winter.

He climbed the three steps to BLUNT's front door.

Before he could push inside, the sounds of an argument drifted from within. Through a window, a middle-aged woman was jabbing a finger at Gale behind the front desk.

Remy hurried inside, putting himself between the women, assuming something had gone wrong with a framed delivery. Clientele were quick to snap at small mistakes.

"Is there something I can help you with?" Remy asked.

"Nothing from you," the woman said. "She's the problem. I can't believe she'd come back after everything. It's an insult."

"And how's that?" Remy asked.

"Did you know Shaun?"

"Shaun?"

"My brother. The guy in her movie. Don't pretend you don't know. Everyone knows," the woman said.

Remy knew Shaun was a local actor. He had been the lead in several plays at the Cape Rep Theater. He'd never made it to Broadway but had done well on the small stage. Remy didn't think anyone from the man's life would show up at his shop, but again, he wasn't good at gauging the severity of online notoriety.

"I told you I was sorry. I don't know why he did it. What else do you want me to do?" Gale said, stepping around the desk, hands flexing at her sides.

"You don't know why he did it? Are you kidding?" the woman asked, stepping back from Remy. "Maybe the whole stringing him along then breaking his heart thing?"

"I never did that."

"That's not what he said, and it's not like we can ask him about it anymore, can we?"

"He might wake up," Gale said.

The woman looked like she was going to swat Gale, to reach across the distance and tear her face off. Remy had seen it happen at bars, fingers raking flesh, swaths of red furrowed into cheeks. He repositioned himself again, arms out, making space.

"I'm going to ask you to leave. This is a private establishment, and I'd prefer to not have to call the police," he said, hands shaking.

"You're going to call them on me? You literally have a murderer working your front desk," the woman replied.

"She didn't push him."

The woman's eyes went wide. She shook her head, told them to *fuck themselves* and stormed off, slamming the door. There was a moment of silence, both Remy and Gale staring at the door, waiting for the woman to stroll back in with another stream of profanities, but the dust settled, and they were alone.

"Do you know her?" Remy asked, as the two found chairs behind the front desk.

"Not personally. She was probably one of the people sending me threatening Facebook messages before I deleted my account," Gale replied, a red flush climbing her neck, heat radiating in her cheeks. "I never realized she was Shaun's sister."

"It's pretty low to accuse you. Like I said, you didn't push the guy."

"I didn't, but I don't think I helped the matter. Shaun was a great actor, but I didn't realize how much of the played-at psychosis was actually real-life psychosis. I wouldn't have cast him if I knew it endangered his health."

"You don't have to answer this, but you two weren't involved, right?"

"I'm not exactly into men."

"I'm aware, but you never know. People move back and forth between the two depending on what strikes a chord."

"True. But it's just women for me. I don't know if he couldn't understand that, or what, but he got really angry four-fifths of the way through shooting, and from what his sister said, I'm guessing there were things he wasn't honest about."

Remy nodded, crossing his legs. "And that's not your fault. Just because you didn't return the feelings, doesn't give him the right to…"

"I know. It's just this has happened so many times. No one listened about how creepy he was acting, all those phone calls, all the times he showed up at my hotel room drunk. He got touchy. Overly aggressive. It's all in the movie. I… I didn't know what to do."

"Completely fair. People rarely listen," Remy replied, reaching out for her hand.

A week later, someone threw a rock through the gallery's front window. Shards glinted off the hardwood like slivers of ice reflecting the dozens of photos along the walls. Gale swept up the mess while Remy gave a report to two police officers standing in BLUNT's doorway.

"We had a woman in a week ago threatening my assistant. I don't know her name, but I know she was related to Shaun Cummings, the guy in that video," Remy said, voice low so Gale wouldn't hear.

The two cops shrugged as if they already knew, had decided how the interaction was going to go. They darted glances over Remy's shoulder, hands on hips, fingers running over pistol grips as if a bear was about to emerge from the darkroom.

"We'll see what we can do," the first officer said, flipping his notebook closed before the two returned to their cruiser.

Gale had visited Cape Cod throughout her childhood. Had spent time at her grandparents' cottage in Brewster. That was the line dividing her from Shaun. Summer person versus local. It wasn't hard to see where the cops' loyalty lay.

There would be no returned phone call.

Vandals gave up on rocks.

When Remy went to unlock BLUNT's front door on a random Wednesday in August, he found every window papered with images of a man in a hospital bed, feeding tube down his throat, a nest of wires swarming in and out of his body. The words *HE'S STILL HERE* was written across the top. Remy swore and began tearing down the photographs, hoping to get them all before Gale arrived.

He only managed to remove eight before her footsteps tread the stairs. She didn't say a word as she moved to the window besides his, reaching up, peeling the taped photographs from each pane. She lay them at her feet, stacking one atop the next. They worked like that until all the photographs were removed, the pile shivering in the wind. Gale stooped to pick them up, sweeping through the front door as Remy held it open. Neither flipped the closed sign to open.

"Maybe we close to the public today? Catch up on some darkroom work?" Remy said.

Gale leaned against the front desk, one hand at her throat, eyes staring through the front windows.

"I think things might be easier if I left," she said. "First the rocks, then this. I don't know what they'll do next. I'm bad for business," she said.

"I'm not going to keep you against your will, but I wouldn't fire you over something like this. Let me share a story with you."

He gestured to the chairs behind the front desk.

They sat.

"When I was young, I made my name over a few risqué photoshoots. Twenty-somethings nude in a quarry, emerging from the water and trees, trying to capture a mythic appeal, a real rough version of what I do now. Think water nymphs meet college keg party. Some people loved it, others called me perverted. I had Christian groups picketing my art school. Hate mail arrived every other day. But the photos were good, so I wasn't going to stop. Eventually, the threats dried up. They always do. This is what you're good at," Remy said, pointing back into the studio. "Stick around and I'll let you hang your own work on the walls."

Gale had shown him a number of shots she'd taken of the moon over the dunes, shadows cast over shacks hunkering by the Atlantic. She had an eye for Cape Cod gothic, or so he called it. Just the day before she showed him a photo of a whale beached by Rock Harbor, ribs exposed, the glint of sunset caught on its moldering skin.

Remy knew all it took was one person to show faith.

Gale's eyes lit up, lips twitching into a smile.

"Really?" she asked.

"Of course. Let's get through fall. Come winter we can make some space and put together a show."

"Other people would kill for that. People who worked much harder than me."

"You've got talent. Don't think too much on this."

"I won't," Gale replied.

Is Gale still at work? The text flashed on Remy's phone. It was from Gale's girlfriend, Zelda. The three had shared drinks at a handful of bars over the past months. Occasionally they played Scrabble at their apartment. He'd sprung for theater tickets during the Tennessee Williams festival. Texts weren't uncommon. *She won't return my calls.*

Remy was at his own house in Truro. As far as he knew, Gale said she was going home after five o'clock. He texted back. *She left hours ago. Did she mention an errand? Some meeting?*

Nothing, came the response. *I've been worried she's going back to the base.*

I doubt she'd do that. Remy typed hesitantly.

You'd be surprised. Her mind's always going there. Why wouldn't her body?

Maybe she went back to the gallery. That makes more sense. She was working on her photos. Maybe she had a moment of inspiration, Remy replied. *I'll check.*

Thank you so much. I'll try a few places myself. Tell her to call me if you find her. She's the worst at remembering to charge her phone. Zelda replied.

Remy got into his Subaru and headed north.

For the past months, all through winter, Gale had been hesitant to share work with Remy. She'd spend hours in the darkroom but swept her developed stock from the drying racks before he could see.

One afternoon, when she'd left for lunch, Remy dug a roll of negatives from her desk, holding them to the overhead lights. The shots were clear, black and white thrown into sharp contrast. They appeared to be from the base of steep dunes, a hunkering steel building on the horizon, someone's silhouette blackened against the sky. Remy didn't know how she could get the angle, that much clarity with such distance. In one shot, the body belonged to a woman. In the next, a man. In a third there was just empty space, cloudless sky, the lens trained on something beyond the viewer's sight.

Had she been working with a partner, he'd wondered, hurrying to stick the roll back where he found it.

He'd thought she'd been doing better, had pushed the matter from her mind. Rocks stopped raining through windows. No one plastered BLUNT's facade with worrisome images. The negatives said otherwise.

As he slipped the canister back into her desk, he noticed the writing on the side: *STILL THERE.*

The cover of the Cape Cod Times from that morning featured a photo of the abandoned air force base. According to the article, it was the anniversary of Shaun's fall. A hundred devotees to Gale's film journeyed to the base to pay homage. They built a shrine, burned candles, and recited his lines from the script. Locals had gotten word and taken to their Jeeps and flatbed trucks. There was a confrontation, fists and pepper spray, a knife in the ribs. Three people had been injured. The article said they'd approached Gale for comment, but she couldn't be reached. Remy considered tucking the paper into the recycling right away, but if the reporter had already contacted Gale, what good would it do?

He scrapped it anyway.

She didn't need to see the hateful protest signs, promises etched on cardboard.

Two lights burned inside the gallery. One over the front desk, the other by the darkroom. Remy swept the building, checking each closet and bathroom. They never left lights on, but he couldn't find Gale anywhere.

He did find the Cape Cod Times spread on the front desk, open to the image of the air force base, all those men and women with their signs and sneers. The words *CAN'T LEAVE* were scrawled in black Sharpie across the photo. A small man had been drawn in the upper corner, face featureless, peering over the crowd. Next to the paper were dozens of film canisters, all with the words, *STILL THERE*, written across their sides. Remy couldn't bring himself to touch them, to pull out the negatives and hold them to the light.

"Oh god," he said as he hurriedly stepped into the night. The moon was full, the streets mostly empty. The sounds of conversation and music drifted down the street, the lap of waves somewhere beneath it. He jogged towards his car, mind sprinting through where she could be, when someone whistled across the street.

It was Gifford. Remy forgot he'd had a show opening earlier that night.

"Can't talk right now," Remy called.

Gifford didn't reply, only pointed towards the gallery's steeple with a shaking hand. Remy followed the gesture, finding a woman's silhouette blackened against the white boards.

He didn't know how Gale got up there. There was no ladder or stairway, no access point. Without looking back at Gifford, he ran around the building, standing beneath Gale, the moon almost blinding, wind picking up. She stood above him, her peacoat tugged by a gust, hair streaming, eyes on the sky.

"Gale, just stay there. I'm going to call the fire department. We're going to get someone out here," Remy said, dialing 911.

The phone rang as she spoke.

"Do you know how many views it's up to?"

"I don't, but it doesn't matter. Don't do this to Zelda. Or me. Just hang out and we'll figure this out, nothing's worth…"

"Thirty million views. It's insane. It was supposed to be a short film a hundred people saw. Nothing like this. I can't stop the spread. There are too many eyes. His eyes are always there…"

Remy lost her trail of words as the operator picked up. He quickly begged them to send a ladder truck. *Ten minutes*, the operator promised.

"That's fine," Remy almost yelled into the phone before shoving it in his pocket.

"People will get bored eventually. Trust me, I know," Remy called to Gale.

"You aren't right about this. When it's out there, online, it's out there. I can't take it back. Everyone sees it, everyone knows it's my fault. I tried to bring him back, but there are things you can't change. I need to go," Gale called into the wind, words unraveling, drifting one into the next.

"It's not your fault. We're getting a ladder. Zelda's waiting at home. Just take a deep breath and…"

Gale screamed.

"Too many eyes. Too many eyes," then she stepped back into a space Remy couldn't quite see, the steeple's shadow swallowing her form.

Remy hurried, calling to Gale, listening for the sound of a slip, feet sliding over shingles. He rounded the corner, trying to catch a glimpse of his assistant outlined against the moon. When he reached the far side, Gale was absent, the roofline vacant, steeple pale against the black-blue sky. He continued to call to her, searching the ground, searching the roof.

Too many eyes, reverberated in his ears.

A text message from Zelda illuminated his phone screen.

Did you find her?

Then another question mark. Then another. They seemed to go on forever, scrolling down his screen.

He didn't know what to say. He hadn't found her. Not really.

The EMTs and firefighters failed to locate her body as they swept the grounds. Gifford and the gathering crowd did little better. Not a single camera pointed at the steeple resulted in an identifiable image, just the moon and the building, the spread of stars beyond.

Over the next week, dozens of clips would appear on YouTube, all of the steeple, red and blue lights flashing over the spire, sirens wilting in the night air. There'd be a flicker, an undefinable shadow, something most would miss. Comments sprawled below, speculation of a silhouette, someone there but not, someone just out of reach. It might have been a bird, a cloud, a face. There was no consensus, but the views continued to climb, millions upon millions staring at their screens, faces just inches away, never truly seeing.

While police joined the search, Remy tapped his own phone screen, responding to Zelda the best he could.

I think my eyes are failing. I don't know how I could have missed so much...

A single question mark came as a reply.

Thought Experiment

Jacob Derin

"I feel empty."

This statement rang out into the silent air, the oppressive stillness parting for a moment before returning once more. Nature abhors a vacuum, after all.

That place was never truly silent, actually. Along with the constant *hum* of the noise machine, designed to make listening in to our conversation impossible from the outside, there was the steady *tick*-ing of Dr. Schuman's clock. But, when I say silent, I mean silent to me. I had learned to tune these things out.

"And what does 'empty' feel like?" Dr. Schuman asked.

Dr. Schuman asked me questions like this often, and never seemed to be deterred by my lack of a satisfying answer.

I shrugged.

"It feels like nothing," I told her.

Again, silence. I took this opportunity to study the wall behind Dr. Schuman. It was covered in peeling wallpaper which was adorned with small sailboats. I didn't like the sailboats.

"And what does 'nothing' feel like?" She put a peculiar emphasis on the word "nothing", as if this particular phrasing was very important.

For a long time my only reply was to stare at her intensely. I tried to make it look as if I was gathering my thoughts, but I knew that I really didn't have any answer to that question.

"It feels… empty," I clarified, at last.

Dr. Schuman opened her mouth to, probably, ask for more specificity when a small timer placed on the desk directly to her right rang sharply. She reached over and switched it off.

"I'll see you at the same time tomorrow," she said, extending her hand, which I took in mine. After a brief, awkward, downwards motion, I released it and walked back out the door and into the waiting room.

The waiting room was full of dour people. Some were flipping through the boring magazines which litter doctors' offices. Some were playing on their phones. Some even stared out into space, entirely motionless. I passed them and continued on to my car, turned the engine over after several unsuccessful attempts, and began the drive back to my apartment.

Dr. Schuman always did her best, and I appreciated the effort, but these sessions did not seem to be progressing towards anything. I had not experienced the epiphany which the layman seems to think is the goal of psychotherapy. I assumed the fault lay with myself.

The radio was playing a debate between a Christian and an atheist over the existence of God. I listened, found myself unconvinced by either side and switched it off. Afterwards, there was nothing with which to occupy myself but the white snow and monotonous rhythm of the traffic. My mind was blank until I arrived home.

I didn't like the way my apartment looked from the outside. I couldn't really tell you why; I just didn't like it.

When I stepped through the door my girlfriend was waiting. She kissed me on the cheek and asked how my day had gone. I shrugged and told her that nothing had happened. She told me that something must have happened. Something is always happening. She repeated her question. I paused for a minute, thought hard, and replied that I had gone to my appointment with Dr. Schuman after work. She asked me how that had been and I told her that it was fine.

She accepted this and we ate dinner together, mostly in silence. Afterwards we watched TV for a while and went to bed. We had sex and then set the alarm clock and went to sleep.

"How are you feeling today?" Dr Schuman asked me.

I shrugged.

"I feel empty," I told her.

"And what does 'empty' feel like?" Dr Schuman asked.

I told her that it felt like nothing.

"You've been feeling that way a lot since your father died, haven't you?"

I nodded. "I haven't been feeling much since then, I guess."

I could tell that she was about to ask for further clarification when a strange expression crossed her face and she seemed to change her mind.

"Have you heard of philosophical zombies?" she asked me.

"No," I replied.

"A philosophical zombie looks exactly like a human being from the outside and displays all of the characteristics of one. They eat and talk and answer questions, but they're not conscious. Hence: zombies."

I nodded.

"You, Philip, are not a philosophical zombie. You're feeling something right now."

This was a joke. I laughed a little.

"Would you know if I wasn't?" I asked her.

"Probably not," she shrugged. "The whole point of the thought experiment is that they act exactly like a normal person."

"Interesting," I said.

It was interesting.

The next day at work my boss yelled at me, but there didn't really seem to be that much anger behind it. It almost seemed like a chore to him, something he just had to get out of the way. There was this queer emptiness behind his eyes, like nothing was there.

I told him I was sorry for misfiling my report and that it wouldn't happen again. He walked away.

Karen from accounting asked me if I was okay. He seemed pretty mad, she said.

I told her that everything was fine. He wasn't really that mad; I could tell.

She left with a concerned look on her face, but I could see that there was nothing behind it.

My girlfriend wasn't happy when I got home. Apparently, her sister had said something insulting to her aunt, despite knowing that the two of them (my girlfriend and her aunt) were close. They weren't speaking now (my girlfriend and her sister that is). I told her that I was sorry and she said it was okay, that she just needed to vent. I nodded and went back to typing on my laptop.

I had set myself up in front of the TV which was off. I didn't want it to distract me, but since the conversation with my girlfriend had already done that, and since I needed a break anyway I turned it on.

The President was giving a speech about a mass shooting. Twelve people had died. He was devastated. He offered his deepest condolences. He promised that "something will be done." But there was nothing behind it; I could tell.

That night, as my girlfriend and I lay next to each other, falling asleep, I looked at her and wondered what she was feeling.

Maybe she's not feeling anything I thought to myself. I looked into her eyes. She looked back. I saw nothing there.

"Is something wrong?" she asked me, after this continued for some seconds.

Dr. Schuman's words echoed in my mind: "They eat and talk and answer questions, but they're not conscious."

After I didn't respond, she put her hand on my arm.

"Are you okay?" she persisted.

"Yeah, I'm fine," I told her.

That night, I dreamt of zombies.

My next session with Dr. Schuman wasn't until the following week. Nothing happened in the interim, really. She asked me how I was doing, and I told her that I still felt empty.

"It might be time to try other methods, Phillip."

She took out a piece of paper and scribbled something on it.

"This is a prescription. I think it might help. Give it a shot and if nothing changes in a week or so, we'll know that it's not for you."

I reached out and took it.

"Thanks," I said.

On the way home, I stopped at the drugstore and tried to fill the prescription for the first time. They told me it wouldn't be ready for a few days.

My girlfriend told me she was going to visit her parents and would be back later in the week. I said goodbye and she walked out the door.

That night, I dreamt of nothing.

The next morning the TV was playing the Presidential Debate. One candidate promised equality. The other responded by promising a balanced budget. The first said that the country wasn't doing enough for the poor. The second insisted that we couldn't allow rogue nations to acquire weapons of mass destruction.

And never the twain did meet.

Work was not going well. Fixing my mistake with the report was taking longer than I anticipated and Doug wasn't happy about it. He wanted the corrected report on his desk by the end of the day, but I knew I wasn't going to be able to do that.

I told this to Karen, and that worried expression crossed her face again.

The same one.

Exactly the same.

"What are you going to do?" she asked.

I shrugged. Somehow, I wasn't too concerned.

When I brought what I had managed to finish to Doug at the end of the day he was furious. I'd never seen him so angry. His eyes were wide and people on the other side of the office could no doubt hear his tirade.

But I remained calm. I knew there was nothing behind it.

The next night, my girlfriend returned and asked me how my day had gone. I told her that I had been tired. She dropped the plate she was holding and spun around to look at me. I pushed past her to retrieve the broom and dustpan, then bent down to begin sweeping up the shards she had created.

"What do you mean you were fired?" she asked in a shaking voice.

"I mean that I don't work for Walton Chemical anymore," I told her.

She knelt and put her arms on my shoulders, stopping me from continuing with my work.

"How are we going to pay the rent, Philip? What about food and car payments and... medical expenses?" she guided my hand to her stomach. I was confused.

"Medical expenses?"

In response, she held up a pregnancy test. It showed positive. I took and examined it quizzically.

"You're pregnant."

She gripped my shoulders tighter. "Is that all you have to say? After losing your job and finding out you're going to be a father?"

I continued sweeping.

"Well?!" she yelled, shaking me. This was annoying.

"Could you move your foot a little?" I poked at her left shoe with the handle of the broom.

"What the fuck is wrong with you?" her voice was rising in volume. It was beginning to hurt my ears.

"There's ceramic on the floor," I murmured, gently moving her foot to get at the piece of plate trapped beneath it.

A loud *crack* reverberated around the room as her hand connected with my cheek. I was surprised at how much it hurt.

"Why'd you do that?" I asked, holding the side of my face.

"To wake you up, Phillip! Jesus Christ! We have to talk about this. We have to *do something*! We can't support ourselves on what I bring home, especially not with a baby on the way."

"So abort it," I shrugged.

She looked as if she were preparing to hit me again when, instead, a resigned expression crossed her face, and she stepped out the door.

I went back to sweeping.

The next day my prescription was ready. The pharmacist handed me a small, colorless bottle. Later, I took my first dose, with food as the bottle had instructed. Though both Dr. Schumann and the internet suggested that no effects would be apparent for several days at least, I instantly felt something shift within my mind.

I was growing to hate my own cooking. So, the next day, instead of making myself food as I normally would, I ate all three meals at the McDonald's down the road. It was hardly more expensive.

When I remarked on this to the cashier he just nodded and handed me my order number.

It was usually a quiet place, but as I entered the building for the third time, I saw a little girl sitting in the middle of the floor and crying loudly.

I crouched in front of her.

"Does anyone know who this girl's parents are?" I asked.

No response.

I spent a few minutes just looking at her, examining the way her tear-stained cheeks rose and fell, how her little chest danced erratically back and forth.

The salty droplets traced rivers and valleys on her skin. They reminded me of rain whipped against a car window. I thought of the canals on Mars.

Still, no one came to help. After a while, her voice grew hoarse.

She looked for all the world like a broken android.

I was walking to McDonald's again when a loud *pop* drew my attention. A man with a gun was walking away from a female figure lying on the sidewalk. Blood leaked from its mouth and onto the ground.

Many people walked past her. A fair number were even forced to step over her torso or legs in order to continue onwards. Yet, nobody made any attempt to render aid or stop the murderer as he evaporated into the night. In fact, nobody other than me even acknowledged the dying woman.

I knelt and clasped her hand in mine, looking deeply into her eyes as the life drained out of them. I wanted to see if I could find the instant when they passed from humanity to objectivity.

She smiled at me as I attempted this, as if she were glad to be of service.

Eventually, it became clear that she had died with that smile still upon her face.

I never did figure it out.

The next day was the election. That night, as the results were announced, I mused vaguely that I had forgotten to vote. It was at a dreary bar on the other side of town that I watched the tallies from the various states trickle in.

The candidate of change pulled ahead, and I felt an electric wave of excitement wash over the room. It was quenched suddenly when the candidate of the people took the lead and held it until the end.

As the victory and concession speeches played, I saw anger and confusion explode from the people sitting across from me. Their faces radiated frank horror.

Then, a deafening *bang* sounded directly to my left and I turned to see the man sitting next to me slumped in the chair, his recently discharged gun held in a limp fist. Blood trickled to the floor.

Then, another *bang* rang out, and another and another until most everyone in the bar met the same fate, and by the same means. The few who remained calmly raised their glasses back to their lips and continued to drain them one sip at a time.

The floor was slick with blood and viscera.

I got up, only to slip and tumble back down. I had fallen next to a young woman with a self-inflicted gunshot wound to her chest.

She reached out to me, and I put my hand on her cheek, whispering soothing words.

"It's going to be okay," I told her, again and again, stroking the side of her face.

"No. It's not," she whispered back.

I almost thought that I was witnessing the destruction of a human soul, amidst the mire and blood, in the bullet's wake. She almost succeeded in convincing me that there was such a thing to destroy.

As I looked into her dimming eyes, I saw their evaporating existence as nothing more than a facade wrapped around the unyielding void at the bottom of all human life. But, still, her heartrending final gasps and bloody caresses, which I received with gravity, were truly lifelike.

Later that night the President-Elect gave a speech about the incident. He promised that "something will be done," and offered his deepest condolences, but there was nothing behind them. I could tell; I could always tell.

Every time I visited the library that room was closed. At 3 PM, no earlier and no later, I would walk up to the librarian and politely ask if the room was open today.

"Not today," she would tell me.

The day after the election, however, she smiled at me instead of giving her customary rejection.

"Yes, today it is open."

I nodded sagely.

"Take me there, please."

She obliged, taking up a lantern and leading me into the space behind the librarian's desk. We moved slowly, hobbled by her ancient legs.

"Why, today, is it open?" I inquired.

"All things closed must open eventually, elsewise they are not really closed, they do not exist."

This was a reasonable answer.

"I am not open," I told her.

"Presumably, you have bled at some point?"

"And if I hadn't?"

"Naturally, you would not exist."

This too was satisfactory.

We came to the room, and she left the lantern, the only light source available to me. For a long time, it was the two of us and nothing. Then, a ghastly scream began to echo in the dim chamber. For several seconds it ricocheted wildly, as one would expect in a place with narrow walls. And then the echoes became more and more distant, as if the walls were drawing further and further apart. At that instant, the room was flooded with an unbearable light, against which I screwed my eyes shut, to no avail. It pierced my eyelids like rice paper and became more and more painful until I feared it would precipitate blindness.

And, strange it was, strange indeed, that in the instant blindness appeared certain it came not. Spinning and blue, and green, red and yellow, and indeed all the many particularities of human ocularity came instead, laughing and crying and smelling gorgeous. An eternity passed like this, and then another in reverse. All of this, of course, passed through my eyes, but then, vision inverted itself and I stepped outside the vantage of these globular impediments and saw them instead, especially the pupils, and what handsome blackness they were!

I saw them fold in on themselves, drawing the rest of my formerly useless body along with them, back into the nonexistence which gives rise to us all. Free, finally, from corporeal entrapment, the humor of it all became very clear, and the visions resolved into the form of a woman quite familiar to me: Dr. Schuman.

"And how are you *feeling*?" she asked.

"I feel nothing," I told her.

I ran my hand over Dr. Schuman's body, and at every flinch, every shudder, I suppressed the urge to laugh. She smoothly undid my belt, with quiet efficiency. And then, the rhythm of the act, normally so primal, so *human*, began to grow metronomic and hysterically *precise*.

She let out soundless gasps and arched in perfect stillness, suffering nameless, horrific ecstasy. Her sweet nothings, whispered directly into my ear, were most funny of all, for I couldn't tell whether these responses were born of passion or programming.

Images of violence and savagery flitted behind my eyes, all of them hilarious, putative outrages upon the body. And then, mangled machines: twisted, broken, unused.

Everything dissolved into phantasmagoric splinters, swirling in cosmic uncertainty, and, of course, as above, so below. I couldn't keep it all straight: man, machine, and morality.

Severed limbs, rusted engines, brains, and motherboards. All of this appeared in my field of vision superimposed upon Dr. Schuman's body, still motionless and writhing. And, finally, I was able to stand it no more and the sound
of my laughter exploded against the wide walls as I was forced to wonder,
what difference is there between these things?

forgetting To how I talk am. was Right that?

and yoU aLl; --

It's funny, isn't it?

w0r ds c1n

Ho w

 b**E** so broke,n

St il**L** and so und3rstan;

dable. l1k3 SomUch intHat way**P**eo ple they are Like you
aNd like

ME

A Widow's Field Guide to Fungi

Marissa van Uden

FLESHY TOOTH *Phellodon violascens*

Fruiting body: Flesh is pallid (whitish fawn) with mealy complexion. Shallowly depressed in the center. Many tooth fungi are two layered and change form as they grow. Some individuals will fuse together with others or even engulf them entirely.

Habitat and range: Some tooth fungi grow on the ground, some on trees, but others grow from his gums, where they gleam (yellow) when he smiles in the moonlight, in that way that makes your hand tremble. Those teeth have taken so many sharp little bites out of you, you can't remember what it's like to wake up without dread. Teeth are what you think of whenever you hear his car engine winding its way up the long driveway.

Odor: Disagreeable, especially in the mornings.

Spore print: Leaves bluish-purple marks with greenish yellow margins.

Edibility: Some have been made very ill by them.

SHAGGY SCARLET CUP *Microstoma floccosa*

Fruiting body: Outer surface smooth, bald in center with zone of coarse white hairs, unkempt, grown conspicuously long.

Habitat: His armchair (brown), the leather finely cracked and worn smooth in places, just the cap of white hair showing. You stand behind him, willing yourself to do it.

Texture: Surprisingly little resistance to a hammer blow. Sticky-wet when caved in. The inner parts glisten jelly-like.

Veil: Bright red.

Spore print: Stains dark when dried.

Edibility: Bitter with a lingering sweetness.

FALLEN STARS *Astraeus hygrometricus*

Fruiting body: A globose cap with nearly colorless skin, dull to translucent, opening outward into starlike rays. Six or seven bone ridges form "teeth" around an apical opening. Large central depression with bright red petals where the skin has sloughed back around a gelatinous interior (whitish gray with yellow shadow).

Habitat and range: A shard of bone (bright white) has fallen onto the carpet beside the new stain (cinnamon red). It shines in the light from his mother's old lamp. She gave the lamp to you as a wedding gift and also as an apology. Sorry for him. Sorry for what I bore and set upon you. Maybe she bought a lamp for herself too, to celebrate being rid of him.

Edibility: Not even a mother can stomach this one.

VISCID VIOLET CORT *Cortinarius iodes*

Fruiting body: Pallid, slimy, and tacky, with violet-purplish gills becoming rust-brown. Face: smooth and paling at the lips. Nose: yellowish. Mouth: yawning wide but now blessedly silent. Fists: once hard and quick but opening so gently in death, resting on his lap with palms up, fingers splayed. Eyes: accusing.

Habitat and Range: A quiet room, only the sounds of peaceful birdsong weaving in through the windows.

Veil: Into the fire pit with the dress.

Odor: Increasingly unbearable.

DEVIL'S URN *Urnula craterium*

Fruiting body: Large with heavy, slack limbs. Flesh spongy or even rubbery at first, seeming almost gelatinous after a couple days in this midsummer heat. Outer surface grayish lilac with alternating zones of shiny smooth and matted hair. Attracts loud buzzing flies (black).

Odor: Distinctive and highly disagreeable; often results in vomiting, diarrhea, and cramps.

Habitat and Range: Migrates from leather armchair to the carpet.

Veil: An old sheet

Edibility: Unknown but too slimy to recommend.

Spore print: Salmon pink when dragged across faded gray carpet, a few feet at a time. You can do it. You're strong.

DEADMAN'S FINGERS *Xylaria polymorpha*

Fruiting body: Sausage-shaped, conspicuously clasping. Sticky outer layer peels back like tissue paper. Just underneath, the muscle appears shiny (grayish blue). Remember how it used to push you up against walls, slam doors so hard the house would shake, punch through the drywall to leave dark explosive holes.

Habitat: Under decaying wood and soil in coniferous woods, partially buried. Right next to the big rock covered in yellow lichen, where you were standing when you told him your sister was sick and you had to go to her, and he said *no* he needed you here. He would not feed the animals if you left him alone out here for even a few days. Fuck your sister and her dramas, he said in that hard little voice of his.

Veil: Cold damp soil.

Spore print: Covered over to leave no trace.

Edibility: Edible to worms and beetles and ants. Don't forget to call your sister.

DESTROYING ANGEL *Aminita virosa*

Fruiting body: The Destroying Angel, a strikingly glorious and beautiful species, may appear dull and bruised when mishandled, but brightens again quickly in the right environment. She is often found under old oaks or larch trees, sitting on mossy logs with her sister, or tending the garden and feeding the animals. When near the rock with yellow lichen, the Destroying Angel's surface appears unusually smooth and expressionless, yet the interior shines with rose-gold resilience.

Veil: Made of long membranous memories, but they will fade with time.

Habitat and range: Anywhere you want, now.

Edibility: Deadly.

I-90

Pamela Durgin

ALICE DIDN'T HAVE any paid time off, and her boss was a dick.

"Sure, you can have a day off. I can get plenty of people to take your shift, but I may not want you back…your decision."

The featureless highway allowed her to immerse herself in worry. The November wind howled, flattening endless gold grasses in elaborate patterns and stirring up vortices of dust from the roadside. The sky had been low and gray all day. The twilight, a sliver of purple on the horizon before the dark settled.

By the time Alice pulled into the rest stop it was close to midnight. Barely illuminated, the building was an outpost on the edge of the cold, black prairie. She had been driving for hours, trying to push through to Nevada and, maybe, save her shitty job.

She climbed out of her Toyota truck, pulling her coat tight. The drone and jabber of something loose on the truck still in her ears. Snow was in the forecast.

Two parking lots, one on each side of the building, were vacant except for a small pickup truck, almost identical to hers. The yellow truck was in the far lot on the other side of the cinderblock structure. Alice's truck was the same color and roughly the same model year. Even though it was ten years old, it was new to her. She was driving it home from her parents' house in Illinois.

"Just to help you out a bit," her mom had said.

A reference to her inability to help herself.

Alice had admitted to her mom that she totaled her car after a long shift. She didn't tell her that her shift at the casino had been fueled by crank along with a few shots - to take the edge off - before heading home. Her usual routine but this time she misjudged a turn and clipped a light pole, destroying the front end of her decrepit Datsun. Only, in the story she told her mom, someone else ran a red light and hit her.

Her mom pressed her on whether she was hurt, she wasn't, and then instantly offered up her brother's truck.

"A loaner. I'm sure he won't mind."

Wayne was away at school. He was the responsible one, the one they pinned their hopes on. Alice was seven years older, and ten times more fucked up. She was twenty-seven and had tried and failed at community college three times before landing in Wendover, Nevada. Alice was waitressing at The Nugget Casino while she figured things out.

Her mom bought her a plane ticket to Chicago where her dad picked her up. His silence and clenched jaw making it clear that she was still a disappointment. This wasn't surprising. They had fought bitterly until she left home at eighteen.

Alice had started up the stairs to put her bag in her old room, when her mom stopped her and said, "Oh honey, I think you'll be more comfortable at the Best Western. We've already paid for a room. That way you can get an early start." Her mom, ending her statement on a higher note in her effort to sound casual and upbeat. Alice knew they were both writing her off.

"I thought I'd stay in my old room and, you know, watch tv with you or watch a movie or talk or something..."

"It's just so...tense between you and your dad...it's better this way."

The truck was a gesture, as was the last-minute gift of a bright blue scarf and stocking cap her mom had crocheted. A way for her mom to help and protect her, without acknowledging the stand-off her relationship with her father had become. Her mom had long ago given up trying to negotiate a peace be-tween them. Her and her father were hostages to their own stubbornness.

Wayne didn't care about the truck. He would probably just shrug, dis-tracted by maintaining his overachievements. Sports and business clubs and academic excellence and who knows what. He moved smoothly through the world, never a ripple of rebellion.

A sharp clink brought her back and she looked up at the ragged flag as it flapped and fluttered, shredded by the near-constant gale. A high-pitched ringing from the pole with no discernable source cut through the remnants of road noise and dull hurt and anger still fuzzing her brain. Cold, biting wind scoured her face. She pulled the scarf tight around her neck, tugged the hat down over her ears.

The drone and rattle of her truck had worked its way so thoroughly into her body, she carried it with her. Wind thundered out of the darkness and bat-tered the building. Ringing the chains and padlocks that secured the vending machines and maintenance closets. Finding cracks, openings, and poorly se-cured doors through which the gale whistled and groaned. After hours in the rattling cab of the truck, she thought perhaps the sounds were in her head, prickling and slapping her anxiety into full wakefulness. She was exhausted but the constant assault of discord made her buzz with a need for vigilance but no energy to maintain it.

The crosswinds had been so fierce, the small truck shook and juddered, bucking and seeming at times to lift off of the pavement when, just for a mo-ment, she felt a complete loss of control before being returned to the road. The tingle of adrenaline pricked her arms, her hands white knuckled on the steer-ing wheel. Though it felt good to be on solid ground, the cacophony of sound against the desolate landscape was unnerving. She shivered.

As Alice approached the building, a bug zapper buzzed, misfiring on bits of brush and dirt, blowing into the small "Convenience Center": a cement slab bordered by a block wall with a bulletin board and drinking fountain on one side and vending machines on the other. Two sides were open to separate parking lots and darkness beyond, serving as a wind tunnel and a poorly lit passageway from dark to darker.

Restrooms were in the structure behind the vending machines. The bulletin board, "Information Center," was screwed into the cement block wall. A map, stapled so many times the road and town names were obscured in places, flapped in the relentless wind. An unnerving number of missing persons flyers fluttered, overlapping and faded. Alice couldn't help but pause to look at the board. Most of the photos were of young women, smiling into the camera during happier times. But one showed a girl, probably late teens, looking directly at the viewer, her eyes were haunted, resigned to a fate off camera. Alice looked away.

She glanced at the battered vending machine with ancient looking packs of cheddar and peanut butter crackers, Milk Duds, and off-brand cookies. A dusty shoe print stamped on the front. The soda machine was partially lit, buzzing. Faded logos marked the selections: Fresca, Tab, Coca-Cola, and Root Beer spelled out in sharpie. Alice noted the coffee dispenser on her way to the bathroom.

Before going into the restroom, she took a last look at her truck doppelgänger huddled at the base of the light pole as if seeking protection from the dark surrounding it. She had seen many of them over the years, even the same color. They must have made millions of them. She followed the arrow below WOMEN, pushing the heavy metal door open with a clang.

The restroom was surprisingly large, six stalls down one side of the room and three sinks opposite. It hit her as soon as she entered. The distinct smell of vomit. She knew it well, having spent too many hours hunched over the toilet.

Alice felt a twinge of commiseration. She knew the feeling.

The wind whined and moaned, pushing in through the vents. Under the discord of wind and metal, she heard an intermittent sound, a stifled sob or cough, coming from the last stall. The truck owner.

Was she alone? Maybe someone else was in the men's room.

Alice stopped at the first sink. Polished metal reflected her pale face and smudged eyes. She pushed escaping dark strands behind her ears, and up into her stocking cap, annoyed that she couldn't seem to keep her hair out of her face. Her puffy features framed by the bright blue of her hat, jarred her. Her face was cherubic on good days, now it was just swollen. She felt like shit but at least she wasn't sick. Pulling her scarf out of the way, she washed her hands and splashed cold water on her face. A misguided effort to shock herself into wakefulness.

Rustling, the distinct sound of crying.

"Hey, are you ok? Do you need help?"

Alice took two steps towards the stall but stopped, not wanting to be weird about it. Silence. She quickly went into the stall closest to the door, suddenly embarrassed. The sounds continued but were drowned out by the howling of the wind, the clank and rattle of what she didn't know. Seemed like there were way too many loose parts, untethered and on the verge of a catastrophic failure. This same anxiety plagued her constantly back at home, the drugs and alcohol keeping it to a smolder. But this trip, the family visit, driving the truck - small, insubstantial, rattling across the country - unmoored her in a way she hadn't experienced before. Despite, or maybe because of, the commiserate soul three stalls down, Alice was overwhelmed by loneliness and a bleak inevitability. But then again, she always felt this way coming off of a binge.

Coffee, even shitty watery coffee, would help. She wouldn't be able to get any more speed until Wendover.

Alice felt relief leaving the crying woman in the bathroom. Not that she didn't understand. She had been there many times. Even now, she felt like crying.

The road was as desolate as before except now she was wide awake, even jittery. The potency of rest stop dispenser coffee surprised her. The truck's headlights were overwhelmed by the job in front of them. A vast landscape of black, no moon, no other vehicles, no roadside lighting from a town, gas station, or truck stop.

She was at sea in the badlands.

The wind was howling, banging, and she pictured a creature crouched on the roof trying to peel it off the truck. Whistling through the many crevices and poorly sealed windows.

She turned the radio on. Static. Spinning the dial, she landed on a station playing 70s country western. "Ode to Billie Joe" tumbled from the tiny speakers. She couldn't help but sing along even though the dark ballad further depressed her. Static overwhelmed the signal as Johnny Cash started into "Ring of Fire." Keeping her eyes on the road, she turned the dial again. Static, with some kind of trumpeting. Taps maybe.

Just then she spotted a light out in the darkness off in the brush. *A fire?* She had heard of vicious wind-driven grass fires gobbling up acres of land, consuming anything not able to get out of its way. She had seen them along the highways out west. This was different. It was stationary, perhaps a structure. She couldn't tell the relative size. The dark and her fatigue telescoped everything, as though viewed in a fun house mirror.

The fire was still ahead and far off to the right like a vertical totem. She eased her foot off the gas pedal. Drawing up closer she saw that it seemed to be moving. She realized it was a human figure. As she passed, the blazing effigy raised its arm as if in greeting, or farewell. The rattle of her truck intensified, hitting a washboard section of the battered highway.

Alice stared into the rear-view mirror, unsure she was really seeing a burning figure scampering up to the edge of the road, as if it just wanted a ride.

"What the fuck!"

She pulled over, the truck shuddering to a stop. Twisting on the bench seat, she had full view of the roadside. The darkness lay across the prairie, and she saw nothing but black beyond the faint glow of her brake lights.

The flame was snuffed out and she doubted whether she had actually seen it.

Uneasy turning her back to whatever was out there, Alice shifted in her seat, her foot slipping off the clutch. The truck lurched and stalled.

"Fuck!"

Stepping back onto the clutch, she cranked the key and the engine caught. She eased the clutch out staring in the rear view, not wanting anything to sneak up on her. There were no other vehicles on the road. Alice wished for the usual truck traffic, or some other signs of normalcy, but with the storm imminent she assumed the drivers were hunkered down at one of the truck stops along the highway. Accelerating, putting distance between herself and whatever was along the road, calmed her. Just as she shifted into fourth, she caught movement over her right shoulder. Turning to look, she could only see darkness, but she sensed a displacement, a rippling like the refraction off hot pavement.

Fatigue, and shitty coffee.

It persisted. It looked as if something was running alongside the truck. More an impression than a vision, it was grasping at the side as if to jump in back. Panicked again, she stomped on the accelerator. The truck rattled, whined. A meaty thunk, then slap, slap, slap along the length of the truck.

Alice screamed.

Then just road noise, truck rattle, wind, and the laboring of the engine.

For over an hour, Alice had been working her way back and forth across the AM band, calming herself by focusing on the waves of country western, unhinged talk radio, classic rock and static. Alice had almost convinced herself she was having some kind of withdrawals.

The pitch black of the road ahead was interrupted by the hazard lights of a semi-truck pulled off to the side. She moved into the fast lane to avoid side-swiping it, easing off the accelerator.

As she passed, she was surprised to see the yellow truck from the rest stop on the side of the road. *Maybe a different one?* The semi was nosed up to the back of it and there was a man on the far side bending down. He was wearing a cowboy hat and a plaid shirt, and it looked like he was struggling with something. She wondered if he was trying to jack up the Toyota to fix a flat. The truck cab was bright purple and there was some kind of script on the side that she couldn't make out.

Alice didn't think anyone had passed her and she would have remembered her doppelgänger...or maybe not. She was so tired. Maybe she had dozed off while driving. The blasts of adrenaline and bad coffee were fucking with her perception. *The other truck had still been in the lot of the rest area when she left...or was it? Maybe the woman had been left there.* She thought of the missing person posters again.

The vehicles receded in her rear view.

The massive sign for Truck Inn truck stop towered over the lot where thirty or so rigs were parked. Lot lights shown into the night sky causing the glow Alice had spotted several minutes before she came to the off-ramp. She turned into the front of the station and followed the CAR signs to a gas pump. As she turned off the ignition and picked up her wallet, she thought she should look to see if maybe she had run over something. Maybe it hit the side of the truck before tumbling off into the grass, and in her fucked-up state she imagined the rest. Her stomach clenched thinking of a hapless prairie dog or coyote. But there was no sign of a dent or fur or blood.

The rigs filled the huge lot behind the Truck Inn Convenience Center. Harsh lighting muted the colors. Blue, gold, white, red, orange, black; some sparkly, some pearlescent. Some with graphics: flames, Yosemite Sam, screeching eagles, and script declaring love for Angie or Bella or Connie or Jesus, scripture, and patriotism. Despite the cold, people walked around in front of the semis, lingering to examine the trucks or to smoke, plumes of tobacco and breath fluttering up and around bulldog hood ornaments. Women wandered between the rigs, some of them clearly drivers and some more likely sex workers. A small city, temporary, but comforting. A beacon in the vast howling darkness.

Alice entered the brightly lit convenience center, loud with conversation. Laughter competed with the blaring of the TV, a meteorologist somberly reciting the latest forecast of extreme weather: imminent blizzard conditions. The loudspeaker intermittently broke in to call a mechanic to the back bay or a driver to pick up his order. The vast interior housed a deli counter and small cafe. Toiletries, stereos, flares, air fresheners, oil, crow bars, tire thumpers where all arranged in the logic of need and impulse sales.

In the corner a service counter for truck parts and repairs was doing a brisk business. After paying for her gas and coffee, Alice lingered, comforted by the light, small talk, and normalcy. She stood off to the side observing the flow of people while she finished her cup of coffee. The brief respite from the rattle and buzz of the truck cab cleared her head a bit but didn't lift the fatigue. It was too deep. After a few minutes, reminded again by the TV weatherman that she needed to make it back home, she returned to her Toyota, still parked at the gas pump.

While she was inside, the semi had pulled up to a diesel pump two aisles over. The truck she had seen along the road. In the blast of gas station lighting, she could fully appreciate the garish sparkly purple paint. Elaborate white script under the driver side window read "BEN." As Alice stood pumping gas, she noticed movement in the small port hole window of the sleeper as if something was pressed against it, fogging the glass for a moment.

Loudspeakers blared announcements: "Rich R your order is ready" "Ken to the service bay, Ken to the service bay."

It was 2:40 a.m. and Alice's mind was numb, her baseline anxiety droning, reminding her of her troubles. Her stomach roiled from too much caffeine and not enough food. She rubbed her face occasionally just to get the blood flowing. She would probably have to stop and sleep for a few hours but wanted to try and beat the storm.

As she stared at the purple semi, lost in her thoughts calculating the time to Wyoming, again she noticed a shape pressed up to the window of the sleeper. A light flesh tone, fogged glass, the impression of blinking, bugged out eyes, a smudge of gray across the face. Dark hair and a flash of bright blue as the shape shifted. Not sure what she was seeing, she tried to fit it into something logical but couldn't. She sensed a plea, desperation.

A man came around the side of the truck, watching her. He was stocky and wore a plaid shirt and faded jeans. A cowboy hat cast shadow over his face, the lenses of his glasses reflecting the gas station lighting. A slight smile on his face as he stared at her.

Her gas nozzle clicked off, making her jump. Shaken, she screwed the gas cap on and hurriedly climbed into her Toyota. As she pulled away, she watched the truck driver in her rearview mirror. He swiveled his head, following the yellow truck, before slowly climbing back into his cab.

The heater pumped warm air from the small dashboard into the cab, making her drowsy. She cracked the window to blast some cold air into her face. The truck shimmied as wind gusts jerked the steering wheel in her hands. Static and snatches of conjunto on the radio. The darkness all around. No other traffic. A light dusting of snow started to swirl out of the darkness, making her press down on the accelerator. She was trying to outpace the storm, willing the dawn to come. Her watch read 3:45. She needed to sleep.

REST AREA NEXT EXIT. Alice pulled into the lot and parked on the far side, under the only working lot light. Now the snow was coming down harder, flurries carried on the wind. She could just make out a cinderblock building and the ubiquitous rest stop flagpole. *They all look the same.* Pulling her coat tight and digging under the seat for her mittens, she coiled her scarf around her and pulled the stocking cap down over her hair. She had to pee. She hadn't eaten since the day before and her stomach roiled.

She headed for the bathrooms. Once inside the bright lights shocked her awake, and she ran to the last stall. As she pushed the door open, she vomited. The rush of hot acid made it into the toilet, mostly. She barely caught her breath before another hot stream burned her throat.

She was in the presence of a void, a black hole drawing her in. She was utterly alone. She put her cheek, hot with fever, against the frigid tiled wall and slid down onto the toilet, so sick, not caring that vomit now coated her pants and back. She started to cry.

CLANG, wind whistled through the open vent, water running.

"Hey, are you ok? Do you need help?"

Alice stopped, stunned by the familiarity of the voice, putting her hand over her mouth, unable to move. After a few moments, rustling, someone peeing. Clattering, clinking of metal, the wind, the door clanging.

Emerging to an empty bathroom, Alice stumbled back out to the truck, attempting to flee the ghosts, the void.

The snow was coming down harder and the cab of the truck was frigid. She could smell herself, reeking and sour. She drove as long as she could, then pulled to the side of I-90, turning off the engine and watching her breath gather and disperse in small clouds. The truck rocked, groaned, and creaked in the wind, the sound of a thousand lost souls pushing and prodding.

A small orange light appeared far off in the darkness. Alice rolled down the side window. The blast of cold and snow like a slap across her face. She stumbled out of the truck and walked to the edge of the highway. The glow amongst the swirling of snowflakes was like a star emerging from another galaxy. Growing larger as it approached from the prairie, the sounds that followed her continued, perhaps on the wind, perhaps she carried them within her.

Clatter and clang of metal on metal, flagpole or padlocks or her truck, her reality shaking loose coming apart. All familiar but other, alternate. The lonesome, mournful cry of the wind rose and fell. Like a scream lapsing into a whimper, the screamer going hoarse with exhaustion. Alice stared and listened. Words, pleading, sirening up into a wail carried on the wind.

The light moved closer. She knew she had been here before. The light now clearly moving, gliding, a form with limbs, flames, so close the heat melted snowflakes as they sought to cling to Alice. Fire pulled at a crusted coat, pants, mittens. The clothing sluiced off in fiery sheets, the skin blistering, duct tape peeling away taking flesh with it, hair and stocking cap curling and fluttering away, embers mixing into a swirl of snowflakes.

Alice stood transfixed as the figure raised a limb, black and cracked, towards her. The combustion of skin, fat, and muscle glowed and smoked. Alice felt the heat of it, the smell: sweet, nauseating, and inevitable. She reached out in recognition just as airbrakes from a purple semi hissed the rig to a stop behind her small yellow truck.

The Customer is Always Lost

Karley Pardue

THE YELLOW BAG of cat food was eleven dollars cheaper. Liz still wasn't sold though. For the last five minutes, she'd compared two different brands. Tito, her domestic shorthair, was used to a pampered life. All the budget cuts and recent "restructuring" around the office, however, meant Liz's paycheck could only stretch so far. Cats probably didn't even know the difference between the yellow bag and the luxury brand. The ingredients were mostly the same. Both had happy felines on the front. The contrast was in the price, and cats didn't understand the economy. Eleven dollars would be worth it. Liz grabbed a sixteen-pound bag and put it at the bottom of her cart.

One of the wheels squeaked as she went past the entertainment section. The stereos played "Stay" by Rihanna and she hummed along while choosing a pack of batteries. The music faded as she walked into the grocery department. Liz had a list, but she went up and down every aisle just in case she missed something. She grabbed a pint of mint ice-cream as a treat.

Liz filled the cart with supplies for her party on Friday: cases of IPAs, bottles of wine, snacks, and dips. Luckily, the chips were on sale, and she snagged four bags for the price of two. She hadn't heard back from the usual "Need anything at the store?" text to her roommate. When Liz checked her phone, it was dead. Maybe she forgot to charge it or something.

Her cart rattled as she wheeled into the line for self-checkout. She hated waiting for an employee to help her. They all looked like they'd rather be anywhere else—completely zoned out. Whatever happened to customer service? Eventually, she scanned her things, paid, and moved on. A red-haired employee checked her bags and receipt on the way out, and then she walked through the sliding doors marked EXIT.

The yellow bag of cat food was eleven dollars cheaper. Liz still wasn't sold though.

She grabbed the brand she usually bought and looked at the ingredients. Then she looked at the ones on the yellow bag. They were pretty much the same. The cats on the front looked happy enough with their respective meals. Tito probably wouldn't even care or notice if she saved some money. She put a sixteen-pound bag at the bottom of her cart.

Liz should've grabbed a different cart because the squeaky wheel on hers was annoying as hell. Too late now. She went past the stereos, blaring "Stay" by Rihanna, and grabbed batteries. The song was everywhere, and it wasn't bad, but she was a little tired of the repetitive piano. She went out of hearing range to find food for the party on Friday. Liz stocked up on mint ice-cream, booze, and snacks. The chips were on sale—two for the price of one. She couldn't see if her roommate needed anything because her phone was dead. She paid at self-checkout, got her receipt looked over by a dull-eyed redhead, and left.

The yellow bag of cat food was eleven dollars cheaper. Liz still wasn't sold though.

She dimly remembered buying a sixteen-pound bag of food the other day. Why did she need another one? Was Tito not eating it? She should probably call her roommate to double-check in case this was like that time they'd ended up with five tubs of mayo in the fridge. Unfortunately, her phone was dead for some reason. Liz grabbed an eight-pound bag of the expensive brand she usually bought. She might be set on cat food for the next month at this point.

"Stay" by Rihanna played in the distance, but she didn't want to go near it. Hadn't they been playing it last time too? She'd grab batteries from the front of the store. Liz tried kicking the wheel of her cart so it wouldn't squeak, but it didn't work. Instead of wandering through the grocery department, she only took what she needed for the party on Friday. Then she went toward self-checkout, but the people waiting stretched to the rotisserie chickens. The twenty items or less line shuffled forward at a quicker pace. The familiar-looking checker gave her the stink eye but didn't say anything as he scanned her stuff. She juggled the plastic bags and left.

The yellow bag of cat food was eleven dollars cheaper.

Liz grabbed the smallest bag. She'd bought food for Tito just the other day and the time before that too. Why was she here again? And why didn't she remember that she didn't need cat food before coming down the aisle? That seemed silly. Her memory had never been this terrible before. It must be the stress from work. She put the cat food in her cart and collected the other things she needed before leaving.

The yellow bag of cat food was eleven dollars cheaper.

Liz backed away from the stagnate smell of pet food. What had she been doing before this? What had she done after her last trip to the superstore? Nothing came to mind. She reached for her phone, but it still wasn't working. Maybe something was wrong with her head, some kind of amnesia or something, and it was causing these blackouts. She'd never had problems like this before.

She wheeled her cart away from pet supplies and toward the front. She should go to the hospital; this could be serious.

"Ma'am, are you okay?" the redheaded checker from the other day asked.

"I'm fine," Liz said. "I just remembered I have to go."

His nametag read Tim. "You haven't bought anything."

"I know."

Tim let her go, but his eyes followed her as she walked out the sliding doors.

The yellow bag of cat food was eleven dollars cheaper.

Everything before this moment was a black hole in Liz's memory. Why did she only remember things when she was in the superstore? Had she gone to the hospital? Why did she always wake up in front of the cat food? She leaned on the cart and the wheel let out a loud squeak. It was the same cart as before and before that, and however long she'd been having these blackouts. She dug through her purse for her phone before remembering it would be dead. Liz abandoned the cart.

For the first time, she noticed the people around her. Shopping alone would be weird, but she'd never paid attention to the other customers. They were background, unmemorable, unremarkable. The store was crowded with men and women, boys and girls, people of every kind shopping, their carts in various states of fullness. A woman to Liz's left was looking at cat litter.

"Excuse me?" Liz asked.

The woman turned with glazed eyes and shook her head. "Yes?"

"Can I borrow your phone?"

"My telephone's at home. Why would I have it with me?"

Liz walked to another person. "Can I borrow your phone?"

The same murky gaze cleared a little as the man handed her an outdated Nokia. It was odd, but it would have to do. When she tried to turn it on, however, the result was the same as hers.

"Sir, do you know what time it is?"

He looked at his watch and shrugged. "The battery's dead. I came here to get a new one."

Every person she ran to had a dead phone, a dead watch, or neither. Someone was watching her, but no one came to help. Even the empty-eyed employees with their slow, plodding steps ignored her, and their unnatural smiles kept her from approaching. Liz rushed to the office supplies and tore open a package of markers. She scribbled her name, phone number, and the words 'I am sick. Help me' on her arm. Someone outside would take her to a hospital. At least one person had to have a working phone.

She went toward the exit, and the same employee, Tim, was waiting again. "Can I assist you, ma'am?"

He knew something, she could tell. "Do you have a phone I could use?"

Tim shook his head. "Sorry, customers aren't allowed to use it."

"Fine then." She walked outside.

The yellow bag of cat food was eleven dollars cheaper.

Liz yelled, grabbed the nearest bag of the shit, and threw it on the floor. The bag burst open, spilling little fish and chicken-shaped bits onto the gray concrete, and she yanked another. The woman to her side looking at cat litter glanced up, eyes widening, but didn't say anything. Liz threw a few more bags at the floor before catching sight of her arm.

It was blank.

She ran out of the aisle, leaving her purse and cart behind, as she pushed past people and toward the doors. This wasn't possible. She had to remember what it was like to be outside. She had to know what time it was or even what day it was. There had to be more to life than cheap fluorescents and Rihanna and the same yellow and blue bargains. The party on Friday could've been months ago. Where were her friends? Did they know about her blackouts? Why wasn't anyone helping her?

Tim stood at the front again, in his khakis and polo shirt, with those knowing eyes.

"Can I help you, ma'am?" he said.

"Yes, you can. Call the police. Call the hospital. I need help."

"May I ask what's wrong?"

"I keep getting lost," Liz said.

"If you need help finding something I can point you in the right direction. Have you been to our entertainment department? We have Rihanna's new CD."

"I need to get out of here!"

"Then go." Tim frowned. "No one's stopping you."

The yellow bag of cat food was eleven dollars cheaper.

This time Liz didn't scream or throw the food. She left her cart and purse, and calmly walked toward the doors. A little red lever was easily accessible on the wall, so she pulled it. Then she sat on the ground and waited. If she had to stay in the superstore to hold onto her mind, then she would. The fire department would come and then she could explain the situation to them.

Tim and a man in a suit walked towards her. The redhead kept wiping his palms on his khakis. The well-dressed man's expression was a mask of false sincerity. It reminded her of when they'd held the company-wide meeting and her boss had explained about the pay cuts and hiring freeze. Her boss had said, "You'll just have to pick up the slack." Maybe this was a nervous breakdown and a sign she was long overdue for a vacation.

"Ma'am, is there a problem?" the man in the suit said. "I'm the store manager."

"I'm waiting for emergency services," Liz said.

"Why? There isn't an emergency."

"I need medical attention." Liz chewed her lip. "I'm waiting for them."

The manager's voice was cloying. "Why not wait outside?"

"I'll forget if I go out there."

"Oh, will you?"

Tim shook his head side to side with wide eyes. He was the only person who had noticed she was continually in the superstore and always in a panic. He'd be able to back up her breakdown. "He knows," Liz said. "I keep coming in here, don't I? And I can't remember anything before or after that."

The manager turned toward his employee with a smile that didn't meet his eyes. "My boy, you saw a customer in crisis and didn't help them? And you didn't report it to me? That's protocol."

Tim's face paled. "No, sir."

The manager's dark gaze turned back to her. "I understand you must be *so* frightened, and we apologize for the inconvenience. Ideally, we want our customers to have a blank and blissful shopping experience, to be a place they can return to again and again. That's our company policy. Would you say your experience reflects that?"

"Oh, it's…It's not your fault." Right? They hadn't done anything to her. She was stressed and must be losing it. That made more sense than some sinister store where time didn't exist, employees were basically drones, and customers bought without thought.

"We noticed a change in your purchasing habits," the manager said, accepting a paper from a shaking Tim. "Are you, by chance, worried about money?"

"I guess so."

"The company would be happy to offer product recommendations to better suit your new budget if you wish to continue shopping with us." The manager's smile was sharp and white. "Or, if you'd rather, we have a new opening. The pay is competitive and I'm sure you'd be happier here."

A job? That didn't make sense. She was in the middle of a medical emergency and this man wanted to offer her a job?

"I didn't fill out an application."

"You're more than qualified. We like our employees aware of the store's rigors."

Fire trucks or an ambulance should have arrived. Liz couldn't hear sirens or aid coming to her rescue from outside. "Can I think this over?"

"This is a one-time offer. Did I mention our benefits package, including premium health insurance?"

"Sir, I do apo—" Tim started to say.

"Let the poor girl think."

Tim fiddled with his lanyard and its numerous pins: five years of service, ten years of service, fifteen years... He couldn't be more than twenty-five, though, or he had a hell of a dermatologist. Liz has worked at her office for three years—three migraine-inducing years—and all she had to show was a tiny cubicle where the only personality she was allowed was a pitiful succulent and a cat calendar. If Tim could stay here for fifteen years, then this had to be a decent place.

"Okay," she said, "I'll do it."

The manager helped her up and they shook hands. "Remember, kid, customer service is a feedback loop. If they're happy, we're happy. So don't screw up."

The customer was buying the yellow bag of cat food, a sixteen pound one, and Liz scanned it with practiced ease. She didn't know how long she'd been working for the superstore, but it had been a while now. "Stay" by Rihanna played through the loudspeakers. She hummed along as she scanned the man's other purchases: car magazines he'd never read, beer he'd never drink, and bleach for clothes that would never be cleaned. The man paid while she bagged and left without saying goodbye.

She had a customer after that, and another, and even more after that. It was an endless line of products and oblivious people and never-ending shifts where all she did was scan and ask how others' days were. Her phone was in her pocket, charged and ready to remind her she was still on the clock and always would be. As long as she didn't mess up and upset the manager. She'd been hired because of an opening, because some employee hadn't followed protocol, but she didn't think much of it. Her life before didn't really matter anyway.

"Thank you for choosing our store. We hope you'll come back soon."

DECADENT FEARS IN
THE KING IN YELLOW

Richard Snowden-Leak

[What follows is the transcription of a livestream a streamer gave last year originally titled, 'The Horror of the Self in *The King in Yellow*', which is released here as a transcript by S and is now retitled 'Decadent Fears in *The King in Yellow*'. The original stream, which was meant to last only for thirty minutes, has been cut down from its 6-hour run and is presented here in transcript form. While most of the rambling has been cut, S asserts that some of it is important to 'the process of interpreting the void'.]

S: I have long wondered what made *The King in Yellow* by Robert W. Chambers so terrifying to people, as for me it never really was scary. But having found this painting [S holds up painting to camera: see appendix 1] called 'Hildred Regards Himself', a depiction of a scene in the first story of the collection, I think the horror comes from a fear of Decadent art in the fin de siècle. Kenneth Hite, in an annotated edition of *The King in Yellow*, writes, 'as a bourgeois art student with typically American beliefs in progress, romantic love, and nature', 'Chambers and the Decadents were natural opposites.'[1] Arthur Symons, too, writes that in Decadence there is 'an intense self-consciousness, [...] an over-subtilizing refinement upon refinement, a spiritual and moral perversity', surmising it as a 'new and beautiful and interesting disease'.[2] Regenia Gagnier also writes that 'Modern Decadence was identified as the choice and fantasy of the individual psyche, detaching it from the social whole.'[3] Looking at this 'Hildred' piece, I see this 'disease' in the painting, and I also see this fascination with the self, both in its style and in its subject matter (a man painting himself in a self-portrait over a mirror). Chambers is writing in response to Decadence, then, for it is this 'fantasy' of 'the individual psyche', this 'intense self-consciousness', that takes center-stage in the Chambers stories, a beginning of a world fascinated not just with the self, but of its detachment from 'the social whole'.

For Max Nordau, a physician at the time, this intense self-consciousness is indeed a kind of horror that effects the formal elements of art. He said 'impressionism' was an 'atavism' which 'carries back the human mind to its brute-beginnings', where 'artistic activity' devolves to 'an embryonic state', as the impressionistic writer 'gives himself the air of a painter', 'professes to seize the phenomenon, not as a concept, but to feel it as a simple sense-simulation.'[4] When I look at this painting, I see that the artist is purposefully leaning into that style, of a world made of impressions—though it does also feel expressionistic in how the skin of the hand is a nicotine yellow, and how its palette doesn't differ all that much from the tones of the rest of the piece. It's this

---

[1] Kenneth Hite, 'La Decadence', in *The King in Yellow: Annotated Edition* (Arc Dream Publishing: Chelsea, AL, 2019), p. 193.

[2] Arthur Symons, 'The Decadent Movement in Literature', *Harper's Monthly Magazine* 87 No. 3 (1893), p. 859.

[3] Regenia Gagnier, *Individualism, Decadence and Globalization: On the Relationship of Part to Whole 1859–1920* (Palgrave Macmillan, London: 2010) p. 88.

[4] Max Nordau, Degeneration (London William Heinemann: London, 1898), p. 485-486.

painting that made me think of the fears that Chambers and Nordau address, this terror that was felt in response to the turn toward the self.

This turn toward the self is something Chambers draws upon in 'Repairer of Reputations', the story this painting is inspired by, as the entire story is unreliably narrated. Hildred, for instance, is wearing 'the diadem' which he perceives as a 'golden jewelled crown', when in actuality, however, the golden diadem is just a 'brass crown'; he looks in the mirror, 'absorbed in the changing expression of my own eyes', because the 'mirror reflected a face which was like my own, but whiter, and so thin that I hardly recognised it.'[5] Him painting over the mirror in this painting, then, is not only demonstrative of how unstable one's own perception can be, but how, in a way, to see one's self is to immediately make some sort of unconscious judgement, or painting, over the you that you see. Hildred, after all, hardly recognizes himself, and this dissonance between perceived-self and felt-self (the self one feels they are) is all that Hildred feels in the moment.

Nordau's worry about the writer giving themselves the 'air of a painter' here might be said as well for how one perceives their own reality, then, as Hildred, in looking in the mirror, can be regarded as an act of creation on par with painting. This connection is bridged also by Oscar Wilde's assertion that 'Lying, the telling of beautiful untrue things, is the proper aim of Art.'[6] Perhaps it's because Chambers is directly drawing a parallel between perception and creation, as if to perceive the world is to create it, to make it 'beautiful' yet 'untrue', just as Hildred does. Hildred envisions himself as someone who will 'secure the happiness and prosperity of a continent', for instance, because he can't face the reality of living in an asylum for the criminally insane.[7] There is a melding of life and of art in Decadent literature, then, of making content out of your existence—which again reminds me of another Wilde piece, *The*

---

[5] 'Repairer', p. 21.

[6] Oscar Wilde, 'The Decay of Lying' in *Intentions* (New York: Brentano's, 1905), p. 17.

[7] 'Repairer', p. 19.

Picture of Dorian Gray, when Harry says to Dorian that 'Life has been your art.'[8] But if one's life becomes one's art, what can be said of Symons's remark, 'What Decadence, in literature, really means is that learned corruption of language by which style ceases to be organic, and becomes, in pursuit of some new expressiveness or beauty, deliberately abnormal'?[9] Furthermore, if one considers Wilde's assertion that life imitates art, then Chambers sees the horror in a world where everyone tries to live their lives in the pursuit of that art, fearing that the conflation of art with life will lead them to living a life 'deliberately abnormal', and so the art they create would be horrific.[10] If Hildred's life is being lived out as if it is his own art, his own impression of the world around him, then that leads one to believe that he could even pursue a 'new expressiveness' that's 'deliberately abnormal'. No wonder, then, that Hildred has grand ideas of becoming the new king of the 'Imperial Dynasty of America', as Chambers supposes that art unhinged from morality will fabricate deranged ideas in those who should consume it.[11]

[S looks over notes again. This goes on for twenty minutes.]

Perhaps it might be useful to look into Wilde for a moment and his ideas, so that we can properly assess what Chambers is also reacting too, this fear of life conflating with art. In *Picture,* Harry replies to Dorian's assertion that he was poisoned by the yellow book: 'As for being poisoned by a book, there is no such thing as that. Art has no influence upon action. It annihilates the desire to act. [...] The books that the world calls immoral are books that show the world its own shame.'[12] Even if decadent literature is self-obsessed, even if it

---

[8] Oscar Wilde, *The Picture of Dorian Gray* (Oxford University Press: New York, 2006), p. 182.

[9] Arthur Symons, *Studies in Prose and Verse*, (London: J.M Dent, 1904), p. 149.

[10] Wilde, 'The Decay of Lying', p. 16.

[11] 'Repairer', p. 28.

[12] *The Picture of Dorian Gray*, p. 183.

pursues what Harry calls 'extraordinary sensations', it does not incite these actions.[13] And even if Wilde espouses that art is the telling of 'beautiful untrue things' whilst simultaneously showing the 'world its own shame', its very creation took place only for the pleasure of the artist. What happens after that is up to the reader and the reader alone. Art, then, reveals; it does not beget.

To Chambers, however, it's the opposite, because he is particularly attracted to this connection between self-consciousness, the conflation of art and life with regards to the self, and also the fallibility of the senses. What I'm attracted to here, in how Nordau and Chambers can view Wilde's ideas as horrific whilst Wilde does not, is this colliding of two differing perceptions of one thing. What I mean to ask is how can one person find something beautiful, and another find it horrible? [S picks up painting.] The horror is no longer just at how we as subjects create the world we see, then, but with how there is no stable, objective reality we can reach, or even perceive, and therefore no way of verifying our ideas, our preconceived notions, our perceptions. Hildred, when discussing the Play that drove him insane (which is also titled *The King in Yellow* in these stories), remarks that 'No definite principles had been violated in those wicked pages, no doctrine promulgated, no convictions outraged', only that 'human nature could not bear the strain, nor thrive on words in which the essence of purest poison lurked'.[14] The horror comes from the idea that there is something humanity cannot comprehend, and so it alludes to something, somewhere, outside, just beyond our horizon, to an objective reality.

[Twenty minutes of S staring straight ahead, caught in thought.]

And so this horror of subjectivity comes with the horror of not being able to communicate—

---

[13] Ibid.

[14] 'Repairer', p. 6.

[S looks tired. Begins muttering to himself.] I think—I think there's an idea of something beginning to form. I think... I feel...

[S spends a few hours writing away in a darkening room.]

Sorry. Just needed to collect my thoughts.

Now—I feel a little closer to this idea, that there is a horror manifesting itself not just through a reaction to Decadent literature and its conflation of art and life and the fallibility of the self, but to the idea that there is something outside of us that binds everything, a Truth, as it were. One thinker that might elucidate some of the more disturbing parts of *King* (and hopefully the painting) is Arthur Schopenhauer. Schopenhauer proposes that one can never find an objective reality, because 'The world is my representation'.[15] Schopenhauer goes on to say that one can never get past these representations, '*from the outside*', and that 'no matter how much we look, we find nothing but images and names.'[16] On this painting, Hildred regarding himself indeed seems to echo this kind of idea, with him seeing only a world he is painting for himself. Furthermore, what lies beyond perception for Schopenhauer is what he calls will, a constantly striving force that embodies everything.[17] The Play does allude to a reality that 'human nature could not bear the strain' of, and so to read this Play is to try and go past the world as representation, to perceive formless will. Schopenhauer, too, says that the 'artist allows us to look into the world through his eyes', and it's this flagging of ownership, 'his eyes', that gestures toward this inherent instability (and fallibility) of reality as we experience it.[18]

---

[15] Arthur Schopenhauer, *The World as Will and Representation*, trans. and edited by Judith Norman, Alistair Welchman, Christopher Janaway, (Cambridge University Press: Cambridge, 2010), p. 23.

[16] *World as Will*, p. 123.

[17] Ibid., p. 17.

[18] Ibid., p. 219.

We have in 'The Mask' another artist who tries to show us the world they see, but this time the artist looks to capture life as art. The artist in question—the narrator's friend, Boris—has a chemical formula that can turn any living thing 'to the purest marble.'[19] After demonstrating the effects of the formula on a flower to Alec, the narrator, Boris remarks, 'What sculptor could reproduce it?'[20] Here, Boris, through his art, wants to bring the world he sees to life by inversely taking life away from things and turning them into art. Every depiction of something, then, comes with a cost. Meanwhile Alec, who is also a painter, returns to his muse who, 'unwillingly dawdling through a series of poses for [the painting], today refused all bribes to be good'.[21] After sending the boy away, Alec says, 'it took me the rest of the afternoon to undo the damage I had done'.[22] In comparison to Boris's instantaneous transformation of something living into a piece of art, the painstaking process of painting appears tedious and taxing, and not nearly as efficacious as Boris's process. Chambers knows that this process is tempting to a sculptor, as the process merely solidifies whatever the artist wishes to depict—a dream, I imagine, for Alec and his fidgeting muse. Here is a world, Chambers asserts, that allows the artist to present the world as they see it, even if it means solidifying lifeforms to achieve that beauty. It's no surprise that the story's love interest, Geneviève, should come to submerge herself in this pool of liquid, then, as a kind of Faustian cost to the deal.

[S takes a few minutes to think].

I didn't, on initial reading, see the relevance the love triangle between Geneviève, Alec, and Boris, other than that of a cautionary tale, of course. But

---

[19] 'The Mask', p. 33.

[20] Ibid.

[21] Ibid., p. 37.

[22] Ibid.

now I realize that, in conjunction with the title, 'The Mask', Chambers is bringing us back to this subjective element, but in another way, offering that when life imitates an art intensely 'self-conscious', people can treat everyone's actions as artistic expressions to be interpreted. To explain what I mean, I think we'll have to look closer. Why Geneviève jumps into the pool in the first place is that she falls ill from having to choose between the two men, saying to Alec, 'I love you, but I think I love Boris best'.[23] Geneviève becomes 'quite out of her mind' after choosing Boris, alluding to the fact that she never actually did love 'Boris best'.[24] After this she is found 'at the bottom of the pool, her hands across over her breast. Then Boris shot himself through the heart.'[25] From the evidence here I would wager that Geneviève was in love with Alec, but that's the issue Chambers might be picking out, for when life collapses with art, other people's lives and actions can be interpreted as artistic expression.

[S goes to notes again.]

At this time, too, authorial intent is beginning to wane in favor of interpretation. In a testimony James Abbott McNeill Whistler gives during a trial defending one of his paintings, he remarks on this very idea: 'As to what the picture represents, that depends upon who looks at it. To some persons it may represent all that I intended; to others it may represent nothing.'[26] Not only does this gesture to unstable realities, in that we all each are isolated from one another in our perception of something, but it works also with the potential fallout of a world where people are the artists of their own lives, and if they are, then Alec—just as we readers do—must interpret what people's actions mean.

---

[23] 'The Mask', p. 41.

[24] Ibid., p. 42.

[25] Ibid., p. 43.

[26] Linda Merril, *A Pot of Paint: Aesthetics on Trial in Whistler v Ruskin*, (Washington, DC: Smithsonian Institution Press, 1992), p. 150.

Chambers points out, then, that this disruption between authorial intent and perceived meaning can only mean the worst for a society that mimics the art it creates. At one instance, Alec narrates that Geneviève, 'refusing to take up our usual bantering tone,' 'murmured a hospitable commonplace and disappeared', leaving Alec to ask, 'I had better go home, don't you think?'[27] Who knows, is what I'd reply to Alec, because her refusal could be due to a many number of things, all of which are equally as valid, all operating at once, in a sort quantum superimposition… And even if we did know we'd never truly know no matter what Geneviève said, because we're not her—and so Chambers asserts there's a dangerous blurring between the lines of art and life, where people's actions can be left up to interpretation. Authority and agency are taken away from a person whose every action can be treated as an artistic piece that can be challenged or even reinterpreted against their own will. And so we revisit Geneviève's 'I think I love Boris best', paying special attention now to 'think'. Geneviève didn't know—and it's this inability to be sure that leads to her falling ill for having made the wrong decision and subsequently trying to escape the awful situation she found herself in.

The Play, then, might drive people insane because of how it addresses this conflation of art and life when it comes to the representation of one's own thoughts to others and to themselves. We can see this idea foregrounded in a rare excerpt from the play:

> CAMILLA: You, sir, should unmask.
> STRANGER: Indeed?
> CAMILLA: Indeed it's time. We all have laid aside disguise but you.
> STRANGER: I wear no mask.
> CAMILLA: [terrified, aside to Cassilda] No mask? No mask!

---

[27] 'The Mask', p. 35.

The King in Yellow, Act i, Scene 2[28]

The stranger, wearing no mask, terrifies Camilla who has 'laid aside disguise', because the stranger's existence flies in the face of everything Camilla knows, that people act. To wear no 'mask' is to live outside of representation—it's to live without a fiction of the self. And so the Stranger appears almost like an embodiment of this objective reality, this unmasked, true place no one can perceive. The Stranger's very existence gestures to these masks we wear, then, the masks that are so ingrained in us that to think of a life without them is terrifying. After Alec reads the Play he says, 'The mask of self-deception was no longer a mask for me, it was a part of me' when talking about him hiding his 'sorrow'. and so we realize that the Play taught him the same lesson, that we see how easy it is to lie not only to the world about how we feel but also to ourselves.[29] And so we can't even be sure of how we ourselves feel...

[S speaks now at break-neck pace, but for the sake of clarity, the rest has been punctuated.]

Hildred and Alec, they saw a world that none should see, they saw, like Camilla, that reality is a mask, a collection, a composite even, of 'beautiful untrue things', and that the mind is its own artist imagining the spaces around it... [Streamer picks up the painting again] Perhaps it is fitting that in this painting there is no face—whether or not Hildred painted over his face or is yet to paint his face is no matter—because this painting tells me that, like how all colors combine to make white, all my masks combine to make void. 'Hildred Regarding Himself' is a piece in dedication to Hildred's discovery in that 'book of great truths', that when we look at ourselves we see the world as 'representations' far more clearly, and so all artwork concerned with the self in

---

[28] Ibid., p. 33.
[29] Ibid., p. 40.

Decadent literature is in pursuit of that ultimate, sublime pleasure, what Schopenhauer says is that 'painless state that Epicurus prized as the highest good and the state of the gods', for when we contemplate the beautiful in art, 'for that moment we are freed from the terrible pressure of the will.'[30] It's will. It's all will. Everything. Nothing escapes it. 'The world is my representation', and from that one can feel the power of that possessive 'my', a 'truth' in it, as for what I now read is not just that the world is a representation of will, but that the world I see is mine and mine alone. And there is still another layer past 'my representation' of this world, and that I can never truly see it. And that horror resides in myself, too, for the only way to communicate the world I see is through the life I lead—the art I make—and that can be interpreted and reinterpreted however way a person wants. I have no control over anything. To blur life with art, even if it becomes 'deliberately abnormal', is to abate these Decadent fears, this 'terrible pressure of the will', and to live in clear acknowledgement that the world we live in is a world of masks, of representations, and no matter what I can do I will never escape the horror at the heart of it all: that the world I experience is not real.

[S laughs, repeating 'I am a blank page in that book of great truths' until the stream is cut off and it ends.]

---

[30] 'Repairer', p. 22; Schopenhauer, *World as Will*, p. 220.

References

Chambers, Robert W., 'Repairer of Reputations' in *The King in Yellow* (Wordsworth Editions: Hertfordshire, 2010).

—, 'The Mask' in *The King in Yellow* (Wordsworth Editions, Hertfordshire: 2010).

Gagnier, R., 'Decadent Interiority and the Will', in *Individualism, Decadence and Globalization Language, Discourse, Society*, (Palgrave Macmillan: London, 2010), 87-115.

Hite, Kenneth, 'La Decadence', in *The King in Yellow: Annotated Edition* (Arc Dream Publishing: Chelsea, AL, 2019).

Merril, Linda, *A Pot of Paint: Aesthetics on Trial in Whistler v Ruskin* (Washington: Smithsonian Institution Press, 1992).

Nordau, Max, Degeneration (London William Heinemann: London, 1898).

Schopenhauer, Arthur, *The World as Will and Representation*, trans. and edited by Judith Norman, Alistair Welchman, Christopher Janaway, (Cambridge University Press: Cambridge, 2010).

Symons, Arthur, 'The Decadent Movement in Literature', *Harper's Monthly Magazine* 87 No. 3 (1893).

—, *Studies in Prose and Verse* (London: J.M Dent, 1904).

Wilde, Oscar *The Picture of Dorian Gray* (Oxford University Press: New York, 2006).

—, 'The Decay of Lying' in *Intentions* (New York: Brentano's, 1905).

Appendix 1:

The Triumphant Bellow of the Room

Ukata Edwardson

a light splays through my curtain to cast a split of three shadows on my floor,
one like a stretching arm, another like a stretching arm, and the other resembling
a little boy. i hear a whimper in the background of my ears, three words woven
in my mother's medical voice: i want you; like my body is a spice necessary for
a concoction. the darkness in my room moves like mist, lays its cold hands on my
skin, and clothes me with goosebumps ridged like heavy boils from a possession.
and then i see her by the door, wrapped in only her skin, ordering my body to leave
to its mother. and her voice is a shilling bribing my bones, and my body begins
to carry me to her, and we fade into a room. slight men begin to crawl out of the
walls, cracking like nuts, dropping as paste on the floor. ants colonize the ceiling
and become a sea, and her voice begins to deepen into a bellowing crowd as she
orders my body to touch its mother. touch your mother, she says, crying streams
of blood. touch your mother, she says, her silk skin breaking into glass and slowly
shooting forth green shrubs, and grass, and trees, and algae. touch your mother,
she says, a car with screaming people tumbling over in her eyes and making her
shriek. her voice multiplies and multiplies and multiplies and her breasts begin
to leak milk that floods the room and begin to drown me. touch your mother, she
says, and i am screaming and suffocating and taking my father's name by death.
and my father presses my head against his chest where he has his own injury
from grief, locked in the profanity of mature memory, and says it is only a dream.

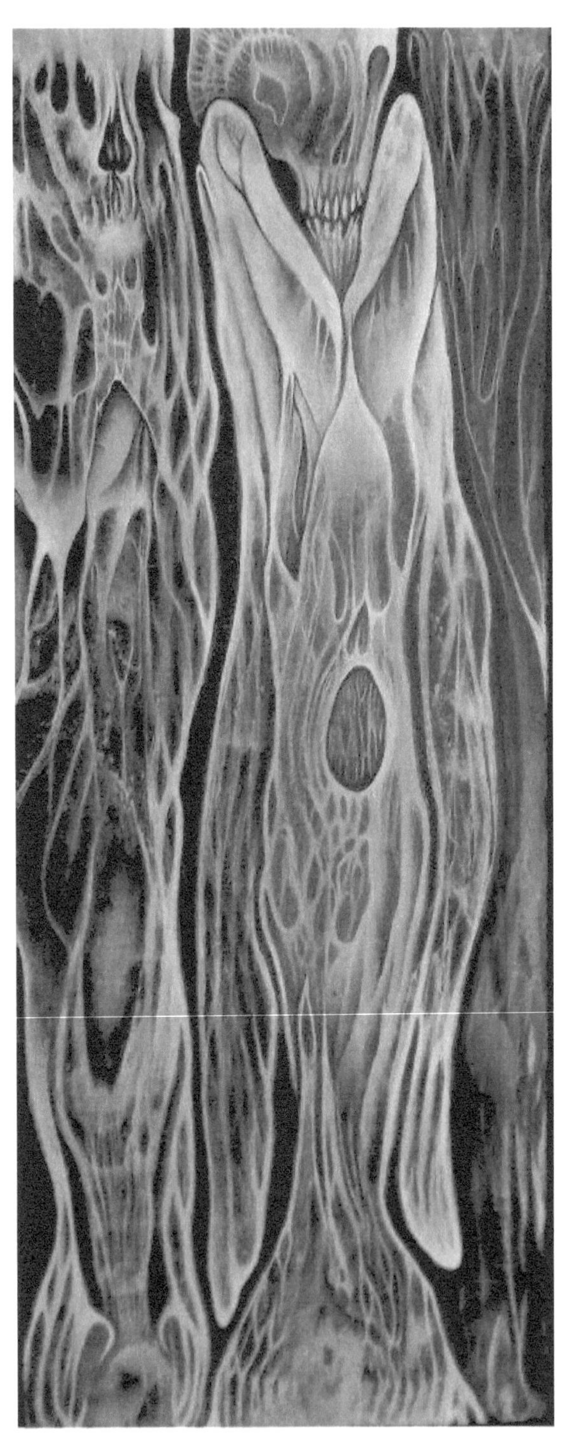

ART BY JESSE PEPER

THE VOICE FROM NOWHERE

Andrew Koury

ACK WAS A biloquist. He insisted on the archaic word because he only threw his voice, there was no dummy that borrowed it. His newest endeavor was throwing his voice near peoples' mouths, making them appear to talk with his own voice. I joked that this was flesh and blood ventriloquism, but he said, "Ventriloquism is the illusion of a person through a dummy. This is the realization that there is only the voice." We had been living together for a few months, and I was beginning to find him pretentious. Despite that, he had an admirable sense of purpose that I lacked.

I didn't know how to spend my days. While at work, I felt an ache to be home and while home, I felt adrift, hoping to one day be stricken by the idea that there was something more to life. And for a brief period, there was. Zack, the biloquist himself, was my first serious boyfriend.

I even came out at work. Results were mixed. It was the same hollow environment, but now everyone thought they knew everything about me, like I was an open book they had already read. The guy next to my cubicle used to print out insipid articles about how businessmen can better weather generational differences, about how millennials like me think. Now he printed out insipid articles about LGBT people 'disrupting 'corporate culture in a positive way. He handed these things to me like trivia he had gathered that I would be happy to talk about. But he never wanted to talk. It was never a conversation starter; it was the whole conversation.

I came home from work to see Zack rehearsing his newest project, a one man show. He was absorbed in the process, staring into his script. He shifted between several distinct postures, trying them out like clothes, to find the one that fit this performance. Without changing his gaze, he said to me, as if right next to my ear, "Given any thought to performing with me? Or acting at all?"

"Maybe someday. Not yet."

"Not yet, not yet, people die with a pocketful of 'not yets'."

"I like watching you more."

Zack didn't smile. He looked through his script.

"You know you were good at performing. If you want to be part of a show again, it wouldn't be hard for you."

"I don't know. I don't know what I want."

"Yeah, I can tell."

I walked to the bathroom and washed my face. Just left the conversation. That's something you can do in a long-term relationship, I guess. I stared at my reflection. I used to love contorting my face and making myself laugh. It's what every actor starts with: performing to amuse themselves in the mirror. Today, I just stared.

On Grindr I used to able to put 'Discreet' and nothing else and that was enough to meet up with people. Now I had to think about if I'm more masc or femme. Why did I let my wrist go limp? Is that something I've been repressing, or something fake I've added to a performance? Every action, from how I run, to how I stand, to my voice—am I talking higher or lower, what's my real voice even feel like—has been taken from me and replaced with the fucking articles that my coworker leaves for me like treats for a caged pet.

I opened the door and Zack was right there. I looked mean, which brought a smirk to his face. We kissed and then more. I took charge and lifted him to the bedroom.

He maneuvered on top of me and said, "Say you want it."

I opened my mouth—and it was honestly to say the word yes, I swear I think I was going to say that—but something else escaped my lips when I felt my lungs squeezed by something cold, like a doctor's hand. The pocket of air slithered up my throat and emerged from my open, unshaped mouth, as my voice said, as naturally as possible, "Do it. I want it."

I was unnerved but things were progressing. He entered me and I moaned in shock. He had a fierce, stony look on him as he stared right into—almost through—my eyes. And then my mouth. His lips parted microscopically, and I was made, or maybe encouraged to say, "Harder." It was all so quick and fluid, like a true parlor trick that I can only try to convince myself that it was all him, that I wasn't encouraging the act or moving it along like an unwitting audience participant. I began to question if something was happening with my limbs. Sometimes these movements feel automatic and sometimes deliberate, but rarely so clearly both as I made a show of gripping the bedsheets in pleasure and pain.

I opened my mouth to say something of my own, nothing important, anything to feel like I still had my voice, but he covered my mouth with his hand, and then he came more than he had in weeks.

Lying in bed after cleaning up, he had his hand around me. He took up most of the bed in his sprawled posture. It was unlike us. But then he turned to me with the sincerest smile I had ever seen from him, and I knew things would be good, at least for a while.

"Here's what I'm working on," Zack gestured to the big show curtains in our unfinished basement. On the walls were community theater *Les Misérables* posters and costumes from *The Phantom of the Opera*. Scripts and props in nearby boxes from fringe shows no one else had ever seen. All of the detritus from my earlier career as an actor. "I want you to tell me what color the curtains are." He bounced on his heels in boyish excitement.

"Okay. They're red." And they were. They must have been.

"Now hold still." Zack closed his eyes and I felt that touch inside me again, but more careful and precise. The word "blue" was massaged up my throat and into the world.

"Blue," we both heard me say.

"Now, what color are the curtains?" Zack asked.

I was wrong before. They were blue now and always had been. I hadn't been the one to declare them blue, but now that my voice had it was impossible to see anything else.

But they had been red. I squinted at the curtains and little pockets of red poked through, like glitches of unreality that I could never quite focus on. I shifted my stance and heard my shoes peel off the sticky, stone floor.

"Answer me."

"I need to think about it."

"No. Thinking about it is only emasculating your perception." Zack stood straighter than normal, a posture I would likely see in his show. "Action is beautiful in and of itself and must be taken before or without previous reflection."

"Blue." As the words left my mouth there was no doubt that the curtains were blue. But I was not certain if saying so was Zack's voice or mine.

I went to work and watched my list of tasks shorten as the day progressed, but I couldn't tell you any details. I pretended to skim an article my coworker sent me titled 'Queering the Work Ethic, a Faggot's Guide to Maximum Productivity.' I watched my hands type words on my computer. Type letters. My fingers were moving quickly in arranging those letters into words. It was all perfectly normal, but the bending of my joints alienated me with their automatic movements. My phalanges were wrapped in a tight suit of skin with little hairs on them. The arm with more hair and spots. My elbow twitched, the skin and muscle gave a shudder. Who told it to do that? Who told my body anything?

I stopped typing and gazed at my fingerprints. Or tried to. I could not quite make them out without squinting. I felt adrift. I returned to my house from work early, but it didn't help. I did not feel at home in myself.

I saw Zack before he saw me. He wasn't rehearsing. He was staring at a mirror and moving his mouth in slight little aberrations. His index fingertip placed against the mirror. He swayed as if he might fall, but the finger on the mirror anchored him, like that was his center of gravity. His mutterings were far away.

I strained to hear. I just made out the phrase, " …mbs. Let me walk you into the world." It was not Zack's voice, and it was not mine.

"Zack!" I shouted.

He whipped around and glared at me.

"What?"

"What's going on? What were you doing?"

"I was rehearsing. I try to do that when I can get some time alone."

"What's that supposed to mean? I'm at work all day."

"But when you're not, I have to put on this whole show for you so you feel special, don't I? Talk up your past so you can trudge through your future. Sorry."

Those were the words I can sort of remember. But they don't trigger any rage inside me. Speaking honestly, I don't remember them as a conversation I had, but as someone else's distant memory.

I felt acid reflux. It clattered around in me, stretching and scratching my insides like a sharp fingernail. The sentence, "Forget about it, I'm the one who's sorry," emerged from my mouth with sincerity, my breath suddenly sour.

I felt a prickling in my fingers, like they had fallen asleep.

"Why did you do that?" I said.

"Do what?"

"You did something to me. To my voice. I don't know."

"I didn't do anything to you. You're impossible."

"Why are you like this today?"

"Why aren't you like anything? There's nothing to you and you don't want to be anything."

Zack stormed out of the house, script in hand. Later, he texted me he was staying with a friend. The details were maddeningly vague. But he said if I wanted to talk again, I should see his show in the coming days.

I first met Zack at a show. It was at a dingy basement in a bar home to the local avant-garde theatre productions, a regular haunt of the artistic underworld. He was part of the audience, that amorphous cloud of judgement or validation. I played a fanatical preacher overtaken with the spirit of the Lord. My big scene was begging for forgiveness from God for what my character did in his night of religious ecstasy. Zack praised me for the choices I made as an actor, how a lesser performer would have gone huge with it instead of restrained. I never told him that wasn't my instinct, that my main talent was following direction. But the director was the one who introduced him to me, so maybe he knew all along. Regardless, I surged with pride when he looked at me that day.

Thinking back over our fight, there were not gaps in my memory, but some things were more opaque than others. My feelings about it all were slippery.

I sifted through all the cast photos in the basement. Looking at the different people I had been. I had worn a lot of faces. Every cast photo was a family that felt like it would last forever, which made its broken promises of post-show connection over drinks after the curtain call.

I closed my eyes. The prickling sensation in my hands was gone and my stomach had settled. Breathing in and out slowly, like a meditation, I felt heavy and leaden. I missed the prickling and the acid burn inside me. There was nothing there in their absence.

I couldn't live my life as my own director. A relationship must be a performance, and I wasn't playing my role. I would see him perform, and then he would see me perform after the show. It was packed but not with the usual crowd. Instead of the drunk old college friends and the supportive amateur illusionists, there was a strange assortment of people that I had seen but never talked to. Faces I recognized but never heard speak. Fellow grocery store shoppers, gas station workers, businessmen from my building but from different floors, and people I would see on the bus, all apparently part of this one group together sharing in some uneasy camaraderie before the curtain lifted. The only seat available was in the center and I caught the audience's flickering glares as I claimed it. Right before the curtain rose, I registered that it was not blue, but red, and this filled me with an inexplicable panic that arrived too late to be useful.

Zack performed an unexpectedly tender one man show. It was about longing in many variations through different characters. One of whom seemed directly inspired my life. I hadn't seen this kind of sensitivity in Zack for a long time.

But the longing was never fulfilled for any of the characters he played. It would be difficult to show that fulfillment given the format of a single actor performing to a crowd, but the narratives left everyone hanging in increasingly frustrated moments. This was a performer who had brought us in and gotten us to spend our empathy only to feel cut short and spurned. The crowd was growing frustrated. Angry. At our lowest point as an audience, the voice made its appearance.

"Welcome to truly being. Become a part of something greater." I didn't hear it so much as feel it leave Zack's throat. It disseminated like a noxious gas, filling the container of the building and everyone in it.

I didn't realize how much empty space was in my lungs until I felt the voice invade me. I could feel my organs slosh when I moved, but they weren't fragile, they were heavy and strong like steel. The separation between my skin and the air around me was sharper than it had ever been. I sliced through reality with each step I took, and I deserved to do so. But even before I moved, I knew where I would step, how I would move my hands, what I would say. I knew my possibilities and the choices I was fated to make and that they were good. All I had to do was let it out; speak the voice.

But I kept my mouth shut and felt the voice beating against my lips like a gust of wind. I panicked at the sense of completion it gave me. Maybe I was afraid of an ending, I don't know why I didn't give in. I looked at Zack on stage to see him ignoring the chaos around us. Of people rapturously opening their mouths to speak the voice. It was a cacophony of a single tone. He extended a hand to me and only me, his expression unreadable. I wanted him to see me open myself to him. Hopefully, he would know I wanted nothing but for him to speak through my mouth. I parted my lips.

The voice that was neither mine nor Zack's shot out of my throat. If I listened carefully, I could hear my own vocal utterances blending and mixing with the otherworldly voice. But it was not an equal partnership, the voice from nowhere was in charge. My vocal cords were creating words I did not think of. I said things I will not repeat here. Something between a manifesto and treaty on the falseness of life and hollowness of the soul. The longer I sat there, listening to myself say these things, the more I became convinced of their validity.

I locked eyes with Zack. We were saying the same things in perfect synchronicity, an expression of terror on his face. He was not offering his hand. He was pleading for help that I failed to give. The play was so big neither of us could comprehend its totality, only the small parts we played. The piece of direction that intermittently spurted out of throats was *Be one of my limbs. Let me walk you into the world.*

I fled the theater, flanked by Zack and the entirety of the audience, shouting with a confidence I had never known. A confidence that was fully me, regardless of my own wishes. Each of our special, individual struggles and pain were for a greater power we could not comprehend. But it easily comprehended us and that was more than enough.

We unmade the town. If you make the mistake of entering where it used to be, you will see nothing but ashes, debris, and a great many footsteps of variable and unnatural sizes and shapes. But if you squint, you may be able to glimpse ghosts of houses and phantoms of roads, but the greater reality will overcome your perception. This may seem like madness, but you will have the opportunity to judge this yourself, for this show is a traveling production. Arm and arm we are walking across America—each of us, a confident link in the chain—bringing true lucidity to an empty world. Be ready to join the chorus.

Echoes of a Former You

Christa Carmen

YOU WAKE IN the house, in the body, you have always inhabited, knowing that something has changed. You are not sure how you could know this; the room is darker than a river bottom, and the creaking of the radiators is as constant and commonplace as ever. You long for oblivion to reclaim you, but delaying your investigation seems pointless, if not imprudent, and so you swing your feet over the side of the bed and lower them to the marble floor.

The hallway is unaltered, but at the bottom of the stairs, you come upon the thing that dragged you from the depths of sleep. The wall that once featured a sizable, arched doorframe and solid oak slab of wood is smooth now, an unbroken plane of eggshell white. You run your hands along the plaster, terror tempered by bewilderment. There is not a single clue that some midnight crew of madmen boarded up the space, no smell of paint or hint of sawdust, neither telltale nail. The door is gone, disappeared as thoroughly as if it had never been.

The other doors! you think and turn, panic spilling forth as if from an overwatered houseplant. You run through the hall and into the living room—the heart of your home—where your fear is realized before the room's other features can coalesce. The slider is gone. The house closes in around you. *No way out, no way out, no way...*

You sprint for the basement, the drumming of your heart drowning out your footfalls, grabbing the waxy cylinder of a pillar candle and a book of matches from a basket on the counter as you go. The depression around the wick is deep enough so that you trust its flame will not forsake you. The smell of sulfur when the match is struck distracts you from your dread.

As you descend into the dark, you picture the house as someone else might see it: a gently sloping roofline and wrap-around front porch, the porch a bit of architecture that must seem strange without a door to get inside. Perhaps, with its well-kept exterior, the house appears inviting, the way some men believe certain women to look. Perhaps it's unexceptional, its nuances—and now, its changes—perceptible only to the one held captive behind its walls. Cupping the candle's flame with a simulacrum of courage, you make your way across the cellar, to the farthest, cobweb encrusted wall.

You are nearing your destination when an explosion of breaking glass comes from overhead. On reflex, you duck. The candle dies an instantaneous death. Blind, alone, paralyzed by fear, *that night* returns to you in a tidal wave of sensations.

The clothes are torn from your body and fists pummel your flesh until you cannot tell one set from another. Consciousness flickers. You are grateful for the blips of blackness and, in moments of awareness, horrified by the certainty that this is all your fault.

You focus on the feeling of your feet upon the floor, and slowly come back to the house, your body, the matches in your nightgown pocket. The first one you strike does not catch. The second, mercifully, does. It is only after you reignite the candle that you see the notebook by your knee. You pick it up but do not open it, then raise your gaze from its cover. The basement bulkhead, the last door out, the final chance to end this nightmare, is gone.

Dazed, abandoning notebook and candle, you make your way back across gritty concrete. Light, inexplicably, uncannily bright, filters down from the kitchen. At the top of the stairs, the air is charged. A sensation of vastness accosts your upturned face.

It is not the doors this time, but the windows. They have not vanished;

you are not that lucky. Instead, they have multiplied exponentially. Dozens, no, hundreds, of windows have been cut into the walls, as if the once-familiar kitchen now exists at the bottom of Alice's rabbit hole. The windows are of varying shapes, and of myriad, abstract sizes. There is one similarity among them all, however, one aspect of their architecture you determine straightaway. Though there are one hundred windows, gaps to see through to the outside world, they have each been installed from the *outside* of the house, so that the locks are inaccessible, the panes as thick as a bank vault door. You are trapped.

And you are on display.

You recoil from the windows and grasp for the doorframe to keep from falling back down the basement stairs, back to before you knew you were a specimen beneath a microscope. There is a pair of eyes on you for every window that has erupted, and those eyes invade and undress you as certainly as you stand. They penetrate your nightgown and sear away your skin and crawl over your teeth and hair like maggots across a corpse.

Whether it is one beast with one hundred pairs of eyes or one hundred creatures each with a single, menacing set, you cannot be sure, but guess it does not matter. The block of knives on the counter comes into focus and you consider extracting one, or all. But what good are knives, chef's, butcher, or otherwise, when the enemy can observe your every move? Facing the windows, you retreat from the kitchen, back against the opposite wall. It takes only a single step into the living room for your hope of sanctuary to be dashed.

The windows are everywhere. Square windows and slider windows, awning windows and port hole windows, windows in varying geometric shapes, bow, bay, casement, and picture windows, windows in every configuration, but none that will accommodate you. In a frenzy, you rush forward and nab a heavy ceramic vase. Too quickly to consider consequences, you heave it at the window closest to the ground, then drop to the floor and cry out after it explodes. Your lovely ceramic vase is little more than powder, but the window at which you threw it has not the thinnest spiderweb of a crack. The thing outside your house, however, growls in obvious displeasure.

With quiet, careful steps, you back away and into the foyer. The creature migrates with you, traveling on what sounds like as many legs as it has eyes, shifting, anticipating, thinking, waiting, satisfying itself—for now—with an unobstructed and unwelcome view.

The radiator starts up again, and you struggle not to sob. That clocks can keep ticking, radiators creaking, that the earth can keep turning strikes you as a flagrant injustice when you are banished to a prison that'd be at home on a Dalí canvas.

You spin wildly for the stairs, ignoring the sleek wooden banister to clear them two at a time. Windows have sprouted along the upstairs hallway too, and the twinkling patterns of light on the runner make you feel like you are in another world. It is not out of the question, given the events of the evening. Perhaps you fell through the wardrobe or were swept up by a tornado. But you feel far less courageous than either Dorothy Gale or Lucy Pevensie, and you dash between the doorframe as if a witch is on your heels.

Before tonight, your bedroom always featured a double-hung window at the center of the space, and you are so relieved that it remains as such, you burst into laughter that echoes wrongly in your ears. With footstool and af-ghan, you obstruct the window, unable to even begin to explain why your bed-room has been spared. You crawl onto the mattress, pull the covers over your body, and reach a trembling hand for the phone next to the bed. The smooth, firm plastic is grounding, familiar. You decide whom you will call.

If your childhood friend who lives up the road will confirm the presence of windows where there hadn't been windows before, maybe she can offer an explanation that doesn't include you having lost your mind. You set your jaw, lift the receiver, and bring the phone to your ear.

There is only silence where a dial tone should be, for the line has, of course, been cut.

You wake sweating and disoriented, the events of *that night* as close to consciousness as they've ever been, and the multiplying windows and disappearing doors return to you like the torment of a ruptured organ. At first you think you will remain in bed, that if you protect yourself with a veil of sleep and sheets, the madness going on around you will cease to carry weight. A combination of thirst and morbid curiosity lure you from your cocoon, and you cloak yourself in another casing: a thick wool sweater and muslin scarf. Protection, however weak, against the monster's gaze.

Wrapping your arms around yourself, you sneak into the hall. Hoping to make it to the stairs without the thing becoming aware you've left your domain for its, you've traversed half of the runner when a traitorous floorboard creaks. Outside, the thing shifts, turning its many-eyed head to the windows.

You race to the bottom of the stairs, slip into the room on your right, and close the door—the interior ones of which have been spared. You'll have no more than two minutes before the monster maneuvers from the front of the house to the back, but you'll need more time than that to accept what's before you, and the migraine that accosts you as a result.

Your glass-fronted shelves have each been shattered, the books they once held in ruins on the floor. A *sea* of books, their level of destruction so severe that a bomb could have gone off without inflicting greater damage. Your lamp is overturned and bent, the cord hacked cleanly in two, its broken bulb ground into the rug like a cigarette on a sidewalk. The well-worn fabric of your favorite armchair is shredded, punctured countless times with an unquestionably vicious blade.

A moan escapes your lips at the sight of your antique roll top desk; its contents have been ripped from nooks and crannies and drawers, papers torn and stained by the soil of an overturned plant. Some of your books and correspondences have been tossed into the fireplace. You can't help but wonder if it's the monster who holds the match. Wallpaper lies in strips beneath the windows, either peeled off by whatever raided your office, or else forced from the plaster when the windows burst into being.

Despite all that has occurred since you awoke last evening (two evenings ago? Twenty?), your mind balks at adding this latest move to the monster's repertoire. It can get in where you can't get out and watch you in your blindness. It can infiltrate your mind as easily as it does your rooms, forcing you to doubt your sanity and second-guess your plans. It can even make you believe you've caused this simply by being you.

If the living room was the heart of your house, the office was your mind, and to regard it in such shambles is like seeing a malignant CT scan of your brain. Gone with the books and papers are the things that made you *you*, and the loss of these threads and memories ignites a white-hot rage.

You open your mouth in fury but before you can utter a sound, the thing is present at the windows, two hundred eyes boring into you, daring you to give voice to your pain.

Though your mind feels as broken as the objects in this room, you suck in another breath. You will close the monster's eyes with the power of your scream, send it away from the house that is yours, and regain your doors with its departure. But like a movie theater in your mind, *that night* is upon you, the empty fairground, the smell of stale popcorn, the pavement against your skin.

In the office, your mouth slams shut so fast your teeth close with a clack, but for all your delayed compliance, the reel continues to run. The taste of beer on unwanted tongues, the sweaty palms on your flesh. The sudden cold, a flash of moon through the trees, the hoot of an owl in the distance.

Silent, you apologize. *I will be silent from this point forward. I won't even think of screaming as long as you promise not to show me* that night *again.*

You dream that you wake in the house you have always inhabited, knowing that everything is the same. The room is brighter than a summer day, and birds chirp from the telephone wires outside. You swing your feet over the side of the bed and lower them to the floor. The marble is cold, but your feet are warm, and you don strappy sandals and a marigold-patterned dress.

You grip the sleek wooden banister as you hasten down the stairs, the dress billowing around your feet and the chorus of an upbeat song in your head. Across the foyer and past the living room, you enter the sun-streaked kitchen, where you lean over the counter to write in your journal while waiting for coffee to brew.

The house—and its prettily-curtained windows, the sliding glass door in the living room showcasing a brilliant blue sky—expands around you, its gently sloping roofline and wrap-around front porch extending out in every direction. You close the journal and pour your coffee. The telephone rings as you take your first sip.

Your fingers close around the smooth plastic of the receiver, and you bring the phone to your ear. "Hello," you say, light-hearted and anticipatory. The voice on the other end belongs to your mother.

"Hi, Mom. Sure, that sounds great, I'd love to meet you for lunch." The dream skips like a scratched CD, and it's your sister-in-law on the phone. "Genevie!" you exclaim, "it *is* gorgeous out. Let's go for a walk."

Another skip, another ringing phone: "What time?" you ask, when a friend from college, Kelly, requests you come for drinks. "Lauren and Elise will be there too? Perfect, I'll see you around eight."

The phone rings, and you answer it. It rings again, and you answer. It rings, and rings, and rings, and rings, and you answer again, and again, and again. The jangling phone and your cheery hellos take on the quality of an anthem.

The phone stops ringing. Your coffee is finished. You place the cup into the sink. As you retrace your steps through the living room, you pluck a light sweater from the back of a chair. Down the hall, and into the foyer, to the wall that features a sizable, arched doorframe and solid oak slab of wood. The door is normal, nondescript, a mere conduit to your plans.

You turn the knob. The door opens freely. You blink in the sun.

There are no monsters. Your body is yours. You smile, and step outside.

The next morning when you open your eyes, you grieve for the loss of your past. That you've dreamed of the time before the monster is the cruelest affront of all.

You dress and leave the bedroom, already wearied by thoughts of what you might find. This time it is the kitchen that has been smashed to pieces: cabinets emptied, appliances upset, glass and cutlery spread across the floor. The tile backsplash you brought back from Italy has been obliterated with a hammer, and the contents of the refrigerator are smeared along the sink.

You take to wandering around the rooms, running your hands along walls, pressing indiscriminately to see if a door will emerge like magic. You go through the house a second time, searching for weaknesses in the windows, panes that might crack or bend or give, where the monster could slip through. You leave no window within your reach unchecked, no wooden frame unrattled, but nothing comes from your frenzied search but broken fingernails and frustration.

You are listless and melancholy. The house taunts you by letting in sunlight. Dust motes are visible in the effulgence, sinking, floating, swirling. It's their tangibility parading as apparition that allows you to see what you've been missing. You are not being tormented by something separate and other, it is your house itself that's haunted. Poltergeists, ectoplasm, orbs, angry spirits; the semantics matter not. No egress is needed to enact destruction when the energy to destroy is within the walls.

This discovery leaves you hollowed out. Fear turns your limbs to lead. The sun changes position in the sky and for a while, you track its progress through the patterns of light in the foyer. Eventually, you rise from where you sit on the bottom step and turn to go up the stairs. The telephone rings as you climb, but you don't bother to quicken your pace. You know by now from the calls before that the line will be dead if you answer.

You release the soggy, rotting banister as you reach the top of the stairs, and walk toward your bedroom along a crack in the marble that began the night the doors vanished and has been widening ever since. Atop the nightstand, by the now-silent phone, your notebook sits, unopened. You pick it up, run your fingers across the cover, and sink to the floor beside your bed.

When your living room became the target of devastation, you figured the basement would be next. You retrieved the notebook from where you dropped it on the night the doors all vanished. Now you flip through the pages, surprised to recognize the spidery script. It seems the handwriting should be different, written by a woman you are no more.

You kept journals since you first learned to write, always a lover of letters. The last entry, dated the fifteenth of June, was the afternoon of *that night*. Exclamation points abound. Anticipation weaves through every sentence. You thought you were in for a night of fun and romance. What you got instead was death.

Not actual death, no. That would have been too final, too easy. But death in every other sense of the word, death of everything as you knew it. Your familial relationships fell apart, followed by the abandonment of your friends. Joy, hope, comfort, security, goals, motivation, the future. Anytime you tried to see beyond the horror, all you saw were scenes from that night.

It was his idea to go to the fairgrounds. You remember that now, reading what you wrote. He was supposed to be waiting for you with a handful of his friends, who were supposed to bring dates of their own. Instead, the men had convened like buzzards. Your undoing was like death on the air.

The fairgrounds were deserted of everything but litter. The previous weekend was its last hurrah. The men quickly morphed from buzzards to monsters, but even as monsters they were merely men. Their eyes glowed red, their mouths stretched open, and they lunged and snapped and ate. You smelled their sweat, sex, saliva drying on stubbled chins. Wild energy rolled off their skin, their impossible muscles, a forcefield like flies around bulls. That they were merely men was more than enough. That they were merely men was hell.

The clothes are torn from your body by the man who was to be your date. He forces himself upon you as if you belong to him. Fists pummel your flesh to keep you silent, pliant. Consciousness flickers, then returns in brilliant technicolor brightness. You feel every transgression against your body. You see his face even in the faces of the others and remember your response a few hours before: "I'd love to come. I'll meet you at seven." You want to die because this is all your fault.

You were wrong, however. Not that it wasn't your fault, because it was. You should have never trusted someone you hardly knew, never gone to a place where no one could hear you scream. It was the last passage you were wrong about. It wasn't from the fifteenth of June. Early on the morning of June sixteenth, one more entry was made. A single line, done in pen, not pencil, scratched into the paper like the inscription on a headstone:

There is no way out of the prison of my body, but unending ways to see in.

Clouds roll past the hundred windows of your empty house and the monster shifts with mindless hunger. Before you realized it was your *house* that was haunted, you imagined the monster as all sorts of things, an option for every set of eyes. A goblin, a goat with the devil's mark between its horns, a dybbuk, a demon, a troll. An alien beast, an angry god, a dragon, a giant, a snake. A horseman, a mutant, a mummy, a yeti, a vampire, a werewolf, a wraith. A zombie, a sea creature, a phantom, a shadow, a spirit, a killer bird, an alligator, an ape. A floating head, a tarantula, a humanoid hunter, a robot, a kraken, an ogre, an undead fiend.

You needn't have gone to the depths of your imagination to shed light on what haunted your home. The movie monsters you feared in your youth are a distraction from the truth. It was always the men, always the memories, always your feelings of shame. The ramifications of that night trapped you completely. You are haunted by what-ifs.

Days pass, and you neither extricate yourself from the covers nor come up with a single reason why you shouldn't carry on lying beneath them. It's possible the house has not succumbed to additional ghosts, but ignorance to the current state of your haunting seems the closest thing you'll get to bliss.

The phone rings constantly now, an ever-present trilling, but your mind continues severing the possibility of connection, keeping everyone that matters away. You think again about Lucy Penvensie and her siblings, how eventually they made their way home. What would they have done had they returned from the wardrobe to find the White Witch ruled their world? You imagine they'd rally to eliminate the evil, because unlike you, they are not alone.

The silence in the house is heavy. You lie in bed. You wait. You tap your finger against the headboard and count the seconds until you can bear the hurt no more.

You wake. You are always waking, but never experiencing the sense of renewal that should come with shedding sleep. While you slept, you must have torn a cuticle, for your skin is stained with blood. Unthinkingly, you place your finger in your mouth; it tastes of cement, of dust.

At first, you think the silence persists, but then you listen harder. The sound—their voices—ripples and pulses, a white-noise hum that has been there all along. It is a sound motivated by hopelessness, by madness, made frenzied by the smell of blood. You know, however, how to quiet them. How to make them disappear.

As you fill the tub with water, you ponder which is worse: having no doors in a house that is haunted, or having one hundred windows? It doesn't matter now, it never did, and you step into the tub. The water is cool, or maybe it is warm, for your skin is not your own.

You sit, unmoving, your thoughts on the past, until the voices surge. This knowledge you have, of the act that will end them, is the sharpest weapon you own.

You unscrew the bottle and drop the lid to the floor. It rolls beneath the sink. The red wine masks the taste of the pills, and you swallow them with indifference. It is thirty minutes (or is it three?) before the pills detonate in your stomach. When they do, the impact is huge. You double over and the foundation splits, like the house is a storybook giant who's swallowed a firecracker. Floorboards shudder. Windows shatter. Outside, the monster screams. You relish in the pain of your assailant, once the monster, now your body. Your home.

Drawing the blade across your wrist hurts less thanks to the pills. The house separates up the middle. The remaining windows explode. You bisect your other forearm along the bluest of veins and black mold seeps from the ceilings. Another sip of wine and your head swims dizzily. Rust-colored water surges through the rooms.

You destroy your traitorous body, this haunted cell, a looking glass for monsters. You will no longer be vulnerable to the vileness of men. It is the brutalist of agonies, to ruin this house, the decaying fortress, to wipe it from the face of the earth. You had to before it could ruin you, before the ghosts dined on your bones.

Better to die than to live in a haunted house forever. To perish while the echoes of your past still sound above the wailing and rattling of chains.

Despair—and the pills—overtake you. You breathe in.

You close your eyes.

The telephone rings. You hear it as if it is an alarm, a reckoning, a signal from another world. It pulls you out from under the weight of your crumbling house, away from the shattering windows and splintering wood. It occurs to you that this time, for whatever reason, if you were to pick it up, there would be someone there. The thought infuses you with something strange. Not quite hope, but something like it. It's a thought like a life raft or the antidote to poison. It's a thought with conviction. With teeth.

You place one pale hand on the edge of the tub and do your best to sit up. The monster howls, more enraged by this small act than by the blade you dragged across your wrists. Its indignation gives you strength, and you heave yourself over the side. You crawl across the bathroom tile, propelled by some deep resolve you did not know you had. If the echoes of your past still reverberate, perhaps it is not too late to reclaim it.

The telephone is ringing from the bedside table in the room across the hall. You make it there in fits and starts, refusing to stop, to rest, to lay your cheek upon the marble.

You grip the cord, hand slick with blood, and pull the phone to the floor. Though your body, the floor, your arm, the walls, tremble, you lift the receiver to your ear.

"Help," you say. "Hello. I need help."

The voice on the other end of the line listens. Outside, the monster closes its eyes.

The Elephant in the Room

Patrick Hurley

Two blindfolded men and two blindfolded women appear in an empty space. They don't know how they came to be; they don't know why. The space, so far as they could tell, has no walls or ceiling. The air hums. They wait.

Though they cannot see, by change in air current and momentary cessation of humming, they can sense when the object appears before them. The blindfolded men and women know their purpose. They place their hands on it, feel its contours and shape.

"It is a pipe!" cries one blindfolded man. He vanishes.

"It's a stick," suggests one blindfolded woman. She also disappears.

"A pencil?" guesses the second blindfolded woman. She has time to wonder how she knows what a pencil was before oblivion claims her.

"A wire," the second blindfolded man claims with certainty. Just as he begins to hope for permanence, he too fades away.

Four blindfolded men and women appear. The object waits for them; they all know their purpose. Each guesses and each vanishes into oblivion.

Eight blindfolded men and women appear. All make guesses; all vanish.

Over and over the cycle repeats itself, with each new iteration of blindfolded men and women doubling. All the while, the humming grows louder, and the great object remains. Finally when only seventeen blindfolded men and women are left out of the 2,097,152 who have appeared during that cycle of becoming, one of the women says in a tired voice, "It is a hair follicle."

And she does not vanish.

There is great wonder in the rest of the blindfolded men and women.

"A hair follicle!" the next blindfolded man repeats.

"A hair follicle!"

"A hair follicle!"

They all repeat the blindfolded woman's guess, and they all remain.

Though they cannot see, they sense when 2,097,135 new blindfolded men and women appear before the hair follicle.

Before the newly created can guess the object, the first blindfolded woman, the savior of them all, shouts at her newly arrived fellows, "It is a hair follicle!"

And this time, she does vanish.

When the others try to repeat her guess, they vanish as well.

Confusion runs amok amongst the men and women. Is this not a hair follicle? What more can be required from the object? Many repeat the original prophet's proclamation of a hair follicle and also disappear, until finally, one particularly insightful man asks, "What kind of hair follicle?"

And he does not vanish.

When a blindfolded woman tries to repeat the question, she does vanish.

The others realize this new prophet has figured out the next question, that their purpose has multiple layers of specificity for the object, which has now become a sacred artifact to them.

"It is a mustache hair!" This blindfolded woman vanishes.

"It's a hair on one's head." The blindfolded man disappears.

"The hair of the armpit!" Another disappearance.

"It's a pubic hair!" This particular blindfolded woman vanishes, though she is remembered fondly by the others, who titter while waiting their turn.

The object is not a forearm hair, foot hair, back hair, or vellus hair.

The blindfolded men and women are beginning to despair, when one of the newly arrived women stands up and says in a calm voice, "It is the hair follicle of an eyebrow."

Nobody vanishes.

Instead, for one glorious moment, all blindfolds disappear. They all watched in awe as the glowing eyebrow hair follicle elevates into the sky, higher and higher until it ascends into glory. And there is great rejoicing among the men and women.

Until their blindfolds return and a new object appears before them.

"Say cheese!"

Wanda Gowen, reporter for *Wired* magazine, smiled as Taryn Nelson, the man she was meant to be interviewing, took her picture with a digital camera and returned to his computer. She was doing a feature on Taryn's start-up Findme for the 2003 end-of-the year issue.

"So, what am I looking at?" she asked as Taryn took out the cartridge from the camera and plugged it into the humming towers on his desk. He pressed a button and several social media accounts appeared on the large screen on the wall behind them. Each of them had Wanda's face on the profile—it had found them by recognizing her face.

"It's the latest in facial recognition technology," said Taryn proudly.

"That is impressive," Wanda said. "How does it work?"

"The math is pretty complex," answered Taryn. "Thousands upon thousands of information bits are channeled into learning algorithms used to identify the correct parts of a person's face. We call it a neural network. It's not perfect yet, but we'll get there."

"Neural network?" Wanda pointed at the towers on his desk. "Does the program mimic the way we think?"

Taryn smiled. "It's just a metaphor for the choice-nodes we've input into the algorithm."

"And you know how these algorithms work?" Wanda asked.

On his desk, the computer towers hummed loudly.

"Of course," Taryn replied, crossing his arms. Though just for a second, as he looked at the humming towers, he wondered if that was true.

Wonky on the Inside

Serena Jayne

THE THROB BEHIND my left eye picked up the pace from a leisurely tapping to an urgent knock. I ignored the horror show happening in my eye by focusing on my latest landscape. I blended oil paints to capture the bloody tinge of sunrise with a childish hope that the scary stuff would skitter back into the darkness. If the two bullet-sized ibuprofen tablets didn't kick in soon, I'd wish one of my boyfriend's beasts alive for a mercy killing.

Byron sketched adorable cartoon abominations. Later, he'd use markers to burst his creations from shades of gray into a rainbow world. He kept his supplies in labeled containers. My brushes and paints, however, were strewn around my workspace. Otherwise, I might panic, thinking ultramarine my only blue option while cerulean and cobalt, phthalo and Prussian, lie tucked away waiting patiently to be summoned to my pallet. Even though I'd taken care to seal the jar of mineral spirits I used to clean my brushes, the kerosene-like stink lingered, as though someone had doused the space with accelerant in an attempt at arson.

The enormous windows, which illuminated the studio with natural light, had sold us on renting the space, but the brightness exposed the dark things darting around inside my left eye. Moving targets raced for the edges of my vision with the speed of scurrying cockroaches.

My glasses slipped down my nose, and I shoved them upward, leaving a crimson fingerprint on one of the lenses. I compared my work in progress with the reference photo I'd snapped during a trip to Lake Erie. The picture evoked a sense of serenity, while the violent undertone of my painting seemed a portent that at any moment, the sky would rain blood.

That morning on the beach, I'd stood shivering, clutching a cup of bitter brew, an ineffective weapon against my dark mood. With dawn breaking around us in a kaleidoscope of color, Byron had kneeled down on the sand and extended a fuzzy jewelry box. "Marry me, Maggie," he'd said.

My heart went into freefall, only to splatter on the packed sand. The wind tousled his sandy hair but failed to blow away his sunny smile or the twinkle in his sienna eyes. Unable to crush his hopes and dreams with my fear and doubt, I'd accepted his proposal and the shackle he'd slid onto my finger.

Later, I returned the ring to its velvet casket and buried the box beneath a pile of panties. The ones with scratchy lace or stiff satin or weird words written across the butt. The ones I'd be mortified to wear on the off chance the day took a disastrous turn and I ended up in the morgue.

Byron added a snaggle-toothed smile to one of his creatures and a pair of horns encircled by a polka-dot bow to another. If cute could kill, they'd be mass murderers.

"Out of contact lenses again?" He raised an eyebrow. "You should go back to the kind that last a whole year. The disposable ones are a waste of money."

I squeezed a tube of cadmium red too hard, and the precious paint squirted out of the tube like gray matter erupting after a headshot. We were barely engaged, and already he tried to tighten the purse strings into a noose.

"Nah, just giving my eyes a rest." I left out the part about how the lenses seemed to magnify the things in my eye. The night before, when I told him about how my eye had turned into a hellish just shaken snow globe, he'd scoffed and said to stay away from Internet medical sites or I'd start believing I had a brain tumor.

I concentrated on my canvas, hoping he wouldn't bring up what had happened at my first solo art show. With symptoms of stabbing chest pain and shortness of breath, I'd been certain I was in the throes of a heart attack. The emergency room doctor had a different diagnosis—panic attack. My new fiancé would have a panic attack of his own if he had any idea how much my anxiety meds cost.

Byron, having grown up the only child of a kindergarten teacher and a florist, tended to see only the positive. I let him think that for me too, the proverbial glass was always half full. I simply didn't reveal that my glass was half full of cyanide.

"Stop scratching." Byron's voice went high-school-principal-stern. "Still dreaming of creepy crawlers?"

I wiped my fingertips, smearing a mixture of red paint and blood on a paper towel. The marks left by the bites alternated between burning and itching. I envied snakes for their ability to shed their skin. "Nightmares starring brain-sucking spiders are the natural reaction to waking up covered in eight-legged creatures. I'm never going camping again."

"Helped you squish them, didn't I?" He reveled in his role of Sir Byron, Protector of Hypochondriac Fiancées and Slasher of Household Budgets, but his real superpower lay in leveraging his artistic talent into illustrating a popular children's book series. A Sunday morning television show was in the works.

"Those little bastards were everywhere. Can't help but worry we missed one or a dozen spiders." I shuddered.

Ever since the ill-advised camping trip, I'd felt the phantom brush of hair-thin legs on the nape of my neck. Tiny teeth nicking my skin. I'd tossed the sleeping bags in a dumpster. I had to, otherwise the fear of the fabric hatching thousands of spider eggs would have driven me mad.

"My happy place is blasting cartoon arachnids into kingdom come." I needed to keep the conversation far away from camping equipment.

"*Spider Island Siege* has shitty graphics." He scrubbed at his drawing with an eraser. "You really should have waited a month or two and bought a used game instead of shelling out the full price on release day."

With my eyes closed tight, I dropped onto my stool and clutched my head.

"What's wrong?" Byron asked. The unsaid word "now" hung heavy in the air.

The strobe light inside my eye kept flashing. "You know those monster movies where a lightning strike illuminates the creepy, dark sky?" My words came out fast, and I barely recognized my voice. "There's a jagged bolt of lightning stuck in an endless loop in my left eye."

"Let's see what your favorite medical site says about your symptoms." His footsteps pattered across the wooden flooring. "Those thingies in your eye must be floaters. I'm checking flashers and eye pain now."

Without giving me a second to rejoice in the fact that Byron finally believed me, the lightning bolts kept coming. I wrapped my arms around myself in an attempt to get my shaking under control before I fell off the stool. "What's it say?"

"Retinal tear or detachment, bleeding or inflamed vitreous, diabetic retinopathy, complications from an autoimmune disorder or eye tumor."

My heart pounded in time with the flashes. Tumor. Cancer with a capital C. The side effects of cancer treatment were as bad as the disease itself. My mother's chemotherapy stole every ounce of quality from her life. She couldn't eat or sleep or breathe. The woman died a miserable husk.

"We going to camp out in my doctor's office until he agrees to see you." His voice trembled. "Shit, Maggie, you could lose your vision. If it's a malignant tumor, they might have to remove your eye to keep the cancer from spreading."

All I had wanted was for him to take my symptoms seriously, but his concern freaked me out. And as though a circuit breaker popped, the disco ball in my eye went dark.

"The lightning bolts stopped." The little girl inside me cheered. Ignoring a problem *could* make it go away. "I don't need a doctor. I'm afraid of the glaucoma test machine." And cancer, I was afraid of a cancer diagnosis. I'd inherited my creativity and my neuroses from my mother. I didn't want to add her diseases to the list.

"You shouldn't be scared of a couple puffs of air." He crossed his arms. "The glaucoma test takes like two seconds and doesn't hurt a bit."

"I can't look into the light inside the machine without blinking. Sometimes they have to hold my eyelids open, but it's like playing chicken with a train that's barreling toward you. And when the machine makes that loud sound, I jump higher than when the can of crescent rolls pops after I jam a spoon inside the crack."

"I had no idea you were such a scaredy-cat." His gaze dropped to my naked ring finger as though he regretted proposing to such a weak woman.

"You still love me, right? Even though I am a chicken and my eye is wonky."

"Sure, you can stop wearing contacts all together. We'll get you some funky glasses from that online discount store. I could get used to the having a hipster fiancée." He stroked my cheek, but when his hand got too close to my bad eye, I jerked away as though some horror could pop out and bite his finger. "Nerdy is the new cool. Anyway, your eye is only wonky on the inside."

After listening to my tales of health woe and examining both of my eyes, Byron's doctor sent us straight to the hospital's ophthalmology department. Elderly patients and their mobility accouterments filled the waiting room. For a moment, I wondered if we'd inadvertently entered a casting call for seniors seeking alien rejuvenation for a *Cocoon* reboot.

A woman, in a faded rose-patterned dress standing behind me, tilted backward. I grabbed her fragile, bird-boned arm to keep her upright. Her scent, with its minty dental adhesive head note, menthol Ben Gay heart note and vanilla-soaked mothball base note, could be dubbed Byron's Grandma eau de parfum. I could almost taste Granny's cookies with their concrete texture and sparse smattering of carob chips.

A middle-aged man with an orange plastic patch over his eye flipped through a newspaper. If not for the bandage that held the patch in place, he'd look like some futuristic pirate.

A print of Starry Night hung cockeyed on the wall. The monsters in his head made Van Gogh hack off his ear, but despite his bouts with insanity, he never sacrificed an eye. I prayed mine would survive the appointment unscathed.

Longing to sneak out the door before someone started digging around in my eye, I fidgeted as though I had ants in my skinny jeans.

Byron decided to stay in the waiting room while the bearded man wearing an unbuttoned lab coat led me into an examination room. Looking at the machinery with its skeletal limbs made my stomach ache, so I zeroed in on his power tie. I coveted the fresh, oxygenated blood color for my sunset. His satin voice was so soft, I needed to lean forward to hear his questions. My fingers twitched, needing to confirm my ears had escaped Van Gogh's blade.

"What brings you here today?" he asked.

"I noticed what looked like a crack in a sheet of glass in my eye along with a gray spot. It wouldn't have been so bad if it stayed in one place, but it constantly moves from the left corner of my eye to the right."

The crack would come and go, a thing that thrived in the darkness and exposed through illumination, such as the brightness of a computer screen or sunlight. The gray spot joined the party days after the crack appeared. At first, I thought a fly was buzzing around my head, or worse yet, a spider had made a web in my hair and dangled in front of my eye. Those damned spiders not only haunted my nightmares, but they also lurked on the edges of my every thought.

"Any other symptoms?"

"It hurts like hell. This is probably going to sound strange, but I had this disco ball or lightning storm in my eyeball for about fifteen minutes."

"Pain is unexpected, but the incident you described is likely an ocular migraine. Be sure to follow up with your primary care physician if you have another episode. Ocular migraines can be treated by a variety of medicines such as those prescribed to treat epilepsy, high blood pressure, or depression." He rooted around in one of the overhead cabinets and removed two small plastic bottles. "I'll dilate your eyes so I can take a good look, and then I'll check for glaucoma."

I dug my nails into the leather armrests of the examination chair, tensing up at the thought of that horrible clicking sound.

"Are you okay, Ms. Rooney?" The doctor's shaggy eyebrows knit together.

Not trusting my voice not to quaver, I nodded and tilted my head back to accept the two rounds of eye drops like they were some magic potion that would protect me from the scary puff of air.

The glaucoma test used a probe that lightly touched each eye, and the machine made no loud pop. Before I knew it, I was alone in the examination room, waiting for my eyes to fully dilate. If the disco ball experience wasn't a big deal, maybe nothing horrible was wrong with me.

About twenty minutes later, the doctor returned to administer more tests. In one, he tilted the chair back and poked at my eyeballs with a stick-like object. In another, he shone a light that lit up the red veins inside my eye and created an odd image on the inside of my eye that reminded me of an electronic bug zapper. The kind with the hatch-marked cage that electrocutes the little bastards who can't resist the lure of the brightness.

The doctor rolled his chair close. "You have a horseshoe tear in your retina. The floaters are a result of the vitreous fluid escaping through the tear. With your extreme nearsightedness, I'd expect to see his type of problem when you reached middle age. Having this condition presenting in someone in their twenties is rare, but not unheard of, especially in someone who does extreme sports."

"The most extreme sport I do is yoga." My short list of talents did not include coordination or athletic prowess in any shape or form. The best I could accomplish was a half-decent sun salutation.

"Maybe you should take a break from the inversions. Anything that places you upside down, such as bungee jumping or roller coaster rides, can damage your retina."

Any lingering namaste was evaporating faster than dry ice.

"So, you'll give me a prescription and the floaters will go away, right?" The thought of the spots and cracked glass thingy bouncing around in my eyeball fluid made me cringe. What if I got more and my field of vision was completely obliterated? My career as an artist would be over before it really started.

"Unfortunately, while the floaters could settle a bit and become less noticeable, there isn't a drug I can give you that will make them go away. They are an inconvenience, but inherently harmless. The real concern is that you're at high risk for retinal detachment."

"Buddhists are all for detachment." I tried to joke, but my stomach was a small craft in the midst of a tsunami.

"Even Buddhists would be against this type of detachment, Ms. Rooney. Surely, they'd see a detached retina as an obstacle on the path to enlightenment." His mouth twisted into a smirk, as though he found me strange, yet amusing. "I'm going to mark the eye I'll be treating." He used a marker to scratch an x on my forehead above my eyebrow.

The x was my version of a scarlet letter, marking me as deficient, unfit for polite society.

He led me to another room, one with a chair and a big white machine. "Relax, this won't take long." He slid on strange headgear and flipped off the light switch.

In the darkness, I squirmed.

I wished I'd been given the option of being knocked out with anesthesia before the doctor played Space Invaders inside my eyeball.

My shoulders tensed and my body went rigid. Breathing shallowly, I shoved the dark fear of losing my sight down past the lump in my throat to my toes. Cancer equaled game over, but so did being blind to a person who considered herself an artist, never again able to paint another bloody sunrise.

"Open your eyes wide and sit still." The doctor leaned closer and zapped my eye with his laser light.

The screech of lobsters being boiled alive sounded inside my ear. Blinking madly, I jerked away. A faint burning odor made my stomach lurch. I prayed my sudden movement hadn't caused the doctor to slice through my optic nerve.

"What are you doing?" My voice came out small. Tight. I longed to curl into a protective ball.

"I'm fusing your retina to the inside of your eye to avoid a detachment. Hang in there. I'm almost done."

Another screech sounded in my ear. Goosebumps broke out all along my bare arms. Like the time I donated blood and nearly passed out once my brain connected the red fluid filling the plastic bag to the stuff that circulated inside me.

I kept blinking to reboot my vision. Everything I saw had a green tinge, as though viewed through a colored filter.

The doctor handed me a business card. "Make an appointment next month for a follow up. In the meantime, if you experience any symptoms of a detachment such as an increase in floaters, flashes of light, or a decrease in your field of vision, call the number at the bottom. We'll make sure you get in right away." He walked me to the waiting room, shook my hand, and handed my file to the receptionist.

Byron returned a dogeared copy of Newsweek to the magazine rack. He licked a finger and rubbed it on my forehead. "With that x, I gotta ask, you dumping me for ole Charlie Manson?"

"Yeah, imprisoned former cult leaders really do it for me. Just kidding. The doctor wanted to make sure he zapped the correct eye."

"Did he go all gunslinger with that puff of air?"

"No, he used a laser to keep my retina from wandering off."

"No cancer?"

"Cancer didn't come up at all." I kept mum about my fear of going blind and that screeching sound that I'd heard while the good doc used the laser. Instead, I covertly scratched my spider bites and waited for him to complain about how much the visit would likely cost.

"I love you, Maggie." Byron held the office door open for me. "Doesn't matter how wonky you are on the inside."

A week later, I abandoned my landscape to paint spiders. Big spiders. Small spiders. Long-legged spiders. Hairy spiders. Spiders. Spiders. Spiders.

My arms were red and raw from scratching. I might have acquired more floaters, but I wasn't certain. Some days, my eye seemed to be full of spots and flecks and spiderwebs. The things in my eye refused to stay still long enough for me to catalogue them. Sometimes, I swore I saw something moving around in my good eye.

Byron was patient at first, but I hardly slept, and I was ever scratching. If I wasn't worried about further loosening my retina, I'd scratch at my eyes and fish out all the bits and pieces that tormented me.

An online search revealed that a treatment for floaters did exist, but it involved emptying out the vitreous like a dirty swimming pool and refilling it with some artificial concoction. Hard pass.

Byron was mad at me for setting off eight extermination foggers in our apartment. I asked him if he still loved me despite my wonkiness.

"Are you trying to kill us and the environment with all those chemicals and ozone-eating substances? Burning down the whole world just to annihilate one innocent arachnid isn't the answer."

I turned my back on him and went back to scratching.

Byron asked for his ring back.

I don't blame him. All I do is obsess about floaters and cobwebs and spiders. All is do is scratch and scratch and scratch.

When I unburied the ring box from its underwear underworld, his face fell. Maybe he wanted me to protest. Maybe he wanted me to beg him to stay. Maybe, all along, he wanted me to be someone different, someone not so wonky.

My right eye turned wonky too. I'm not sure if it happened gradually or all at once. The webs. The gray spots. The cracked glass turned my other orb into a haunted house.

My fingers itched to create. To expel the monsters from my head and onto the canvas. Every so often, the disco ball lit up and spun. In the lightning flashes, a shadow lurked.

Until my other retina was Frankenstein-monster-fused, the wonkiness inside could escape. I kept a mini stapler in my pocket at all times, just in case.

Channeling my inner cartoon Tasmanian devil, I'd flown through the museum, cramming my brain with beauty. I balanced the sketch pad on my knees and reached for a crimson pastel in an attempt to recreate Van Gogh's red willows at sunset.

The drugs I swallowed by the handful to dull the cranium-splitting pain ripped up my stomach and made me cough up blood. Despite the warm weather, I wore a turtle-neck sweater to hide my fingernail gauges and pus-filled sores.

In my dreams, I fingerpainted on the walls using the blood I scraped from inside my empty eye socket. The clots and other bits added the type of texture I usually accomplished using a pallet knife.

After the box I ordered from the Internet arrived, I gave up sleeping all together. The thing emitted a subsonic sound that was supposed to kill every insect within range. While I was deaf to its noise, I couldn't help but hear the unholy sounds whatever's lurking in my eyeballs made.

I rarely left the house these days, but I wanted one last chance to create memories of art to bring me comfort when the evil inside emerged to steal away my sight and my life and my sanity.

I placed my sketchpad to the side and removed the final drawing Byron made for me. The monster wore its swatch of hair in a ponytail, like I did. She held a paint pallet in one hand and a brush in the other. Her right eye was the oogly cartoon version of normal, but the left one dangled from a thin cord of optical nerve. Inside the eye, another creature lurked. I'm pretty sure it was a spider. I longed for the day my monster killed me with her cuteness.

MR. CHESTER

Simon Lee-Price

THE SUN WAS going down, which meant Mr. Chester would soon appear. I stepped away from the window and paced about my study. I was not afraid for myself, but for Sylwia, the young woman who cleaned for me. Mr. Chester was a severe man who belonged to another age.

I could hear Sylwia vacuuming the stairs to the first floor. She usually came in the morning but today, for various reasons, she had started work much later. I sat down at my desk and tried to read my notes. It was hopeless. I kept imagining what Mr. Chester might do if he found Sylwia in the house. She had reached the first-floor landing now, but she still had to clean the bathroom and put fresh sheets on my bed. Foolishly, I'd asked her to clean in the basement as well.

I went over to the window again. I had a view of the front path, which dropped steeply in series of steps down to the gate. In the street, cars drove by with their lights already shining. I had a special name for this restless hour between day and night, which I'd invented as a child. I called it *blue dark*. Blue dark was the time when tea was eaten and children had to put on their pajamas. It was a restless light for a restless hour. Adult voices droned from the TV. The electric fire glowed. Soon the curtains would be drawn. It was during blue dark that Mr. Chester usually called. His loud knock shook the house.

My mother would rise from the kitchen table and say to me: "Be a good boy. Stay here and finish your tea." She would trot up the stairs from our basement flat to answer the front door. When she returned, she seemed shrunken. She walked stiffly and rubbed her back. I never saw Mr. Chester myself, but one night I was roused from sleep by a man's voice directly outside my bedroom. The door opened without warning and the celling light burst on. When my eyes stopped stinging, I saw a hand feeling up and down the wall just inside the doorway. It was a giant hand with wide-spread fingers. I pulled the blankets over my head until I heard the door close again.

"There is no such thing as Mr. Chester," said my mother, when she came to get me out of bed the next morning. I pointed to the wall by the door where he had been feeling with his hand. The wallpaper glistened with damp.

"There is such a thing," I said. "I saw him."

"You just had a bad dream."

Even though it was icy cold, my mother lifted the sash window to let in some fresh air. Pigeons scrambled and fluttered away from the top of the window well. She stood there, gazing up into backyard, rubbing her arms through the sleeves of her dressing gown.

I closed the curtains of my study window and went upstairs to speak to Sylwia. The vacuum cleaner stood silent on the landing, and I found her in the bathroom, bent over scrubbing the tub. She was wearing earphones, but quickly sensed my presence behind her. She spun around, holding the scouring sponge in her gloved hand. The muscles in her face relaxed and her lips stretched in a smile.

"Is something wrong?" she asked, extracting the earphones. She brushed back a strand of hair which had worked loose.

The frosted-glass window had turned violet. I wanted to tell her to leave immediately. To get out of the house while she still had a chance. But how could I warn her without appearing half-mad? I had no clear idea what Mr. Chester would do if he discovered her. When I thought about Mr. Chester, my head clouded with darkness.

"I just came to say it's getting late. You can call it a day once you've finished in here."

"What about the basement?" she called after me, as I retreated to the landing.

"The basement can wait until next week."

I descended the stairs and walked to the back of the hallway. I had not used the basement for years, apart from one room, which served for storage. I opened the basement stairway door and pressed on the light switch, an ancient fixture with a buzzing timer. The bulb cast a hazy yellow light against bare walls. There was no heating in the basement and the dank air always had me coughing before I reached to the bottom step.

The buzzing stopped and the house was silent. I went and stood at the front door, expecting Mr. Chester to knock.

Mr. Chester has not changed in all these many years. My mother is dead, and I have reached middle age, but Mr. Chester is eternal. He dresses like a gent from a century ago and he brings with him the frightful smell of the past. I have never seen him clearly with my own two eyes. However, in a family album that belonged to my mother there is a black-and-white photograph of a man dressed in a dark overcoat, which I sometimes fancy is Mr. Chester. He is posing in front of a roaring fire and raising a pewter tankard. It is the hand I recognize. That huge, workman's paw. It is a shame somebody has scratched away his face.

Sometimes, when they thought I could not hear them, my mother and her older sister, who used to visit us sometimes, would whisper about Mr. Chester. They never used his real name and just said "he" or "him" and sometimes "it."

"How can you live like this?" my aunty Margaret would say.

My mother never answered. I imagined her burying her head in her hands, which was her usual reaction when she could not think how to respond.

Aunty Margaret always left the house as blue dark fell. Sometimes I followed her up the stairs to the front door. I hoped she would take me to her home, where I could play with my cousins, eat ginger cake, and feel warm.

"Is Mr. Chester coming?" I asked. "Is that why you're leaving?"

She tried hard to smile. She would take a coin from her purse and press it in my hand.

"In case the meter runs out."

I spun around to see Sylwia descending the stairs.

"Are you waiting for someone?" she asked. She was carrying the basket of cleaning materials and still wore the pink rubber gloves.

I shook my head and stepped out of her way. I watched her walk calmly to the back of the hallway in her ballet-style shoes. She poked her head through doorway and peered down into the basement.

"It smells," she said.

I came after her. "Really, it can wait until next week."

"I'm here now. Why don't I make a start?" She pressed on the light button and descended, one hand holding the banister. I let her reach the bottom step, drew a deep breath, and followed.

Mr. Chester rarely came down to our basement flat. My mother wanted to protect me from him, which is why she raced to the front door as soon as she heard his knock. But one evening he chose not to knock. We were in her bedroom with a candle lit, keeping warm under the bed covers, when suddenly she fell silent and looked up from the page of the storybook she was reading to me. We could both hear the sound. Somebody was coming down the stairs. My mother leapt out of the bed. She had a look of terror on her face.

Apart from the bed, the only items of furniture in my mother's room were a dressing table and an ancient chest of drawers. She dragged open the bottom drawer.

"Get inside," she said in a piercing whisper.

I giggled at the idea of climbing into a drawer.

"Do what you're told. This is not a game."

I left the bed. I was sure I would never fit inside. It was a capacious bottom drawer, but I was a big boy, almost ready to start school.

It was a struggle for me to squeeze my legs in, but somehow I managed. She pushed the drawer shut and I was submerged in darkness. I couldn't see a thing.

"Stay in there. Don't make a sound."

Sylwia stood in the middle of the basement, clutching the cleaning basket and looking around at the closed doors. Mold had turned the whitewashed walls grey and black. Spider webs hung from the corners, sagging and swollen with dust. I felt ashamed to have exposed to her this neglected part of my house. With each descending step, I fought the urge to cough as the damp air pressed into my lungs.

"It's chilly down here," she said, approaching one of the doors.

"Not that one."

"No?" She smiled at me questioningly.

At that moment we were plunged in total darkness. My chest tightened and I heard myself let out a moan. I was a child, a toddler, my legs too weak to stand.

The ceiling light came on again. Sylwia had her hand on the wall switch in front of me. She had found it quickly in the dark.

"Are you alright?" she asked.

"I nodded and let go of the end of the banister.

"You look faint."

"It's the air down here." I coughed.

The atmosphere had affected Sylwia too. It had extinguished the spark in her.

"Maybe I should wait until next time." She traced a gloved fingertip along the wall and examined the slime that came off. "Yes, you're right, it is time for me to go."

There was a knock like thunder from above. It startled me as much as Sylwia. It has been ages since Mr. Chester has bothered to knock. I had grown used to him using his key and entering the house unannounced.

"Who's that?" she said. She knew at once this was no ordinary visitor. Mr. Chester's knock made your heart stop.

My mother would never speak about the night I hid inside the bottom drawer. I curled up in there for what seemed like hours, and I probably fell asleep. So what I heard and saw might also have been a dream.

When she pulled open the drawer, my mother looked bloodless in the candlelight. She held me tight. Her body shook and she was cold as ice.

"That was Mr. Chester, wasn't it?" I said.

"Never say that name."

I believed that merely to utter his name would bring him to us. I developed a fear of the word Chester and any word that sounded like it. Due to the damp in our flat, I suffered from a persistent cough and, when my mother described it to the doctor as a "chesty cough," and he lifted up my sweater and pressed his chilly stethoscope against my skin, I blacked out and had to be revived with smelling salts.

A chest of drawers is an object of terror for me. I do not have a single one of them anywhere in this house. I keep my clothes on shelves and on hangers in a closet. Years ago, I encountered a grotesque work of art at an exhibition in London – a life-sized wooden sculpture of a reclining man, whose entire chest consisted of three drawers, each one pulled open to a differing degree and exposing its bare insides. I collapsed in front of this abominable effigy. When I came around, I was in the room of the security staff, who gave me a mug of strong, sugary tea. The friend who was with me told me on the journey home that before regaining conscious I had mumbled a lot of nonsense. "Chester made," and "Luck of the draw," I had apparently said.

My nonsense might have meant something to my friend had he ever heard my mother speak. She rushed her words, trying to say everything all at once, and she had a strong regional accent. From her mouth, *chest of* drawers sounded very close to *Chester* drawers. I could never think of that feared item of furniture without also picturing the walled city of Chester, founded on the banks of the Dee by the Romans, with its streets of splendid black-and-white, timber-fronted buildings. In my child's mind, a chest of drawers was like a Dundee cake or an Ulster coat, a creation named after its place of origin.

The front door opened with a rattling sound.

"He's got keys?" Sylwia gazed at me for an explanation.

"Sylwia," I said, "this house doesn't belong to me."

"What are you talking about? Of course this house belongs to you." She tilted her head to one side to better comprehend my madness. "Who does it belong to then?"

I couldn't say his name. I tried but the word got stuck in my throat. I coughed hard. All I could pronounce was "Mr.—."

"What does he want?" She took a step back, staring beyond me up the stairs. "He's come for me, hasn't he?"

She saw the answer on my face.

"Why? What have I done?"

"I'm so sorry," I said. "I should never have allowed you to work so late."

"Will he come down here?"

We both listened. He was walking overhead.

She turned around, shaking. "There must be another way out?"

I thought there might be a window in one of the rooms through which she could escape. I no longer remembered clearly.

"Follow me," I said. My sense of direction was poor, but the door I approached led, I hoped, to the room directly below my study at the front of the house. As I turned the handle and pushed, the light timed out again.

Sylwia gave a little moan, and I heard her fumbling in pitch black beside me. A few moments later her phone-torch lit up. She shone the beam into the room.

I was right. There was a window. A bay window. Black and without curtains.

"It's got bars on it," she said, moving the beam up and down to reveal the extent of the ironwork.

The basement light came on. We both practically tumbled into the room. I shut the door, but there was no way to lock it. When I turned around, Sylwia was taking slow steps toward the back wall, following the beam of her phone-torch.

My stomach tied in a knot. What reared up in the torchlight was monstrous.

It is possible that Mr. Chester is not his real name. My memory of those early childhood days is unreliable. Sometimes, when I think back, I can hear what sounds like another name, faint, submerged, as if it were spoken beyond a veil. It is a rushed blur of a name which, try as I might, I can never bring into focus.

So, Mr. Chester it has always been, and the name suits him better each day. Like the city of Chester, he rises from ancient foundations and affects an outward propriety. He comes and goes, just as he pleases, but never before blue dark. After blue dark, comes black dark, which is when adults go to bed. I haven't the courage to ask him what he wants. I fear how he might reply. Mr. Chester is a rough and shameless man. There is a reason for black dark. Some things should remain unseen.

"What's the matter?" Sylwia turned around and aimed the light at me.

I collapsed onto my knees, pointing a finger toward the back wall.

"It's just a chest of drawers," she said, lighting it up again.

She seemed not to see how massive it was. The thing rose taller than a grown man. It was a chest of drawers built for a giant.

She walked closer, undaunted, and even reached out and stroked the edge with her palm.

"We could both hide inside the drawers," she said. She turned and faced me, and I thought I saw the trace of a grin slide from her lips.

"He'll look inside."

"It's our only chance."

"You get in first," I said.

She shook her head. It was the first time she had ever disobeyed an order from me. "Be quick," she said. "I can hear him on the stairs." She put down the cleaning basket and the phone and, squatting, tugged open the bottom drawer with both hands. "Come on, what are you afraid of? It's just an empty drawer."

I crawled toward the looming object, struggling to bear my own weight. I felt trapped. Helpless. I was back in my mother's bedroom again and needed somewhere to hide. Sylwia had stood up and was watching me. The torch lit her from beneath and made her look like an evil giant. She showed no surprise at my undignified performance. It was as if she knew about my phobia.

"In you get and keep quiet."

I dragged myself into the drawer and she helped me with her foot. I lay on my shoulder, facing toward the front. With a grunt, she shoved the drawer shut and I was dispatched into darkness.

At my mother's funeral, I felt the presence of Mr. Chester. He was not among the mourners in black lining the graveside, but the rumbling thunderclouds told me his spirit lurked nearby. My mother had died a well-off woman, and, at the reception, nobody mentioned the early years in our basement flat with the sour smell of damp and the black mushrooms the size of saucers growing inside the wall cupboards. But Mr. Chester never forgets. He still comes for my mother, just as he did in those days. I sometimes think it was for her own safety and not mine she hid me inside the drawer. Mr. Chester is not the kind of man to trouble himself with a child.

I have never spoken about Mr. Chester to anybody in my adult life. Apart from a hypnotist whom I consulted to rid me of my phobia. Even under deep hypnosis, I could recall nothing of my experience inside the drawer. Regressed, I saw daylight instead of night. I was climbing the steep flight of stone steps, which led up from our kitchen to the backyard. I felt woozy having just swallowed my daily dose of cod liver oil, and the surface of the yard swung into view, a blinding phosphorous white. A huge pigeon puffed out its chest and strutted toward me across this empire of dried shit.

A light came on in the room. It seeped in through the narrow gap around the edge of the drawer. I lay still and listened for the voice of Mr. Chester. To this day, I have never heard him speak, but I know just how he will sound. He is a man of very few words. He barks commands and will not take no for an answer.

It was Sylwia's voice I heard instead. Scarcely a whisper. I could not tell if she was afraid or expressed some other emotion. I wondered how she could bear to face him in the light, gaze at those inhuman hands, one of which had crawled across my bedroom wall all those years ago.

Straining my neck, I pressed my eye against the gap at the top corner of the drawer. With a little wriggling, I could see a section of the room. Not far away stood a figure in a dark coat. Only the rear of him was visible, a pair of broad shoulders and the length of a sleeve. His hand was obscured by the front of the coat. I worked my eye lower down the gap. I saw the calf of his trousers and his polished black brogues. I saw Sylwia too. She was on her hands and knees, scrubbing the floor with a brush. She carried a stick in her mouth like a dog. I shut my eyes as Mr. Chester's hand swung down to strike a blow.

I still remember the smell of mint on my mother's breath when she let me out of the bottom drawer. It is strange I never thought to ask her why she smelt that way. Sometime afterward, we went on an outing to Chester. It was a bright day, but very chilly, and we walked up and down the bank of the river and then through the streets, stopping in front of shop windows but never going in. I think my mother was unwell. We had our lunch in a cafe, and she drank only black tea, even though a man came over and offered to pay our bill. With my spending money, I bought a postcard and a stick of rock, and riding home on the Crossville bus, I learnt to read my first word. The word was Chester. It ran through the stick of rock in bold red letters.

My mother smiled. One day, she said, she would buy me as much rock as I could eat.

I wanted to preserve that souvenir stick of rock. I placed it on the chair beside my bed before I lay down to sleep. The next morning, I found it melted into a sticky white pool due to the damp in the air.

Sylwia helped me climb out of the drawer. My neck ached and my back was stiff, otherwise I felt in good shape. Sylwia, too, appeared unhurt. There was no mark from the blow Mr. Chester had dealt her. Nevertheless, I felt guilty for drawing her into my nightmare.

She let me press her hand, but it stayed limp. The pink gloves had been peeled off and lay in the cleaning basket.

"I'm sorry," I said.

"I'm going."

"I can understand if you never want to come back."

Carrying the cleaning basket, I followed her up the basement stairs and along the hall to the front door. She lifted her leather jacket from the stand and slipped it on. She turned and looked at me. The makeup in the corner of one eye was smudged.

"How can you live like this?" she said.

I had no answer for her. This is the house of my childhood, purchased with my inheritance. But it will always belong to Mr. Chester who comes and goes as he pleases.

I gave her the money I owed her for her cleaning work. She took the roll of notes without a word and slid them in her jacket pocket.

"Thank you," I said, as she opened the front door.

I returned to my study. Through the window, I watched Sylwia, hair untied, descending the steps in the dark. A man was waiting for her at the gate. They hugged one another and then they climbed into a car and drove away southward down Old Chester Road.

I sat at my desk and picked up my pen. I concentrated and tried to write about my day. But my mind turned black, as it always does. The same black as inside the room the night Mr. Chester paid his call.

It Tastes Like Ghosts

Nadia Shammas

IN THE PAINT, in the corners and crevices and *textures* of your plastic horse, smaller than my palm, a choking hazard really if you'd ever choked in your entire life. No, you swallowed toys whole, meat cut too large and boiled too tough to chew, you let it slide painfully down your throat with no resistance. Choking is for anyone who has stopped to think twice. Choking is for the rest of us, hesitant, distrustful of ourselves to either overfill the spoon or not swallow it down. It's about capability. I'd be the one who chokes.

The brown body and black mane dulled. The plastic's hard and sharp, and if I chewed, I'd slice my gums up and then all I'd taste is myself, which I taste all the time. Which defeats the purpose of this.

I recognize how hardened I am, now. I know that the edges of me are different now. Have you ever consumed something that hasn't changed you, even for a little? It's utilitarian to swallow whole, to let things pass through you from one end to the other, untransformed. It's indulgent to taste, to let my tongue wander uselessly over my potatoes, my icing, your pony.

We're back at choking. Because I'm tasting the pony, I'm tasting you in this room, curly-haired and soft. You were a quiet child who threw wild tantrums, which means you were the kind of toddler who it was easy to ignore until it wasn't. Right now, in a cheap cotton dress with an itchy collar, you sat across from this very toy horse. Spit covers your mouth and chin, and you keep your eyes fixed on that pony as you take each of the other horses from that birthday gift set and methodically, one by one, put them in your mouth. You don't chew, never chew, but you work it in your mouth, letting your spit soften it. You were patient, you sat and worked and salivated until you worked your neck hard to swallow the toy. Three times over the hour, you sat and stared at this lone survivor as you ate his family whole. You could have eaten him, you wanted him to know. You could have swallowed him like the rest, but you wanted him to watch, and remember your devouring stare.

You didn't eat him, but you touched him with your spit-soaked fingers and after all these years something of that remained. Or it didn't. I've remembered your gaze, the light bites when we sat, the impartially curious way you watched me writhe beneath you. But I already understood this toy when I found him in your room, long abandoned. Whatever stuffies you had were long rotted, skins abandoned like clothes in the rapture. I know what it's like to be it, so that isn't why I put it in my mouth. I wanted to understand you this time.

I'm going on too long. I said I was indulgent. It's why you left me, probably.

I use my tongue to bring him towards the back of my throat. "It's like taking a pill," I say, or I would say if it wasn't in my mouth. Imagine I said it. I want to keep this memory of you on my tongue. But you wouldn't do this. I position him back first, so his lets don't get stuck on the way down. It's smooth, and a little too big to comfortably slide down, and so I hold my tongue just so, jaw stretching, mouth sore. The strain of it tightens the entrance. It's getting harder now, but you wouldn't choke. I stick my fingers in my mouth and try to push it through. I start to cough, but there isn't even air to cough properly, it threatens to cough the toy out. I push harder and instantly tear up. I think of snakes and, picturing them, picturing you, I work the muscles of my esophagus wide, and down. My shoulders move as I heave, my body trying to force me up, force this hazard out, an exorcism.

The edges of my vision blacken. I think that it would be fine if I died here. If I suffocate, if the pony's sharp legs decide to come to life and trash in my throat, the hard plastic hooves slicing my esophagus. If I choked on my own bile and laid here on your childhood bedroom's floor, would you sense me here like I sensed you? No one has lived here for years. Your presence was too large for any realtor to wave away the strange feeling that you leave in your wake. At some point, everyone gave up on trying to sell it. It stayed abandoned. Teens played pranks to sneak in, they smoked weed and left ashes on the kitchen tile but never once did their footsteps creep up the carpeted stairs. I'm alone here, wheezing like a kettle, trying to finish a job to prove something to someone who walked out of my life without a note.

It's almost down. My eyelids flutter, throat feeling like your long nails have reached inside me and dug in, scratching on their way down. This pony tastes like your fingers. I savor it. This pony is you, has always been you. You've never touched anything you didn't want to consume. You mark your territory with your mouth.

I am what you left behind. I am dying on your bedroom floor. Your carpet is purple. Maybe I'll wake up and find you here after all. Maybe I won't wake up, but you'll be here, trailing kisses down my corpse, stopping at my toes, before you unhinge your jaw and swallow me whole.

I'm okay with that because I've done what I've come to do. I've taken something of yours. Your pony is inside me, now. I swallowed you whole first. You know how it feels, now.

Grandfather's Coat

Shenoa Carroll-Bradd

"Do it. Put it on, I dare you."

Ellison shoved hard between my shoulders, pushing me into the living room where our grandfather's coat lay draped over the arm of his favorite chair.

It was the brown tweed coat with the worn-through elbows, the one he never let Mama patch. The one that always smelled like old man and pipe tobacco. The one he was buried in, no longer with him just as surely as he was no longer with us.

The coat appeared on the back of his sag-seated chair two days after the funeral, smelling as musty as always, unchanged except for a single smudge of dirt on the left cuff.

No one touched it. We all stared, but then just let it be.

We were busy. Unlike him, we still had lives to lead.

But when we didn't pay attention to it, the coat started wandering. We found it on the attic stairs, rippling down the risers. We got up from doing homework on the couch and it was there, lounging across the cushions, sleeves outstretched like old arms inviting a hug. It hung itself on open doors and towel racks, anywhere its lived-in skin could perch.

Mama suspected Ellison of playing a prank, and she whupped him good one night to make it stop.

But the coat kept moving after that, and not even Ellison was that bold.

The coat didn't like being folded, and it wouldn't let itself be put away for long. Any attempt to hide it would only last until you left the room. Then there it would appear again, draped on his chair like it never left.

I licked my lips and inched across our braided rag rug. The way the coat lay, one sleeve hung right above the pocket, and the shadows from the standing lamp made it look like a fist bulged under there.

"Go on," Ellison hissed.

Easy for him to say as he hovered at the edge of the room, like that was safe. Like the coat couldn't hear him if he just kept his voice low enough.

After the whupping didn't work, Mama got so tired of the coat sneaking around the house she pinned bells to its collar, like a little cat.

Grandpa's coat sulked for days afterward, throwing itself in a noisy heap whenever we left the room and making a mournful racket in the hall once everyone had gone to bed. The memory of bells tinkling past the bedroom door still haunts me. Not that there was any comfort in the silence once she took 'em off. The sly rustle of creeping fabric was worse.

Closer now, I saw the lapels rose and fell a fraction of an inch, the movement so subtle it could have been nothing but the pulse of blood through my eyes. I hadn't seen the motion from farther away, which meant Ellison wouldn't see it from that distance, either. It was only moving for me. Grandpa had chosen me.

I grabbed it by the shoulders, the fabric rough and familiar, uncannily warm, and I slung it around my skinny frame. My arms swam in the tattered-elbow sleeves, and the weight of it pressed me down.

Down.

Down.

Out went all the lights.

The enormity crushed me, and the air grew so cold it shocked my lungs, worse than jumping into an icy lake. It was an inside-out kind of cold, like never being warm again. The room closed small and empty and silent around me, and I couldn't make my neck turn to see if Ellison was still behind me or not. I didn't feel him back there. I didn't feel anything, except loneliness and cold. And all I saw was black, and all I smelled was dirt, wet and sticky with clay. The kind of dirt where things were planted but never grew.

And then hands were on me, dragging off the weight. Light flooded back in. I was in our living room once more, with the smiley faces drawn in dust atop the TV and our grimy sneakers shoved under the couch legs.

Ellison had me by the shoulders, his eyes too wide for his face.

"Where'd you go?" I murmured, half-dazed and sour, like he'd shaken me awake.

"Where'd *you* go?" he countered. "You went all stiff, with your eyes rolled back. I thought you might start shaking and bite off your tongue."

We looked at the pile of tweed around our ankles, both seeing something different. Both certain my brother just saved me.

After I wore it, Grandfather's coat never moved again.

Ellison and I never brought it up.

Mama was finally able to tuck it away in an attic trunk, and after a time, the family just...forgot.

Except for me. As the years creep by, I can't keep my mind from slipping back to when I put my arms in the sleeves and felt the grave surround me.

He could always find the tarnished lining, our grandpa. He only ever read out the worst bits from the newspaper, the murders and the accidents, and never let a burnt crust escape without remark.

I've kept it to myself because who would ever believe me? But I think Grandfather's coat was only alive long enough to pass on his final bit of bad news. No glowing afterlife awaits. No grand, loving reunion with all we've lost.

Just a final inheritance creeping down the hallways of time, coming to wrap me up, to weigh me down.

To turn out all the lights at last.

Quid Pro Quo

Paul L. Bates

Multiple Possible Beginnings

I NEED TO get this all down before the *crisis*. I mean crisis in its most primitive application: that inevitable triumph of chaos over routine. My inability to remain asleep has caused the steady erosion of the barriers between dreams and whatever else there might be. Or perhaps it is my inability to remain awake. Whichever it is, I continually *awaken* from one nightmare into another until I remain so wide-eyed that sleep becomes impossible for what seems like days without number.

This task I am undertaking is hampered by my reluctance to accept the veracity of any single version of reality under the circumstances. In truth, it is only when one of the random nightmare sequences continues without aberrant mutation that I begin to suspect I am truly awake. However, the experiences are inevitably without euphoria as I know the next little victory, so to speak, will inevitably offer an altogether different perspective. Consequently, I tend to remember the past selectively, and in so many contradictory versions that all have become suspect. And to make matters worse, these unwelcome dreams are, for the most part, permutations of one another. All involve my various imprisonments within this monstrous house.

The origins of my predicament are open to interpretation as well. In one version I arrive on foot at twilight, a stranger, lost and seeking refuge from an impending storm. Winds howl and circle me like spirit wolves. My only safe haven is the decrepit crumbling manor upon which I have stumbled, seemingly by chance. I have no idea from whence I have come. In another, I stand upon the gravel driveway on a sweltering summer's afternoon. Sheltering beneath the portico, I stare at the imposing entryway fondly remembering the old house from my childhood visits. Distortions caused by heat rising all around me make my head spin as I sway like a sapling in a gale. Once again, I have no idea from whence I have come. In the next version, I rush past the butler to open the many paneled door to greet the young cousin I have not seen for a decade who is standing timidly upon my doorstep. I embrace him fondly and welcome him back into my life—a life that in nowise exists before this precise moment.

I am by turns the master of the house; a welcome guest; a servitor attending the brooding specters who wander the dark corridors often unaware of one another; an illicit lover, desperately awaiting my next opportunity; a secret prisoner, with no chance of reprieve, starving in one of the many locked cellar rooms, chained to the wall while hungry rats gnaw with grim determination beyond the thick door. Each dream memory is as vivid as the next, all are equally insubstantial. All are bizarre and utterly improbable perspectives for someone with my creative temperament. During these episodes, I behave as best I can, never certain if any of it is even remotely real.

There are times when I have no idea who or what I am, seemingly bound to wander the dismal corridors and dusty rooms for eternity. I once found an ancient telephone in my wanderings, an awkward black stem with a sluggish dial and two hard black daffodils for voice transmission. I struggled to remember a phone number, any phone number; dialed digits at random, listened to a distant buzzing, as if a small wasp were trapped within the earpiece. In another dark and dusty room on another floor I heard the listless jingle of an identical telephone. At first the sound was distant, then near at hand, then both simultaneously. Tentatively I answered, *Hello?* Downstairs I responded with *Hello?* Soon *Hello? Hello?* was all I could say to myself on both ends of that desperate and depressing conversation.

Nowadays the ancient mother-of-pearl push-button light switches rarely work, and when they do, they produce the palest amber glow in which flecks of dust drift while objects loom as vague shadows, layered one upon the other receding in the distance. On occasion moonlight pours through open draperies skewing hard edged crisscrossed patterns of the Palladian window muntins across cold black and white checkered marble floors. The worn stairs creak, the threadbare carpets reek of age, the textured wallpaper hangs in tattered shreds. Odors come and go without relationship to their surroundings. They vary, from mildew to the merest suggestion of rotting meat, from the acrid smell of unwashed flesh to the crisp perfume of a freshly extinguished candle. From time-to-time distant sounds penetrate the usual pall of silence, drifting from other parts of the manor. I recall hearing a scratchy record, playing tinny music, a man's ridiculously cheerful voice through a megaphone; a bath being drawn, the tap barely up to the task of filling the tub; the clink of crystal glasses, silverware against bone china; the titter of a woman's polite laughter against the dull roar of male conversation; the clickity-clack of an old-fashioned film projector; distant heartrending sobs in the night.

Sometimes, during the day, I try to read. There is a vast library, heavy bound books, red, black, and burgundy with flaking gold letters obscuring the titles, an antique rolling ladder for reaching the dusty upper shelves, dark leather covered armchairs cracked and veined with age. I'm certain I'm dreaming when the books turn to powder in my hands or some wriggling segmented abomination emerges from half eaten pages silently demanding I leave it in peace. When the words make some semblance of sense, I suspect I am awake. Other times I sit staring at page after page of rambling nonsense or just random symbols, unsure if I am dreaming or simply losing my mind.

Most of the roles I assume in haphazard rotation are utterly dispirited. Perhaps the most painful of these personas is that of the butler, for he is the only one who has full reign over this palatial tomb. The other specters either answer to him or are dependent upon his formal ministrations. It is with stubborn determination and authority I traverse the vast hallways in this unbending role. Even the callous withered crows who peer down at me from the bleak portraits that line the dim passages seem to envy me my usefulness. Yet it is all sham and pretense. The other servants are little more than wraiths, puppets barely comprehending my instructions—caricatures I rarely, if ever, occupy—going about their menial tasks by rote. The master and his guests are equally lost, if only slightly more substantial. Their needs remain much the same, save during those delightful times of chaos that upend the dreary stability of our routine, times when anything is possible.

These inevitable disruptions always involve the same regular visitors to the house, those calculating vultures who circle the mire of our misery at a safe distance save for their occasional appearances meant to maintain the illusion of their indispensability. And in truth, as they are the only major players in this household whose roles I never assume, I must admit they are indispensable, if only to convince me I yet live, however deranged. And perhaps even more importantly, they give me hope that I might eventually make some sense of the rest of it—that the impending crisis which looms ever larger might actually be mitigated.

DOCTOR NOHOPE

The quality of the light changes abruptly whenever the good doctor arrives. Whereas I can usually depend upon all physical manifestations within this prison to appear dim and indistinct—in some wretched state of dissolution save when I strenuously concentrate upon them—this is not the case when Dr. Nohope is about. He possesses an irresistible nimbus which imbues him with the power to illuminate whatever is in close proximity to him. Dr. Nohope's tailored suits are impeccable, his cravats freshly pressed, his face is always flushed and jovial. His elongated round head (which reminds me of an egg) is adorned with a thinning fringe of white hair, and his stubby fingers are deft and agile. Nothing whatever discourages the man. And while his visits inevitably involve some implausible treatment for my agonizing array of conditions, he is overtly careful to avoid naming either my complaints or his fantastic cures as he goes about his task of maintaining his seeming indispensability.

Sadly, his presence causes me such anxiety that I inexorably experience his visits from so many chaotic perspectives I remain uncertain as to what actually transpires between us.

I usually greet him at the door as the indifferent butler, safe within my usefulness. The grey foyer suddenly takes on the aspect of brilliant color near him, like a floodlight breathing life into death within a small sphere centered upon his person as we exchange pleasantries. Dr. Nohope slips me the elixir which fuels my purpose, makes no mention of the fact. He then assures me he knows the way and that I need not announce him. He tells me to take his heavy black bag to the library. He leaves me holding his hat and coat, with the black bag at my feet as he bounds up the stairs, humming a catchy lilt, like a child eager to play with some new toy. I hang the hat and coat in the foyer closet, struggle to lift the bag with two hands that he has carried effortlessly with one.

Suddenly I hear Dr. Nohope's firm knocking at my door. He arrives in a whirlwind, spins to my bedside before I can welcome him. I beg him for something to help me sleep. He insists I sleep like a baby, regardless of my dreams—that what I need is to get out of bed, to enjoy life. The next thing I know he has plucked me from my cocoon of sheets and blankets. Humming like a freshly tuned engine, he begins marching me back and forth about the bedroom, faster and faster, up and down the halls, then down the stairs.

Lurking in the shadows I watch the sinister doctor push the old man into the library. My mind is clouded by the capsules he gives me to control my rampant insomnia. The library door shuts with an ominous thump, like the lid on a coffin. It is not my business, I tell myself. Nothing that happens in this madhouse is my business. I am a guest, only a guest, a fortunate passerby—who am I to pass judgment on the eccentricities of this ancient household? My back pressed hard against the wainscot, I slide down the paneled niche whimpering, my hands over my ears, my eyes shut tight when I hear the muffled voice of the old man reacting to that which the doctor subjects him. I abandon all dispassion when I hear the doctor's harsh laughter, try desperately to piece together the specifics of the old man's endless protestations, but he is strangely unable to articulate his words.

That madman my cousin has let into the house is pounding on my door again, blathering nonsense about Dr. Nohope torturing the old man. I rub my eyes, certain we have had this exact conversation before, although I cannot remember when. Warily, I admit him to my room. His face resembles a stringy bed of kelp, undulating in the tide; his voice sounds like a loose shutter banging in the wind as he rants on and on. Something about stopping the medical madness in the library. How can I oppose the doctor? Who else will secretly leave those vials which maintain my energy and composure? Frantically the fool grabs my hand. He has summoned a Herculean strength one would not expect to look at him. He pulls me down the stairs, stands at a distance pointing at the library door like a prancing idiot practicing pantomime. Failing to move me, he draws near, whispers in my ear, demanding I listen. I put my other ear to the many paneled door, hear the plaintive grunting within, like that of a trapped pig, or lovers consummating their lust. Curious, I open the door, enter the room.

Dr. Nohope is sitting at my cousin's desk, helping himself to the cigars in the humidor, stuffing them into his jacket pockets. Merrily he bites off the end of one and lights it. He looks up, eagerly waves me in. His large black bag is open and empty beside the desk, gaping like baby hippopotamus. He has, I surmise, assembled the ungainly contraption that constrains my poor cousin, who kneels trembling before the desk, his arms restrained behind his back. My cousin's head is firmly secured within an aluminum framework that is anchored to the desk by means of large suction cups. Various claw-like appendages hold my cousin's mouth wide open while a small clamp affixed to another suction cup keeps his extended tongue fixed to the desktop. I circle my cousin guardedly, move cautiously until I am standing beside the doctor, staring aghast in disbelief. Something dark brown and glossy is crawling deliberately within my cousin's open mouth. I catch only glimpses of the thing until I realize it is a long and segmented body with tiny twitching antennae, countless short feet that wriggle in tandem. My cousin protests piteously. Dr. Nohope evidences no concern whatever, drags deeply on his cigar, blows thick grey smoke into my cousin's face, stuffs more cigars from the humidor into his inner jacket pockets.

"It's to increase the level of his discomfort, you know," he explains casually before I can ask. "Like the restraints on his arms. Either he must come to grips with his condition or else he must reject it completely. Either solution, however implausible, is acceptable."

The madman, who has remained cowering at the open doorway watching us, can no longer restrain himself. He barges into the room demanding how I can listen to this dithering claptrap and remain unmoved. He slaps me hard across the face, screaming, *Wake up,* showering me with spittle. His actions have the desired effect. Together we free my cousin, who spits out the arthropod crawling about his mouth before he curls himself into a blathering ball of jelly at the foot of the desk, where he shivers miserably, completely unresponsive to our entreaties.

As one, we turn on Dr. Nohope, who has already captured his pet and dismantled his contraption, placing everything back within the black case. Incensed, we beat the doctor repeatedly with our fists, knock him down, kick him without mercy, fully expecting him to collapse in a bloody heap at our feet, but he takes it all good naturedly. "It is to be expected from *laymen*," he says, as jovial as ever, when, at last, we are too exhausted to pummel him further.

Dr. Nohope stands admiringly before the foyer mirror, straightening his cravat, shirt and jacket, his round face beaming. Once again, as the butler, I help him into his overcoat, hand him his hat. He leaves humming the same ingratiating tune, taking what little light there is within this dungeon with him.

ATTORNEY GLADHAND

Like some elegant stork, all bare legs and long distinguished nose, Atty. Gladhand treats her surprise visits to the house like some absentee landlord making certain her property is being suitably attended by those entrusted with the task. In her presence, the members of that shambling cast of shadows become wretchedly jealous of one another. And I tremble with expectation in whatever role I find myself.

She arrives with the squeal of tires, the spray of gravel, parks her sleek black coupe beneath the portico. As the butler, I take her briefcase, welcome her to the manor. She caresses my cheek, like one might a dog, and I whimper uncontrollably with joy.

"Assemble the staff," she commands.

Together we march off to the back of the house. In the kitchen she confronts the cook who is forever devising some dubious concoction. Atty. Gladhand struts about, sniffs and murmurs her approval. For the dimwitted maids she runs her finger through the layers of established dust, mixing biting insults with irrepressible glee. As the footman—a role I rarely assume—I watch her send the butler on some fool's errand before she seizes my hand and pulls me eagerly into the butler's pantry. She hops onto the narrow counter, lifts up her short skirt revealing her lack of underwear, her unabashed readiness. She unbuckles my belt, deftly draws me into her whispering endless profane encouragements into my ear.

When she is finished with the servants, I can hear her footfalls echoing throughout the house as she seeks out the other occupants. By now I am frantic with perceptions. As the houseguest, I hear her clomping down the hallway like a marauding Clydesdale. I am certain she is pacing back and forth beyond my door simply to torture me. Without knocking she abruptly enters my dark and tiny room, shuts the door behind her with a snap like the cocking of a pistol's hammer. Unhurriedly, she surveys the grey surroundings with abject disapproval, wrinkles her nose, scowls.

"Well?" she demands, after a tortuous pause.

I shrug, hoping the gesture is enough.

"What have you to tell me?" she presses.

"Nothing ever changes," I say, uncertain what else will appease her.

She stares at me with contempt.

"You forget," she announces, "I know who you really are."

"Who am I?" I plead.

"That will remain our secret. Now tell me about each of them."

Sadly, I recount all the nonsense I can remember, not certain if any of it is remotely relevant or even coherent. She paces nervously to and fro during my monologue, filling the dark cramped space with her impatience. Eventually she stops, stares at me for a while before nodding, signifying her satisfaction with my rambling report. She exits my room without another word, leaving the door ajar behind her. I follow her timidly, shutting it as quietly as I can.

On the second floor she pounds frantically upon my locked door. I hastily scoop the scattered pile of empty vials and used syringes from the dresser into the top drawer. I stare at the haggard visage in the mirror, wonder how I sank this low, glad for the dim lighting. I open the door, pull her roughly into the room, lock it behind us. She reeks of sex and sweat.

I peel her jacket and blouse away, watch her wriggle from her skirt, kick off her shoes. She climbs onto my rumpled bed, her rounded buttocks toward me. I caress her thighs, her back, her small breasts, her button nipples swelling in my hands. I rub, caress, and fondle her until I hear her approving squeals, then leisurely slake myself again and again.

Afterwards she assures me everything is in place. I am the primary beneficiary. It is all beyond reproach. Dr. Nohope is doing his part, in return for a large bequest. "The old man isn't likely to last much longer," she tells me, "and even if he does, we have the run of the place, my love. Besides, should push come to shove, you can always help him on his way, I'm sure."

I lay on my back staring into the swirling darkness beyond her. Dizzy and fading, her harsh features already out of focus, I do my utmost to remain awake under the circumstances—at least until she is gone—listen to her endless whining assurances, schemes, fantasies, and conjectures—her painfully tiresome voice devoid of all grace and music.

Again, I hear her stalking the distant corridors, moving about like one hopelessly lost or at least lost in dark thought, the sounds growing gradually closer. Eventually, following a short pause, she enters my room, after a polite knock to announce herself, without waiting for my response. Half asleep, I dream a hungry anaconda slithering purposefully across the faded carpet, rearing its enormous head ominously beside my bed, its flicking black tongue tasting the air inches from my face.

"Are you awake?" she whispers.

I push the sheets away and gasp, stare into those bulging eyes on either side of that long pointed nose. As always, I can smell my cousin all over her.

"I have some more papers for you to sign," she says at last.

I grip the blankets, wondering if she is here to kill me.

"This won't do at all," she declares.

She kisses me on the forehead before moving down the bed, pushes her head and upper body beneath the covers. I feel her cold hands fumbling at my pajama bottoms, pulling them down, her mouth, moist and hot suddenly enveloping me. I shut my eyes, grit my teeth, and cry.

Afterwards I sign her papers. She assures me there is no need for me to read them.

The Prisoner in the Cellar

A special hell, one that remains quarantined from the others in that no one else within the household is actually aware of it, is that one room dungeon in which I occasionally find myself, starved and filthy, chained to a dank stone wall listening to the rats. It is only when I can no longer identify with any of the other members of that dismal cast of deteriorating characters that I can remember that room. That is not to say I am aware of playing multiple roles when I occupy any of them; simply that in each of the other roles I am aware of the existence of the other members of the household save for the man chained to the wall in the cellar.

Now that I have written it, it seems like a complete contradiction, doesn't it?

It is at this point I must stop and reflect.

It is at this point I must consider the crisis that is surely almost upon me.

I sit here, in this dim gray world, watching the great cloud of hovering dust, thankful that I hear nothing, smell nothing, feel nothing save the depressing weight of my body. The pen and this pad of paper remain in clear focus, albeit in shades of grey. The desk on which I write and the chair in which I sit press painfully against my arms, back and thighs, like bullies invading my space. The gray light from an overcast sky I cannot see glows at the grimy window, diffuses across the page on which I desperately scribble these haphazard thoughts, mindful that at any moment I might awaken elsewhere or else fall into some catatonic stupor from which I may never return. The remainder of the room is indistinct, shadows and suggestions of furnishings. These sensations and memories, such as they are, are as real as anything else beyond the desk.

The specific memories of being chained in the cellar are the most focused. The stone wall against which I lean is dank, cold, gritty. The stone floor on which I sit is much the same. The half-light which illuminates the room seeps through the paper-thin slit beneath the massive door. The air is foul with accumulated feces and urine. There is at least one large rat gnawing at the other side of the door. Whether he comes seeking meat, or he imagines he is escaping something, or whether he gnaws to sharpen his teeth for lack of anything else to do occupies my thoughts generating hours of agonizing internal debate I cannot control.

I clearly remember once being terrified by the sound of the rats, but not anymore. I remember the merciless hunger pains ravishing my stomach, that awful growling, but not anymore. I remember shivering, sobbing, screaming, tugging at my restraints to no avail—but not anymore.

The thing that haunts me most when I remember being chained in that dark, cold and putrid cellar room is the interminable length of those episodes. Compared to them, wandering this desolation trying to make sense of it all seems like heaven.

Someone once told me *regardless of however bad it is, it can always get worse.*

They're right.

Epilogue

My god.

I've just discovered this document secreted beneath the writing table in my room. It is unquestionably in my handwriting, although the quality of my penmanship varies from page to page. The manuscript begins in my strongest hand, grows ever more agitated while discussing the visits of Dr. Nohope and Atty. Gladhand. It nearly fades away while struggling to accurately portray the so-called *prisoner in the cellar.* I must admit I'm absolutely flabbergasted by the extravagances of my own imagination.

I live in a single room within this building, although in truth I don't re-member if it is my house, a hospital, a prison, or simply an institution for those beyond caring for themselves. The Dr. Nohope I have described resembles only slightly the physician who attends me on a more or less regular basis. I have no memory of any treatments and certainly nothing as audacious as that which I have described. I do, however, remember that it was he who suggested I write down my dreams and recollections, both for my own edification as well as his.

There is also a Ms. Gladhand, and she does have power of attorney over my estate. She visits me from time to time to discuss the immediate specifics when the doctor calls to tell her I am lucid enough to understand. We may have been lovers at one time, I cannot be certain. I suspect that former intimacy might be the root of the various sexual fantasies I have woven about her. Surely the intensity and the bitterness of the fantasies suggest that such was the case.

There are other similarities between the document in my handwriting and that which constitutes my life. I do not, for example, remember the details of my arrival—if I entered at twilight before the onslaught of a tempest or if I stood before the walls on a summer afternoon so hot as to addle anyone caught out-of-doors. The manor house about which I incessantly rant may in fact exist—if in a more pristine state than I have described it—or it may simply be a metaphor for this institution (if such be the case,) as indeed may be the various versions of my coming here. I have no clear memory of anything beyond the walls of this room, save for those vague bits of information concerning my relationships with Dr. Nohope and Ms. Gladhand.

However I am happy to say the room is clean and bright; the adjoining bathroom is spotless; but the corridor door is locked. I have just attempted to open it. The food, while bland, is nourishing. The single small window does not open but it lets in plenty of sunlight which in its own way obscures the pedestrian furnishings. The darkness on which I have harped exists solely within my mind, save for the evening hours, the natural course of the passing day.

Could this seeming clarity I am now experiencing be the crisis I feared? It does, it seems, utterly terminate the persona who composed the document in my handwriting. Perhaps he feared his own demise. That is a reasonable supposition.

Wait.

I hear someone coming, walking ever so slowly—as if to give me time to acclimate myself to their impending presence—the sound of their footfalls is unnatural, noticeably too loud, too slow. They approach from what I take to be the far end of the corridor beyond the door to my room. Is someone attempting to frighten me, or simply spare me the fear of their silent sudden appearance? I suspect this is routine. If only I could remember... I'm all but certain they're coming to this room; coming here to see me. The odd manner of their approach must simply be how they announce themselves.

I must return this notepad to the manila envelope taped beneath the table before they arrive. I mustn't let anyone else read this document, regardless of my reasons for composing it.

The one thing I take from that deranged *fantasy* I've just read is the absolute conviction with which it was written. Considering everything from my present perspective of cold logic and safe distance, I must conclude that it is altogether possible, however improbable, that what I am now experiencing is simply another delusion. That the truth may be *I* am merely another persona, no more real than the rest, quite possibly what the author termed *the prisoner in the cellar,* while that altered state of rambling awareness and vivid dreaming he has struggled to described in such explicit detail is, in fact, the reality— a reality, however compromised, however fractured, I must, at all cost, respect and protect.

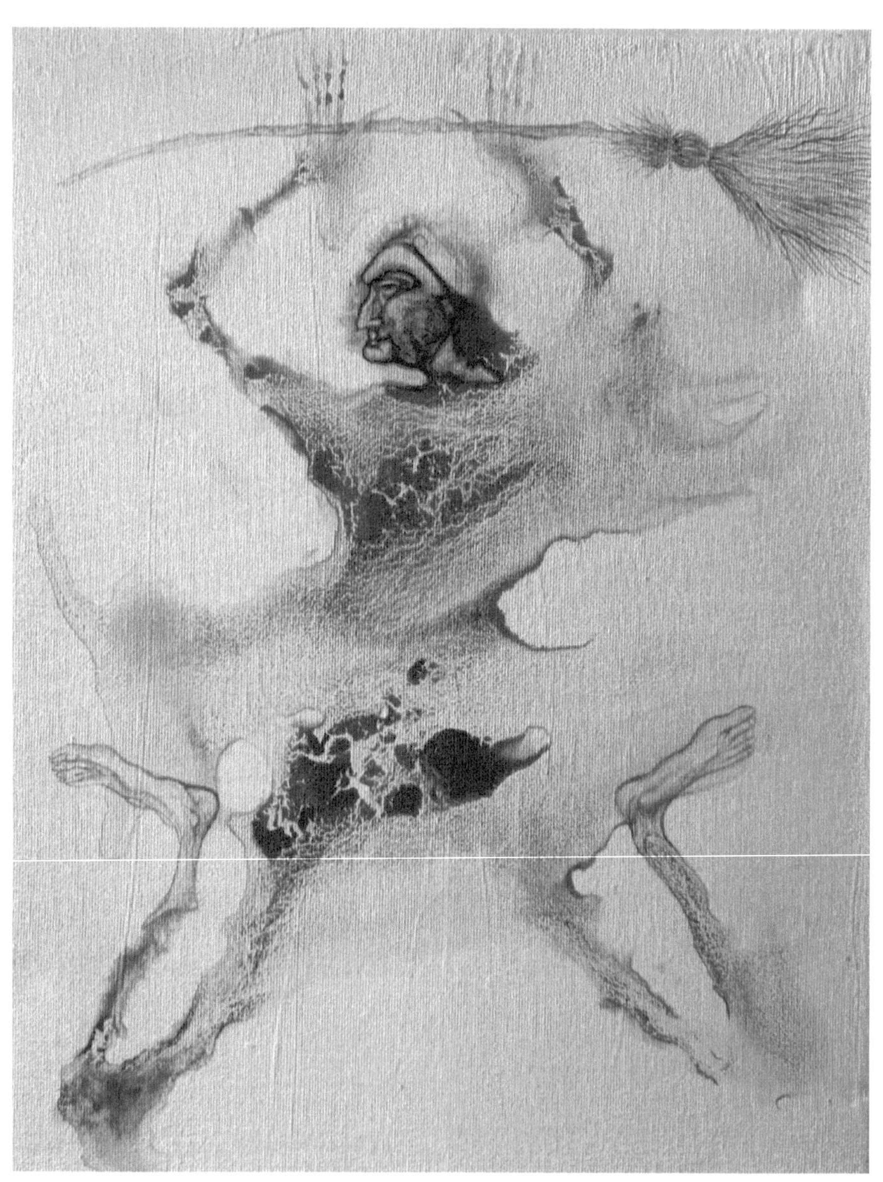

ART BY JESSE PEPER

The Witch in the Dream House

Dr. Raymond Thoss

DREAMS. DREAMS AND Reality. Dreams and Consciousness. Dreams and Darkness. Dreams.

The doomed mathematician/occultist Walter Gilman once said that "math is the gateway to a higher reality." But it wasn't math that killed him. It was his dreams. Early onset psychosis? A fatal manic phase indicative of undiagnosed Bipolar I? John Nash is an obvious parallel example. But Nash did not die from his work.

This is my point. It wasn't math that changed Gilman's reality. It was his dreams.

I believe Gilman looked in the wrong place. Consciousness, not mathematics, is primary. Yes, mathematics is essential, critical even, to unlocking said higher reality, to finding and opening the gateway so to speak. But Pythagoras began his work on mathematics millennia ago. We are light years from the old mystic. Plato and Aristotle outlined all the essential points of consciousness. That was where we stayed until Kant. And then stopped again. Steady millennia of progress in math vs. the scientific equivalent of trying to finish the assignment before it is due the next day in consciousness studies. Gilman, if his notes are taken at face value and not dismissed as psychosis induced ramblings (which I believe is an egregious error made in the decades since he died), believed higher mathematics was the key, the Rosetta Stone, to unlock Reality with a capital "R." Right idea, wrong path. It was not occult theory and advanced mathematics that was the path. It is occult theory and advanced *psychology*. Does this not fit much better? Math and occult theory. Yes, there is precedence. Destreza for instance with its occult geometry (and I suspect this was used mainly to contain the occult, not to expand upon it). But a much stronger and more common thread is consciousness. The mind is what the brain does, as our cognitive psychologists would say. Cognitive psychology. Clinical psychology. Neuropsychology. Psychology of altered states. This is the well needing to be tapped, the path needing to be tread. In Gilman's defense, quantitative methods will keep the "bumpers on the lane" so to speak. After all, as Hegel so wisely noted, the tool examining the subject is the exact thing being examined. Consciousness examines consciousness because what other tool is not "tainted" by said consciousness? Mathematics. Gilman was wise to use this as a barrier of sorts, epistemological PPE so to speak.

All this is prima facie valid and obvious. What garnered looks, and later outright vitriol, was the seriousness I invested in this mission, this project. Moving into the flat that Gilman occupied. Reading the *Necronomicon* at Miskatonic (quite a drive from Brown). Recreating Gilman's study habits.

It was the scientific equivalent of method acting. I admired the man. It was hard not to. Such single-minded focus. Such vision. Visionaries are often wrong in key aspects though. Kant, again, is an obvious example. So, I tried to . . . improve where he could not have at the time. Cameras. Live streaming. Security protocols. Admittedly, these measures were Pascalian in nature. I did not believe in the "Great Old Ones," but why take the chance should I be proven wrong. That was another thing that I found to critique. It always struck me as odd, even intentionally obtuse (no pun intended), that Gilman, while trying to connect the ancient rites of witches and warlocks to higher mathematics, took care in his equations but not in his handling of occult rites. Why even risk it? I know next to nothing about poisonous mushrooms but *because*

I know next to nothing, I would take *more* precautions. Not less. Gilman knew that mathematics was his strength, the thing he brought to the table so to speak. Why did he not take measures with the other discipline he was attempting to mine? The answer is simple: He did not respect it. It was this lack of respect that I believe was his ultimate undoing. Not the vicious attack he suffered. No, his demise came long before then. Like a narrow minded white Western scientist, he did not respect the alternative epistemology. I decided to not repeat the mistake of my predecessor.

This may all seem unfairly critical of Gilman, but did not Schopenhauer critique Kant brutally (though fairly) in his *World as Will and Representation*? Schopenhauer raked Kant across the coals *because* he respected him. Not the reverse. Because he wished to improve upon Kant's ideas. He believed that Kant was right in all his core essentials; it was the remainder that needed to be tightened. I am not comparing myself to such a great mind as Schopenhauer. But I do understand him.

Because I understand my predecessor, both in his virtues and in his failures, I took precautions. Some may seem ridiculous (the iron for instance). Some may seem macabre (human remains usually are). Some may seem legally questionable (growing up in a community of great violence taught me that two 45mm's to center mass stop a great number of things). Ironically, I did not do this for my protection. I did it for the protection of the work. The Great Work. I understand that I am only a small, insignificant part of this Great Work. Work whose larger, more substantial "gears" include such luminaries as Einstein, Tesla, Curwen, etc., etc. But even a small gear that does not serve its purpose in the grand machine can do great, irreparable damage. At most, I was the syringe the medicine is delivered through. Nothing more. Nothing less. Despite appearances to the contrary, hubris and arrogance are not my flaws. Such flaws were literally beaten out of me by my father. Focus. That was what took its place. In Walter Gilman, I saw similar focus. Identical focus from his notes. Not ramblings. Focus. But just as intense light blinds, just as intense sound is deafening, intense focus appears psychotic, manic, etc.

Again, he was right. He had "ahold of the right end of the stick," so to speak. It took me years to discover where he erred, so close did he get. Minds, not numbers. Consciousness, not equations. Psychology, not mathematics. He got them out of order essentially, put the cart before the horse. I rearranged both cart and horse. Thus, why my Ph.D. was in clinical psychology with sub-specialities in both neuroscience and quantitative psychology. HPA Axis and S.E.M. I knew I needed both to break the code.

But I did not forget to study the sibling of the pair. Many hours in Miskatonic's notorious Special Collections. The NSA even sent a dubious duo to "talk" to me. I think they left more worried, not less. Even now they may be monitoring me. I hope they are. Someone must know. At the end, someone must know everything. The Great Work, you see.

But I digress. I spent hours poring over the primary texts of the occult. I took Gilman's notes and made a reading list and went through them one by one until I checked them all off. OCD tendencies, ASD traits, I learned to make them serve me well, MMPI be damned. I dove even deeper than that. I expanded my studies to Gilman's contemporaries. The private notes of Crawford Tillinghast kept at Miskatonic led me to the true culprit. Thankfully, I discovered this early on. If not, I may have veered too far from my mark. Tillinghast's notes were disturbing. But enlightening. As I suspect the man himself was. What shone clear as daylight was that consciousness was the lynchpin, the entry point, the true gateway that Gilman had been looking for and almost found (by accident admittedly). Fortune favors the prepared and the NASA acronym L.U.C.K. (Laboring Under Correct Knowledge) was confirmed by this early discovery in my work.

The commute from Providence to Arkham was not punishing. I grew up in the American Southwest, so we measure drives in hours when traversing those eternal silences and infinite spaces that frighten so many. No. I moved to Arkham not because of distance but because I wanted to immerse myself. Focus at all costs. The chances of success were slim. A lack of focus would annihilate such a narrow window altogether. This entire project was about focus and narrow entry points. I would not give away any advantage. I did not give away any advantage. Of that I can attest, and if you believe nothing else from your unreliable narrator, believe that.

It took me some time to locate the exact flat Gilman rented. The interim between his death and my birth brought inauspicious activities towards that place both by people intent upon destroying his work and people intent upon unlocking his work. I never presented myself as an original thinker. My entire career, nay life, has been built on the custom, the principle, of being the dumbest person in any room I'm in. I knew others would have tried before. They did. And failed. Some failed in macabre ways (Aldo Sax's case may be the most gruesome). Some failed in hilarious ways (the couple who thought they could engage in "sex magic" a la Crowley but failed to bring the apparently necessary Cialis and got caught breaking and entering). The decades brought secrecy and misdirection. There IS a spot in Arkham designated the "Gilman Lodging." This is a ruse, an intentional misdirection. That place has been burned down at least three times in my lifetime. No one occupies it. It is a hated place. But the keepers of the secrets of Arkham are wise. They know if a sacrificial lamb is not given, one will be made. Most do not do their homework. Because from the notes alone it is obvious that this is not the correct place where Gilman lived.

But I found it. It was a room for rent above an Indian restaurant in one of the rougher parts of Old Arkham. Unsurprisingly, the room was difficult to rent out for longer than a few months. Several suicides (and my suspicion is that most were not actual suicides) over the years. This was the perfect place for me. I had cut off most of my external non-Work-related contacts. Family was the easiest, as they were the most dangerous. No more being forced to be at a family reunion with the cousins who molested me and the uncle who watched. No more being asked for money to support my siblings drug addiction. No more being told that I thought I was better than them because I'm a doctor. I *am* better than them. But so is dog shit. "Friends" were harder but by no means impossible. Save the exception of two. One of whom still persists.

(Dear, dear Eva, will *you* be the one to find this manuscript, this elaborate, baroque suicide note?)

As a good student of the Buddhists, I shed all attachments. My needs were/are minimal. My books were my only possible luxury. A good carpenter needs their tools, n'est-ce pas? A small bed in the corner. Refrigerator. Work desk and chair. Sink and stove. Coffee maker. Microwave. That about covers it. I simply sat in silence the first week. I wanted to soak in the energy. The state. I needed to attune my consciousness to *its* consciousness. I think this was the literal fatal error Gilman made. He thought the "witch" altered the plane of reality. In a way it/she/they did. But what they really did is alter the reality with its consciousness. The "witch's" consciousness enveloped all. A la David Lindsay's *Arcturus* or W.H. Hodgson's *House on the Borderland*. The intersection of the phenomenal and the noumenal was its focus and source of power. In hindsight, an obvious point, but I can see how Gilman missed it, as it took me years to identify it. It was a misdirection. He should not have looked for either the phenomenal or the noumenal. He should have looked for the *intersection* between the two. That intersection is, and always has been, consciousness. Hegel got that at least right. Consciousness IS the doorway. But it starts as the barrier.

The "witch" was brilliant. The "witch" made a pocket reality in Gilman's proximal environment. In other words, the "witch" made the area of space-time around Gilman a "dream." An externalization of the intersection between phenomenal and noumenal, consciousness made concrete. If this wasn't impressive enough, the "witch" simultaneously made it a doorway instead of a barrier. Consciousness, after all, divides us from the world and from each other. It is literally a barrier everywhere on this planet with few exceptions. That's its job. The "witch" flipped this entirely on its head. The "witch," in essence, made a "dream-house." You have to appreciate the humor in that, don't you?

Eva always told me my humor had an anger to it. I do not disagree with her assessment. I simply find it irrelevant. Not because I dismissed her evaluation. But because it was so obvious. You can tell, can't you? At least by this point in the narrative? Everything I do. Everything I am. It is all *imbued* with anger. It obviously overrode my fear of this place, even of the mission. It is how I transcended, how I succeeded in my specific of iteration of "Aufhebung" as Hegel would put it. Loose translation: sublation. Even looser: Transcendence. I grow angered by this world. It has given me nothing but anger. I think if Gilman had one key failing, it was that he possessed more than enough intelligence, more than enough curiosity, but not nearly enough anger. I cannot speak for my intelligence. I think this manuscript more than attests to my curiosity. But my anger. That. That has never been in question since I was eight years old. My first fight to the death. I didn't win. But I obviously didn't lose either. In my defense, it was my own father who was my opponent.

I wax maudlin. Sentiment is the great enemy of the disciplined mind. Documentation is what you are interested in. Rightly so. After that first week, I began to make the necessary preparations. Both the scientific and the occult. Both the technical and the ontological. The preparations were, admittedly, as far as my plans went. Not due to lack of foresight but due to lack of sight. A hunter can prepare for the hunt, but the animal will do what it wishes. Only parameters can be set and, let's be honest, even those are only educated guesses.

The only time I left the flat was to get food and to take a walk along Whiterock boulevard. It passed Arkham Sanitarium (excuse me, the more current sobriquet is Arkham Behavioral Health Institute), where apparently Gilman's mother died when he was younger. He never made it to the funeral. Such was his dedication. Others called it insanity. Others are small minded. I would walk and pause intermittently to drink my coffee from my thermos and read. Like a good bodybuilder takes breaks to build more muscle, I would intentionally take these walks to pause to gain greater clarity. Eva told me I was happiest when we walked along Blackstone in Providence where we sat together on a bench, under a canopy of trees, reading and eating Madeleines. I would read

Poe. She would read Proust. Thus, the Madeleines. A remembrance of things past only brings pain. I never needed to read Proust to understand that.

Anger. Yes. Back to anger. Frustration would have been a better word after that first month of nothing. Like knocking at a door and no one answering. Frustration does not even begin to cover it. I checked my instruments and tech knowing there was nothing wrong. At some point it was more something to do to combat the seemingly endless ennui. Thus, a year passed in this manner. In hindsight, I realize like a pirate developing a tolerance to iocane powder, the "witch" was acclimating me, "tuning" me, to the correct mindset, the correct "frequency." My frustration clouded my observational skills. That was intentional by the "witch." I'm sure Gilman suffered something similar but paid it no attention whatsoever. I think, ironically, had I not been looking for what I was looking for, the dénouement would have come more rapidly (after all, those who were not seeking what I sought received their revelations much, much quicker). But what is quick is not what is worthwhile in many cases. If nothing else, that year shed me of my ego in a way I could not have shed such a liability otherwise. The search for Recognition is fundamental to the human parasite. Hegel got this right too. When I say "ego," I primarily mean this sickness of seeking Recognition. "Attachment" in Buddhist terminology. My "specialness" was extinguished. I realized during this year that my father was right. I was nothing. I was worthless. I was a piece of shit. Where he was wrong was the belief that this is problematic. I am no-thing. My worth is less. Simultaneously, manure is the basis of all growth in horticulture. More fundamentally, we are ALL rotting meat. We walk through this thresher with only our illusions, only our fragile stain glass window ego, so certain that something so fragile is so stable. When Blake spoke of cleaning the doors of perception, this is what he meant. Annihilation of the "I." It's the ontological equivalent of sawing your arm off to escape the rock pinning you in the mountain pass. And it is what I did over the course of that seemingly uneventful year. Or more accurately, what the "witch" helped me do.

With the preparatory period at an end, this is when the "whispers" began. As with Gilman, it began in dreams. It was subtle. My dreams had been, anti-climactically, mundane throughout this entire time. They remained so when the whispers began. In retrospect, it was my dream of Eva and I along Blackstone in Providence. A shape. A figure. Not ominous. At first. It was simply another background character. Like an NPC on a video game. But I would see a similar figure in other dreams. Again, nothing ominous. In fact, it was more mundane than eerie. There was no terror, only void. In other dreams it was like the resolution was ever so slightly off on the video. Like a pixelation issue on a screen. It was so subtle initially.

That was sleeping. Waking, it began like a song played at a very low volume. Soothing in a way but also simultaneously infuriating. After a month or two I *knew* that there was something just out of reach. In the dreams it was visual. A figure just out of view of my peripheral. Waking it was auditory. A noise, a voice, a melody a decibel below hearing. I still do not know the telos of this. All I can guess it that, like everything else that came before and after, it was/is ritual. Was it preparing the novitiate for entry into the grand arcana? Or was it the maiden being prepared for sacrifice?

Either was a live possibility. But I remembered. I remembered the vow I took when I left my home. The vow I took when I found the power in books, a power not even my father could take away, no matter how many times he locked me in a closet. This vow: Truth above ALL. At the end of the day, I didn't care so long as Truth followed. More accurately, so long as I followed Truth. Gandhi was right. God is not Truth; Truth is God. I can now say I've seen worse gods than that.

The whispers ultimately turned into "echoes." I call them echoes because unlike what one might have guessed or imagined, nothing "talked" to me. Nothing spoke to me. Have you ever read Danielewski's *House of Leaves?* The phenomenon of echoes and echoing recur repetitively (ironically enough). An echo is location. An echo is memory. An echo is acknowledgement of depth, space, and scope. An echo is many things, but these are the aspects relevant to this account. The echoing of location came first if I remember correctly. I think this is the "echo" that is most understandable to one who was not physically (ontologically?) there. The concise description is that it was a type of déjà vu. But there was more to it than simple déjà vu. It was like the feeling one gets when they see an Escher. Space *amplified*, not repeated. It was like a space suddenly existed in more than four dimensions. Like an Escher. It only lasted a moment. Perhaps I could only take a moment, no more. I would be on a park bench and sudden amplification would descend. Then rescind. Like ocean waves. It should have been terrifying. It was exhilarating.

It was also entirely unpredictable. I half entertained seeing a physician about vertigo. But my health care was a joke, and I did not think it was due to a simple biological etiology. I did not leave my flat much. Maybe that was the witch's plan. Maybe it was happenstance. Paradoxically, it occurred not at all in the flat. That made sense to me. You get jet lag when you leave your home-ostatic time zone. The space-time surrounding me in the flat was becoming my homeostasis. So perhaps this was a type of acclimation. If so, it was very effective.

Because the echo of memories began on the heels of what I've just de-scribed. It is simultaneously difficult and easy to describe what I mean by an "echo of a memory." I mean, perhaps *this* is an echo of a memory. Isn't that what all writing is? Echoing. Echoes frozen through time, not space? The very idea of the written word is a bizarre idea. Marks on paper (or screen). Glyphs. Sigils. The stuff witchcraft is made of. Indeed, the very DNA of witchcraft re-gardless of tradition. Wiccan. Voudou. Enocian. Alexandrian. Etc. Etc.

Yet, this is not that of which I speak. Hypnogogic hallucinations are what a psychologist might call them. Echoes are more accurate. My flat became alive. In a very real sense. It was haunted, but this was a given before I moved in. My memories. They were alive, echoing, within that space. The D.I.D. idea is false. More current research shows that "state-spaces" are what they actually are. A state-space is an echo for all intents and purposes. A personality is far, far too limited when talking about severe dissociation. Far too narrow minded.

One would be fortunate if only one's personality altered. There's a stability even in multiple personalities. But entire *realities* shifting within oneself, with personality as only one of many, many aspects that shift due to the dissociation. That. Now that is where the real perdition (perditions?) lay.

That is where I lay. The very reality of the flat altered. I was in the library I spent my teen years in. The closest thing I had to a church. I was in the closet I was locked in by my father. I was in my 9th grade English teacher's classroom, one of only two teachers who did not tell me I would end up in jail like the rest of my family. I was seeing my uncle run over by a truck after being shot in the back of his head by my aunt. All of this should have at the very least unnerved me. All it did was make me smile. Not out of any bravado (the next thing would unnerve me, to understate it). No, it made me smile because I knew all my childhood trauma had finally come in use for one thing. All my life it had been a liability. I can imagine Gilman terrified about going back to the worst parts of his life. Not me. The witch did not know (or perhaps she knew unequivocally) that, dear mistress, I am ALWAYS there. I always have been, and always will be, in those places. The next life, the hereafter, whatever one wants to call such a metaphysic, I know, I *know* that I will wake up in that closet, as if I never left. I smiled because it simply externalized what was internal. What was always internal.

The echoes of the memories therefore made sense to me. But the screams. Oh, the screams were of no-sense. Like most screams there was a pause, however brief, before the shriek. It hit me like a punch. At night because of course. I say scream but obviously at this point in my account you know it was not literal. I say "scream" because if Edward Munch's painting could be externalized into reality across both time and space *that* is what it would be. The psychological effects go without saying. But as modern psychologists know, there is no Cartesian distinction between mind and body. My body was the most visibly impacted. The few times I ventured out for food or medication I was unabashedly avoided. The medication I only got because I needed to prolong my ascent up Everest. I knew I would die. I just didn't care. Die scaling Everest or die strung out in section 8 housing like I was supposed to. It was an obvious decision. I hoped (and perhaps the fact that I made it to write this account vindicates me) that the medication would let me last the remainder of the journey.

Strange bruising. Migraines. Bleeding gums. GI issues a daily occurrence. Muscle spasms. Vomiting. My body was deteriorating from the assault. Or more accurately the acclimation. Hair loss was not unexpected but still disconcerting. That was when I was awake. Sleep was worse. I entered the Dreamlands. I know, I know with absolute certainty, that *this* was when the shift occurred. In hindsight this was it. The house exited reality and became dream in a literal sense. My metaphysic when I slept was what was real and my metaphysic when I was awake was what was fantasy. (Was *this* what Chuang Tzu actually meant?)

Ah yes, the Dreamlands. *The Scream's* concrete form was the Dreamlands. Man is a fool. Of this there is irrefutable proof now. As if there ever needed to be. The proof is that Man cannot hear the piercing shriek of the noumenal. One would not only have to be deaf; one would have to be willfully ignorant to not experience it. I, as of the race of Men, did not hear it until this moment. I was a Fool. I am now a Sage. The forbidden knowledge does not console its possessor; in fact, it kills its possessor.

But it does not kill him just yet.

I would do a disservice to not at least try, to not at least attempt, to describe my phenomenological experience of the Dreamlands. I do a disservice to try to describe it, nevertheless. How does one adequately describe love? How does one adequately describe abject horror? One does not. One simply attempts to.

I say I was in the Dreamlands, but that is like saying I was in Europe. I describe Bucharest and technically I describe Europe, but it is simultaneously informative and impoverished. So please bear that in mind. Onyx. Onyx was the first and most lasting impression. It was terrifying, the obsidian obelisk, the towering pulsating dolmen. It was also, by far, the most beautiful thing I have ever seen. There is beauty in terror, terror in beauty. In hindsight, I discovered this at six years old when I realized I was in a literal hell. Beating after beating. Locked black room over and over again for the most minor of infractions. Hell has beauty. You must look for it. I believe this is actually what Milton meant. He was correct.

I did what I had done since I was eight. I stopped running away from it and went towards it. I believe this was another of Gilman's fatal errors. One never runs away from a snarling dog. One never tries to lean back when a punch is thrown. You stand your ground with the dog. You step forward into the swing of the fist. It's a paradox. It's also the only way to ensure survival. So I stepped into the punch.

The first entry into the obelisk was the most terrifying. And the most formative. It set the stage for all else. The first thing I noticed was a hum, a buzz. Not human or animal. Musical. Like Beethoven. I tried to follow it, but it was so ubiquitous as to make it impossible. So I followed my phenomenology, my immediate inclination of where or where not to venture. "Let your dreams lead you," as someone once said to me in a dream. Gilman, not being a phenomenologist, would not have had this tool at his disposal. The thought of an entity, an inimical entity, being present, waiting to trap me, crossed my mind. I dismissed it quickly. Not because I did not believe in it or because I thought I was above or "protected" from it. No. It was because if a man sets a trap for an ant, there would be no quarter or reprieve. Either the trap did not exist or it did. If it did, then would this not be a more noble death than the one I would have in the waking world. Demon or diabetes? At least I die with panache.

There was no doubt that slithering, skulking things were all around me. I probably intruded upon their perception as much as the rat in the wall intrudes upon the homeowner's perception. This entire time utter terror gripped me. Yet, intense curiosity and fascination gripped me tighter. Beauty and wonder and awe. An aesthetic experience like no other. I mean that in a very literal sense. How many other sentient intelligent creatures observed what I now observed? Of those, how many looked for, sought for, the beauty. The terror was easy. Just like hate is easy. The beauty took focus and intention. Just like love takes focus and intention.

I continued to follow my intuition. Reason, after all, held no dominion here. That was obvious if nothing else. This took me deeper into the obelisk. I could feel myself descending, like how your body feels a plane descending for a landing. I knew this was leading to a crescendo. The only way I could navigate was a phosphorescence amidst the darkness. Barely enough illumination to see the step in front of me. The smells were overwhelming. I vomited and then dry heaved when there was nothing left. It was the smell of dead flesh in the heat. Why did I continue then? Why did I do any of this? I continued because there was no backwards. The general had burned all the bridges; the soldiers only had the option of forward. I was in too deep; literally, in this case. The only way to was through.

The scream impacted me like a punch. It was like a gunshot in a closed space. My head felt the percussion, and it rippled through the rest of my body like waves on a body of water. It sent me to my knees. My hands covered my ears, but to no avail. Even now I cannot explain it, but it was as if the scream came from within me. Not that I, myself, was screaming, but that it originated from inside my own head. It did not, but that was the phenomenological experience. The only saving feature of this shriek was that, after the initial shock, I could tell it had an origin. I could tell it came from a certain direction. Like the madman I had become, I went toward it (step into the punch not away).

It felt like hours and hours that it took me to locate the source. In real time it was probably no more than a few minutes. The palpable pain, and the fact that the shriek rarely broke its intensity and most definitely contributed to this time dilation.

Then I saw the source.

It was me.

I was on my knees, naked. Screaming.

I looked to be in intense, unbearable pain. I looked like I was in the throes of passion. I looked mad. I did not know what to do. So I did the only thing to do. I moved towards myself. I reached out my hand. I tried to put it over the mouth, tried to silence the scream.

I don't know if my hand ever reached the mouth. I'll never know. For at the moment, I expected flesh to touch flesh I was somewhere else and, thankfully, the shrieking was absent. I was sitting. In a booth. I heard noise around me, but it was the noise of a sparsely populated diner. Instantaneously, I knew where I was. I had been here many, many times before. I was in the diner my mother took me to after my father would beat both of us. Never in the face, of course. Must hit where no one sees, but we still learn our "lesson." Never go for the kill when you can go for the hurt, as my father would say. Apparently, the Witch could have taught my father a thing or two (and I hope one day she will). I looked across the table and saw what was supposed to be my mother.

"Well, this is macabre." I said to the Witch wearing my mother's face.

"How did I do?" She sweetly replied.

I looked around, took it all in. "Not bad. You even got the smell down."

"You make me blush." Her smile was filled with menace, yet I knew she did not mean me any immediate malice. At least not in that specific moment.

"Why all this?" I asked, "Gilman was simply ripped apart from the inside out. Why was I not equally replied to?"

A look of confusion. I could swear it. "You have to know the answer to that by this point, mi corazón."

I really didn't. I swear.

"Did you not wish to become a witch?" She asked. Confusion across her face.

"No."

"Then what did you wish for?"

"Nothing."

"Now that is a lie." A smile ever so sly.

"It is not."

"'Truth at all costs'?" She quoted.

"How did you know that?"

"Because of where you are now. All is known. All revealed. Except what you hide from yourself."

I had no response.

"That is what you promised, is it not? In the dark. When you read your first book and knew that though your father may lie, though the people who were supposed to protect you lie, the books did not. Truth did not. Was it not at that moment that you promised yourself, 'Truth at all costs.'?"

Reluctantly, "Yes."

"Truth at all costs. Your life motto, my dear sweet boy. Different words but same sentiment we witches share. So, I ask you again, did you not wish to become a witch?"

Time. I needed to buy time. Why? I didn't know. But I knew I needed to. "Why did Gilman not receive equal mercy?"

She responded quickly; she knew what I was trying to do, yet allowed it. "Two errors. One, who says I give you mercy? Two, and key, Gilman wished for knowledge. Not truth. He mistook order for truth. They are rarely the same. So he was shown truth. The truth that the universe is simply a yawning, gaping mouth filled with razor sharp teeth waiting to devour you."

Reflex, "Again, why did Gilman receive *his* end?"

A smile, a terrifying smile, "Again, you do not listen. You, my boy, know the teeth. You've known since the closet. You are so very dear. We have such hopes for our new novitiate."

The smile.

The teeth.

The dénouement.

"You know what comes next, don't you boy?"

I looked across the diner.

"I go back in the closet. Willingly. That is what a Witch is, isn't it? A child stuck in a closet. Blamed. Hated. Damned. Eventually, heartless. Only the dark to comfort them."

Another smile, "And you've known this since you were six. Now, don't you see why we smile so happily?"

One last delay from me, "Why this place?"

A girlish smile from a thing that had never been a girl. "You tell me. You know already, young one."

"This is where my mother would take me after my father beat us."

"And?"

"And she would tell me so many things. So many promises. Ultimately, empty. She would tell me we would leave. She would tell me he would be better. She would tell me she loved me. Lies. Not intentional per se, but lies nevertheless. No truths were spoken in this place save one."

"Which one?"

"There is nothing to do and there is nowhere to go. There is nothing to be, and there is no one to know."

"Pretty."

"A poem."

"A pretty poem."

"Yes." I said, "I agree."

I looked across the diner again. One thing was different. The door. The entrance. It was not a glass door as it always was. It was hard, unyielding wood. My closet door.

"Final step, young one. Or more accurately, the first step."

Now I smiled.

She looked right at me, "Yes. Yes, we have chosen well."

I looked at her. There was no fear. Fear died in that closet. Fear died when I was eight. Because what came out of that closet was not human. Never was from that point forward. I don't think a human could have looked at her. But I looked at her. *I* did. "And?"

"And tell me, mi corazón, what I see."

"I must choose. That's how this works isn't it? I must choose to become a witch."

"And?"

"And to make the choice, I have to understand it."

"Yes." She said, "Do you?"

"Yes." I said, "I do."

"Lastly, now. Tell me what you understand."

I looked at the door. "The witch chooses servitude. The witch chooses captivity. Forever. Aligns herself with the dark forever, this being tantamount to incarceration. Yet this prison must be freely chosen."

"And why, young one, would any sentient thing commit such heresy?"

"Because all is sick. All is light. And our light is naught but sickness masquerading."

"Beautiful. Simply beautiful."

"And if the world is sick, we must shelter in place. This prison is our shelter. The only shelter there is or ever was. A prison still, but no light, therefore no sickness."

"You see now."

"Yes," I said, seeing the door crack open, "I spent my childhood in the darkness. And when I came out, I knew the sickness of a so-called light that allowed me to even be in that closet in the first place. You chose me because I have always seen the sickness in the light. I was never deluded. Gilman was. Could not help but be. I wasn't. Could not help but be." The closet door opened even wider.

"One last request." The witch said.

"What?"

This. This was the last request. I sit here. Alone now. She doesn't need to be here. My choice is as preset now as the sun rising. She wished me to record all of this. It was never a witch house. It was a dream. I still sit simultaneously in the dream and in the house. When I step into the closet, the dream will end, I will end, but the house will not. This document will stay in the house, and I in the dream. I, the witch. Gilman was not a witch. Never intended to be. Never had the prerequisites to be. The moment my father threw me in the closet the first time, bleeding and weeping; that first moment my path was set as inexorably as if I had been pushed off a skyscraper. Terminal velocity has followed me my whole life. She requested I record it.

Because others will follow. She knows this. I know this. I have no qualms with the fact that this document will draw, like a magnet, those others. I have no qualms because they were pushed off the building too. Brothers and sisters and everyone in between. This is your invitation. We await you. You are home. And you will never be rejected. You will never be sick. For there is no light to infect you here, no light to be afraid of here. Ever again.

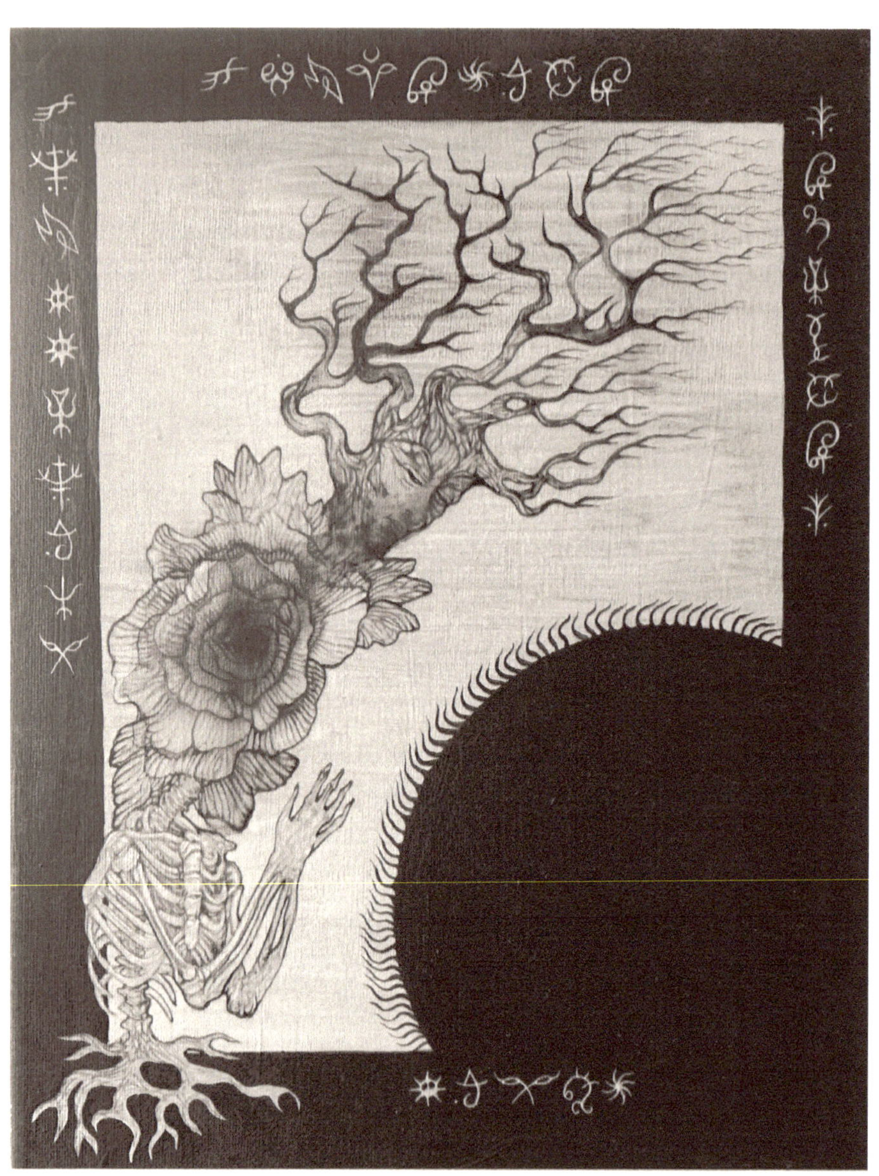

ART BY JESSE PEPER

Horror's Bitter Pill:
Pessimism in Lovecraft and Ligotti

Dejan Ognjanović

THE HORROR STORY SEEMS like a natural, fictional variant of philosophical pessimism: it depicts a world filled with natural and supernatural forces aimed at man's destruction; Evil seems to reign supreme, Monsters are countless and multiform, hope is futile. Victory is rare (often at great cost), defeat highly likely. Suffering and death are omnipresent. Horror is the only popular genre in which the protagonist's survival at the story's end is not taken for granted; quite the opposite. Other genres typically have some sort of uplifting ending. Only in horror does the audience's horizon of expectations include an outcome in which the Monster remains undefeated, while the hero may be crushed – or turned into a monster. To the audience's delight! A hopeless ending in horror – sometimes literally apocalyptic – comes with the territory, and is gleefully accepted, ever since Edgar Allan Poe's "The Masque of the Red Death" and its unforgettable conclusion: "And the life of the ebony clock went out with that of the last of the gay. And

vvv

the flames of the tripods expired. And Darkness and Decay and the Red Death held illimitable dominion over all."[31]

Bleak plots and even bleaker endings seem to be the fundamental parts of the genre's repertoire, and thus horror's proximity to pessimism is practically taken for granted. It is understood as an axiom which barely requires discussion. Many would claim that horror genre's dark worldview deflates the enthusiasm for life promoted by other genres and paints their rosy pictures into black.

Let us for a moment assume that there is what I would call The Big Black Truth: that *our world and our existence in it are a bad thing in itself,* and that this truth is occulted by delusion. If we assume the pessimistic stance, accepting this for a truth, one is left to wonder: is the horror story really its messenger? Is horror merely a sugar coating on a bitter pill which most people either avoid or pretend does not exist? On the other hand, we could go contrary to popular belief and ask: *Can* the horror story even *be* pessimistic, and *how*? This paper deals with these and attendant questions, testing their assumptions through samples from the works of two horror authors in whose writings The Big Black Truth seems to have been most persistently and fully realized: H. P. Lovecraft and Thomas Ligotti.

Horror: A History of Pessimism?

Is horror truly a "pessimistic Trojan horse," as labeled by Ethan Stoneman and Joseph Packer in the paper "No, Everything Is Not All Right: Supernatural Horror as Pessimistic Argument"? These authors argue that horror genre's pessimism-spreading role is obvious. Their article, later included as a chapter in their book *A Feeling of Wrongness: Pessimistic Rhetoric on the Fringes of Popular Culture* (2018), maintains that:

---

[31] Edgar Allan Poe (1842). "The Masque of the Red Death" in: Stephen Peithman, ed. *The Annotated Tales of Edgar Allan Poe.* (New York: Doubleday & Company, Inc, 1981), p. 119.

weird fiction is uniquely situated to convey the spirit of pessimism while avoiding the pitfalls of anchoring: like a pessimistic Trojan horse, weird fiction promises a simple, scary tale while surreptitiously working to invoke in the reader a sense of uncanny fear and in ways that call into question the very nature of reality. Rather than presenting well-reasoned arguments in support of pessimistic claims, weird fiction manifests or enacts pessimism, aesthetically, through the clever deployment of a range of stylistic devices and rhetorical maneuvers.[32]

These authors claim that the sense of uncanny fear shares a strong resemblance to pessimism:

weird fiction does not merely scare its readers but fundamentally disturbs their world-view, moving beyond shock in the pursuit of an indefinable, disconcerting understanding of the world... Weird fiction, by psychically transporting and effectively disarming the reader, seems to accomplish what pessimism cannot achieve for itself via rational (inductive or deductive) argument.[33]

According to their paper, the weird tale creates a sense of uncanny fear, "a feeling of ontological wrongness" and thus "affords pessimism a suitable model of rhetorical effectivity."[34] It is "un-anchoring" the readers' basic cultural optimistic ideas, such as the belief in "the adequacy of rational thought to organize and structure the sensible world of appearance"[35], and it does that

---

[32] Ethan Stoneman, Joseph Packer. "No, Everything Is Not All Right: Supernatural Horror As Pessimistic Argument" (*Horror studies*, Vol. 8, no 1. 2017), p. 27.

[33] ibid, p. 31.

[34] ibid, p. 31.

[35] ibid, p. 33.

by insinuating "that the world is essentially unintelligible, our frameworks of interpretation fundamentally wanting."[36]

While there is some truth in their claims (and they will be further tested below), it must be acknowledged that a brief overlook of horror literature's history reveals its major authors to have been *anything but* pessimist, while their works were motivated by mostly optimistic ideas. Horace Walpole, the father of the "gothic novel," was a conservative politician and dilettante whose single, seminal novel, *The Castle of Otranto* (1764), was a literary hoax with ambition to amuse deploying a marginalized mode (fantasy) and emotion (fear). It was created as a reaction to predominant rationalism of The Age of Reason, although its humble aim was not to crush its opponent, but merely to embellish it with some colorful additions. The author's intention was "to blend the two kinds of romance, the ancient and the modern. In the former, all was imagination and improbability: in the latter, nature is always intended to be, and sometimes has been, copied with success."[37] The genre thus birthed was not conceived to "question the very nature of reality," but to copy nature, taking it for granted as a model, adding to it just a little spice of imagination. Rather than revealing "an ontological wrongness," it aimed to merely widen the socially prescribed limits of allowable perception and artistic expression, without shaking the fundamental societal ontological concepts which were based on the Christian doctrine.

Ann Radcliffe, also conservative, used horror as a novelty spice for her labored romances brimming with pre-Romantic, idealized concepts of Love and Nature. Her notion of the Sublime, derived from Edmund Burke's treatise *A Philosophical Enquiry into the Origin of Our Ideas of the Sublime and Beautiful* (1757) and expressed throughout her gothic oeuvre, did not have a dark, pessimistic streak – quite the opposite. Instead of exposing The Big Black Truth, she used terror in her works because she believed that it "expands the

---

[36] ibid, p. 33.

[37] Horace Walpole (1765). "Preface to the Second Edition" in: *Four Gothic Novels.* (Oxford and New York: Oxford University Press, 1994), p. 11.

soul, and awakens the faculties to a high degree of life."[38] Rather than questioning the "adequacy of rational thought," she confirmed rationality through her mode of "explained gothic," which conveniently exorcised the apparently supernatural phenomena through natural, reasonable explanations.

Even those writers with radical politics and non-conventional views of life (for the time), like the young Mary Shelley, did not write horror in order to convey that the universe is an abyss of nightmares, but to better delineate certain evils in society (e.g., injustice based on class and sex) and in human nature (e.g., Faustian over-reaching and pride). She believed that those evils could be eradicated with a proper application of reason and moral responsibility. "O! If I could only contrive one [ghost story] which would frighten my reader,"[39] she exclaimed in her Introduction to *Frankenstein's* third (1831) edition. And yet, her aim was not to frighten the reader by calling into question the very nature of reality, but to confirm the accepted Christian metaphysics and morality: "for supremely frightful would be the effect of any human endeavor to mock the stupendous mechanism of the Creator of the world."[40] Starting with *Frankenstein* and going all the way to the 21st century's "New Weird," horror has been used mostly as a tool for satire, its subtext basically psychological and sociological, *not* ontological: by criticizing man's and society's ills, it had a positivistic and optimistic aim, to reveal certain faults within The Big Rosy Picture, and thus hopefully lead to its betterment. Horror was basically a bitter (or, more accurately, bittersweet) medicine used with the most optimistic purpose, that of individual and societal improvement, and this view is applicable to most of its practitioners, both conservative and liberal.

---

[38] Ann Radcliffe (1826). "On the Supernatural in Poetry" in: Clive Bloom, ed. *Gothic Horror: A Guide for Students and Readers (Second edition)*. (Basingstoke and New York: Palgrave Macmillan, 2007), p. 66.

[39] Mary Shelley (1831). "Introduction to *Frankenstein*, Third Edition," in: *Frankenstein,* A Norton Critical Edition, J. Paul Hunter, ed. (New York and London: W.W. Norton & Company, 1996), p. 172.

[40] ibid. p. 172.

Those early gothic novels only rarely touched upon the metaphysical, their hints towards the Numinous usually shy, sugary and, implicitly or explicitly, permeated by the rosy Christian views. A rare exception to this rule has been Edgar Allan Poe, whose worldview was much darker than his age was willing to accept and able to digest. However, if his long philosophical prose poem *Eureka* (1848), published one year before his death, is to be understood as his ultimate manifesto, it can hardly be labeled pessimistic, since it expresses his belief in reason, mathematics, natural laws, and human destiny as a part of *cosmic teleology* towards the ultimate unity of all disparate particles. Still, his horror (a minority in his opus, constituting approximately one third, i.e., about twenty stories out of some sixty) evokes an unparalleled sense of doom and gloom. Furthermore, his tales are profoundly tinged with suspicions regarding man's psyche and reason, forever gnawed by the inner psychological demon ("The Imp of the Perverse") and by the outward corporeal corruption ("The Conqueror Worm"). Although passionately devoted to idealized Beauty, his intelligence and temperament still led him, inexorably, back to morbidity, ugliness, insanity, and decay. His major works are too complex to be easily categorized: like the best of poetry (and he considered himself a poet above all else), they remain open for various interpretations, including the darkest ones. Still, one suspects that Poe, a natural born showman with finger firmly on his readership's pulse, leaned towards them more for their dramatic effect than because of his inherently pessimistic beliefs.

All the greatest classic weird tale writers had basically optimistic views. Algernon Blackwood's pantheistic nature-worship, belief in reincarnation and potentials of the human mind and spirit earned him the title of "the most wholesome and cheerful horror writer I know of";[41] the key word of his opus was not terror, but *awe*. For this reason Joshi wonders "why he even attempted to convey fright in some of his tales, as his predominant message is optimistic

---

[41] S. T. Joshi. *The Weird Tale* (Austin: University of Texas Press, 1990), p. 89.

in regard to human beings, their souls, and their place in the cosmos."[42] Machen, likewise, advocated an occult mysticism pretty distant from The Big Black Truth; its key word was *ecstasy*, or "rapture, beauty, adoration, wonder, awe, mystery, sense of the unknown, desire for the unknown."[43] M. R. James, a devout Christian, wrote horror as a diversion for himself and entertainment for his friends, its ambition limited to causing chills in his listeners and readers: "here you have a story written with a sole object of inspiring a pleasing terror in the reader; and as I think, that *is* the true aim of the ghost story."[44] Although a first-rate master in achieving this aim, he was more preoccupied with form, and quite disinterested in his contents' deeper connotations. Neither optimistic nor pessimistic, "they are simply stories: they never add up to a world view."[45]

If we were pressed to derive some sort of sense out of the classic weird stories, it would be the same as in Bram Stoker, R. L. Stevenson, A. C. Doyle, and countless other writers who tackled horror in the late 19th and early 20th century: ultimately, they are all "warnings to the curious." They warn the readers not to stray too far from the safety of reason, logic, science, Christian morality, and one's own sex (male), race and culture (white, British) – or else monstrous Otherness may intrude, corrupt, and destroy the *status quo* of The Big Rosy Picture of "everything's alright with the world." And yet, with the exception of a few stories (like Blackwood's "Willows" and "Wendigo" and Machen's "The White People"), majority of the tales from this Golden age of horror fiction do not depict the world as essentially unintelligible and ontologically wrong, but merely as open to still unrecognized possibilities and forces. Those, however, as their authors believed, could be grasped with human effort, will, reason, and activity (scientific, mystical, or occultist), so that their ultimate

---

[42] ibid, p. 89.

[43] Arthur Machen. *Hieroglyphics* (New York: Knopf, 1923), pp. 18-19.

[44] M. R. James (1929). "Some Remarks on Ghost Stories" in: M. R. James, *Collected Ghost Stories* (Oxford: Oxford University Press, 2011), p. 411.

[45] S. T. Joshi, ibid, p. 140.

result was not pure horror and pessimistic retreat, but quite opposite: awe, ecstasy, and just a bit of "a pleasing terror."

It is thankless to generalize in as rich a field as horror literature, especially considering its growth, wealth and diversity in the second half of the 20th century, but the bulk of modern genre fiction, from Ray Bradbury to Stephen King, is essentially based on the models of romance, adventure, detective/mystery, melodrama and morality play – the morality essentially reducible to slightly modernized warnings to the curious: "Kids, don't do this at home! Obey your elders, respect authorities, walk the well-trodden path... or else!" This is the medieval morality play aspect which Stephen King designated in *Danse Macabre* as his genre's basic attitude: "the horror story, beneath its fangs and fright wig, is really as conservative as an Illinois Republican in a three-piece pinstriped suit; (...) its main purpose is to reaffirm the virtues of the norm by showing us what awful things happen to people who venture into taboo lands."[46] Luckily, there are horror paradigms other than that, which can have both conservative and liberal shadings: "In terms of ideas and values, there are two key approaches to be found in horror: one, described by King, is the *conservative* one, which supports the *status quo*; the other can be called *progressive*, or open-minded, in the sense that it disturbs the *status quo* by questioning and relativizing the communally accepted values."[47] In contemporary horror the Otherness is treated in a manner more liberal than King designated (starting on a massive scale with Clive Barker's *Books of Blood*, 1984-85), so that it is not merely demonized but also understood, embraced, even idealized (in Barker) – but almost always with a liberal, optimistic implication.

Still, regardless of the ideological shading, conservative or liberal, the genre's predominant mode remains *satiric*, which means that its subtext is a critique of societal ills (consumerism, media, right-wing politics, racism, homophobia, xenophobia, gender-based prejudice, etc.). Modern horror mostly

---

[46] Stephen King. *Danse Macabre* (New York: Berkley Books, 1983), pp. 395-96.

[47] Dejan Ognjanović. "The Three Paradigms of Horror," *Vastarien*, Vol. 4, no. 2, 2021, p. 237.

agrees with Hemingway's quote which ends the film *Se7en* (1996): "The world is a fine place and worth fighting for." Even in rare instances where it doesn't agree with the first part of that sentence, it almost always sides with the second. Behind all apparent pessimism, darkness, violence, and monstrosity contained in horror genre, rays of light glimmer with a faint hope. Even the darkest ideas of contemporary representatives of horror fiction rarely call into question the very ontological nature of reality: at most they may imply that the world is a shade or two darker than we think, but any implication of metaphysical negativity is usually counterbalanced and overshadowed by human values (courage, love, family, or romantic relationships) which seem to justify the continued existence in this world.

What would it even mean for the horror story to be pessimistic? Merriam Webster's dictionary offers two basic meanings of the term "pessimism": "1: an inclination to emphasize adverse aspects, conditions, and possibilities or to expect the worst possible outcome," and "2 a: the doctrine that reality is essentially evil; b: the doctrine that evil overbalances happiness in life."[48] If we accept these definitions, then the horror story could only be called pessimistic in the first sense, of being inclined towards adverse aspects and outcomes, because "Horror genre's master narrative details encounters with threatening Other whose intrusion into the consensus reality and its implied normality creates disbalance and fear among protagonists and audience, and therefore sensations similar to fear constitute this genre's idiosyncratic effect."[49] This means that, since the genre's basic aesthetic intent is to evoke feelings of terror, horror and fear, in order for that to be achieved, it is inevitable that it would be inclined to emphasize adverse aspects, conditions, and possibilities and to organize its plots and scenarios so that the audience expects and fears the

---

[48] *Merriam Webster Online Dictionary.* <https://www.merriam-webster.com/dictionary/pessimism>

[49] Dejan Ognjanović, ibid, p. 233.

worst possible outcome. Without this inclination the basic genre requirement would not be met.

However, it could hardly be said that horror stories, as a rule, evoke the deeper, philosophical pessimism according to the term's second meaning: outside of very few exceptions (see below), horror stories usually do not imply that reality is essentially evil or that evil overbalances happiness in life. Evil in horror stories is commonly presented as relative, local, accidental, man-made. It is not a *rule* which governs the entire creation, but an *exception to the rule*. The horror story's Evil does not turn The Big Rosy Picture into The Big Black Picture of ontological wrongness, but only renders its rosiness a darker shade of purple.

After this overview, one could rightfully ask: where can we find all those pessimistic Trojan horses that Stoneman and Packer wrote about? Among the major exceptions to the above (admittedly, simplified) overview of horror literature's approach to darkest themes, two names stand out as possibly the ultimate Prophets of Pessimism: H. P. Lovecraft and Thomas Ligotti. But do they really deserve that title?

Lovecraft's Pessimism?

American author H. P. Lovecraft (1890-1937) would seem to be a perfect representative of pessimism: for him, reality is essentially evil and evil overbalances happiness in life. The memorable opening of "Arthur Jermyn" (1920) intones: "Life is a hideous thing, and from the background behind what we know of it peer daemoniacal hints of truth which make it sometimes a thousand-fold more hideous."[50] The titular character goes on a road of self-discovery, and what he finds out about himself and his direct ancestors leads him to a suicide by self-immolation. In his later stories, starting with "The Call of Cthulhu"

---

[50] H. P. Lovecraft (1921). "Facts Concerning the Late Arthur Jermyn and His Family" in: *The Call of Cthulhu*, S. T. Joshi, ed. (New York and London: Penguin, 2002), p. 14.

(1926), Lovecraft expounded The Big Black Truth through a "mythos," which included a complicated and willfully incoherent pantheon of extraterrestrial and extra-dimensional "gods" which render man's anthropocentric views into a cosmic joke. The Big Black Truth is delivered in this story's opening paragraph:

> We live on a placid island of ignorance in the midst of black seas of infinity, and it was not meant that we should voyage far. The sciences... have hitherto harmed us little; but one day the piecing together of dissociated knowledge will open up such terrifying vistas of reality, and of our frightful position therein, that we shall either go mad from the revelation or flee from the deadly light into the peace and safety of a new dark age.[51]

It could hardly get more pessimistic than this: the truth is bad, and only illusion and lie keep us sane and functioning. And yet, one wonders... Was Lovecraft really a pessimist? If taken at his own words, as expressed in his letters, most definitely not:

> Contrary to what you may assume, I am not a pessimist but an indifferentist—that is, I don't make the mistake of thinking that the resultant of the natural forces surrounding and governing organic life will have any connexion with the wishes or tastes of any part of that organic life-process. Pessimists are just as illogical as optimists; insomuch as both envisage the aims of mankind as unified, and as having a direct relationship (either of frustration or of fulfillment) to the inevitable flow of terrestrial motivation and events. That is—both schools retain in a vestigial way the primitive concept of a conscious teleology—of a cosmos which gives a damn one way or the other about the especial wants and ultimate

---

[51] H. P. Lovecraft (1926) in ibid, p. 139.

welfare of mosquitos, rats, lice, dogs, men, horses, pterodactyls, trees, fungi, dodos, or other forms of biological energy."[52]

In private correspondence he used his stoic indifferentism as a tool for consolation. Matthew Beach finds evidence of success in this regard in Lovecraft's letters to Mrs. Helen V. Sully, his and Clark Ashton Smith's mutual friend. Some of the quotes from his letters to her are bleakly hopeful: "It is just as childishly romantic to postulate an actively hostile & malignant cosmos, as Thomas Hardy did, as to postulate a friendly, 'just', & beneficent one. The truth is that the cosmos is blind & unconscious—not giving a hang about any of its denizens, nor even knowing that they exist."[53] Or let us consider this advice: "The highest consistent and practicable goal of mankind is simply an absence of *acute and unendurable suffering*—a sensible compromise with an indifferent cosmos which was never built for mankind and in which mankind is only a microscopic, negligible, and temporary accident."[54] In all these samples Lovecraft implies that, while the cosmos provides sufficient reasons to be pessimistic, the reasonable attitude to The Big Black Truth is not pessimism, but a stoic shrug, acceptance and "a sensible compromise."

An essential part of said compromise would seem to be creativity, which is in itself an optimistic trait, both viewed individually, for Lovecraft, as a means of sublimating life's evils, and globally, for the readers who find hope in his example: the author as an outsider who made his life meaningful through creation. Terence Blake sees optimism in the fact that "Lovecraft did not go mad like both of his parents. He became a writer of weird fiction. He

---

[52] H. P. Lovecraft (1929). "Letter to James F. Morton," 30 Oct. 1929, in H.P. Lovecraft. *Selected Letters, vol. III* (Sauk City: Arkham House, 1971), p. 39.

[53] H. P. Lovecraft (1935). "Letter to Helen V. Sully," 23 Sept. 1935, in H.P. Lovecraft. *Selected Letters, vol. V.* (Sauk City: Arkham House, 1976), 195.

[54] H. P. Lovecraft (1935). "Letter to Helen V. Sully," 15 Aug. 1935, in H.P. Lovecraft. *Letters to Wilfred B. Talman and Helen V. and Genevieve Sully.* Ed. David E. Schultz and S. T. Joshi. (New York: Hippocampus Press, 2019), p. 428; italics in original.

wrote down his dreams, recounted them in his letters and created many of his stories from their inspiration. This is not pessimism but affirmation."[55] Basically, in Blake's view, Lovecraft was a stoic, creative daydreamer who transcended the darkness of real life through his work: "Far from being a cosmic pessimist or a Romantic nihilist Lovecraft is best seen as a noetic dreamer, an oneiric materialist, an immanent Platonist. The dream, both waking (noetic) and sleeping, is part of our creative engagement with the material world and of our resistance against nihilism."[56] Like his great idol, Poe, Lovecraft also yearned for idealized Beauty (in his case not feminine but related to landscapes and art), yet just like in Poe's case, his mental constitution kept bringing him back to morbidity, decay, and monstrosity.

A deeper look would reveal that there are at least two Lovecrafts: one is the *Letter-writer*, the voice of Reason who advocates indifferentism and a sensible compromise; the other is the *Fiction-writer*, the voice of Emotion, Intuition and Creativity, who depicts the universe as an unceasing nightmare of chaos, terror, and Demon-Gods. Lovecraft himself was aware of this division when he admitted in a letter to R. Michael:

> The cosmos is, in all probability, an eternal mass of shifting and mutually interacting force-patterns which our present visible universe, our tiny earth, and our puny race of organic beings, form merely a momentary and negligible incident. Thus my serious conception of reality is dynamically opposite to the fantastic position I take as an aesthete. In aesthetics, nothing interests me so much as the idea of strange suspensions of natural law – weird glimpses of terrifyingly elder worlds and abnormal dimensions, and faint scratchings from unknown outside abysses

---

[55] Terence Blake. "Lovecraft Noetic Dreamer: From Horrorism to Cosmicism." 2017. p. 3. <https://www.academia.edu/35050840/LOVECRAFT_NOETIC_DREAMER_from_horrorism_to_cosmicism>

[56] ibid, p. 3.

> on the rim of the unknown cosmos. I think this kind of thing fascinates
> me all the more because I don't believe a word of it![57]

This opposition between the Thinker and the Aesthete is somewhat reflected in Lovecraft's fiction: it is reasonably structured yet brimming with the irrational; strangely pleasurable and essentially consoling although its themes are dark and morbid. But how can it be consoling if it is truly pessimistic? We will return to this question, but first let us investigate a somewhat different approach to the same Big Black Truth – in the thought and works of Thomas Ligotti.

Ligotti's Pessimism?

Lovecraft's compatriot and in many ways successor, Thomas Ligotti (1953), sounds even more pessimistic than his teacher. In his story, "The Sect of the Idiot," the hero claims: "Life is the nightmare that leaves its mark upon you in order to prove that it is, in fact, real,"[58] before he undergoes a monstrous transformation – or loses his mind completely. The goal of Ligotti's fiction, as he understood it, was the same as his great predecessor's: "Lovecraft dreamed the great dream of supernatural literature—to convey with the greatest possible intensity a vision of the universe as a kind of enchanting nightmare."[59] And when fiction no longer offered a satisfactory means of spreading The Big Black Truth, Ligotti turned to non-fiction, in his semi-philosophical, semi-essayistic and poetic work *The Conspiracy against the Human Race* (2010), his last major

---

[57] H. P. Lovecraft. "Letter to R. Michael, 20 July 1929." <http://www.yankeeclassic.com/miskatonic/dliterature/authors/lovecraft/bio/autobio.htm>

[58] Thomas Ligotti (1988). "The Sect of the Idiot," in *Songs of a Dead Dreamer and Grimscribe* (London and New York: Penguin, 2015), p. 209.

[59] Carl Ford. "Notes on the Writing of Horror: An Interview with Thomas Ligotti," *Dagon* No. 22/23 (September–December 1988), p. 32.

publication until the poetry collection *Pictures of Apocalypse* (Chiroptera Press, 2023).

Ligotti's views, as expressed through his fiction and elsewhere, do not leave much space for consolation. His nameless characters, like the protagonist of "The Sect of the Idiot," are solitary and homeless, and this quality carries a fundamental, philosophical weight in his fiction: "It is this sense of homelessness, one that arises from within the ontology of dream-like life and condenses from without it as the cosmos makes known its indifference to its inhabitants, that is horror's shadow throne, an uncanny (non-)place that exists both everywhere and nowhere to displace the human race into a 'nightmare of being'."[60] His puppet-like characters are ontologically uprooted and lost in a disenchanted world in which any sort of clean, ethereal Beauty (of the kind that Poe and Lovecraft always longed for) is inconceivable.

The distinction between optimism and pessimism which Ligotti makes is very extreme, literally a matter of "to be or not to be." For him pessimists are those who believe that "life is something that should not be, which means that what they believe should be is the absence of life, nothing, nonbeing, the emptiness of the uncreated." Similarly, "[Anyone] who speaks up for life as something that irrefutably should be – that we would not be better off unborn, extinct, or forever lazing in nonexistence – is an optimist."[61]

When asked whether the term "pessimist" properly describes him, and how he distinguishes pessimism from nihilism, Ligotti replied:

> To my mind, "pessimist" and "pessimistic" are casual designations much like those that describe a number of pre-Socratic philosophers collectively categorized as Stoics, Cynics, Epicureans, and so forth. The traits ascribed to these viewpoints signal certain peculiarities of

---

[60] Brad Baumgartner. *Weird Mysticism, Philosophical Horror and the Mystical Text* (Bethlehem: Lehigh University Press, 2021), p. 32.

[61] Thomas Ligotti. *The Conspiracy against the Human Race* (New York: Hippocampus Press, 2010.), p. 47.

temperament that are often loosely characterized as "philosophies," though they are no such thing in a technical sense, as they are in such projects as Logical Positivism or Eliminative Materialism, which are no more true or real simply because they involve a cognitively technical infrastructure. Sometimes they even described lifestyles, as in the case of Epicureans, whose ambition was to live in such a way that diminished their suffering to a minimum. How anyone might achieve this end is obviously a great challenge, much like that of Buddhists to attain emotional and mental equanimity on the way to an elimination of the ego and, religiously speaking, a state of so-called Nirvana. Both seem to me unlikely to succeed, their value residing more in practice than in triumph. Pessimism is much like Epicureanism in that for the pessimist the great matter of life is that of suffering and the great ambition is that of attenuating suffering, as with Schopenhauer's contemplation of artworks as a means of lessening the pain deriving from what he called the Will-to-live or Mainlander's notion that socialism as a political program might serve as a stopgap measure to minimize the self-inflicted anguish brought about by most other ways of living, though for him the definitive solution to the human predicament was suicide. I think I could be fairly described as pessimist in the Epicurean sense that the matter of most importance in life is suffering. Unlike an Epicurean, of course, a Pessimist—at least in my conception—doesn't believe in a way out of the dilemma of being alive and avoiding all suffering, or even significantly attenuating it on a large scale. Nihilism is more concerned with values that provide one's existence with meaning in some way. As I see it, a nihilist isn't as concerned with suffering as much as he's concerned with his suffering being meaningful, whatever that means. For a pessimist, suffering has no meaning that would justify it.[62]

Obviously, for Lovecraft the possible root of pessimism would be the notion of a cosmos which lacks *teleology* (i.e., development towards a meaningful

---

[62] Thomas Ligotti, personal correspondence with the author, e-mail dated Sept. 1, 2022.

goal) and *care* (i.e., a deity which would protect and guide mankind like a loving parent). His stance sounds rather philosophical and impersonal. On the other hand, for Ligotti the basic root of The Big Black Truth is the same as it was for Buddhists – *suffering*. It is the central aspect of existence which colors everything else; the only goal in life is diminishing and (ideally, though impossibly) eradicating suffering.

Both in the long quotation above and in his *Conspiracy...* where the universe is repeatedly designated "MALIGNANTLY USELESS" (sic), Ligotti's view seems more emotional and personal than Lovecraft's apparently intellectual, stoical poise. As shown above, Lovecraft refused the label "pessimist," preferring to be called "indifferentist"; Ligotti, however, accepts the label "pessimist." How opposed and essentially different are these two standpoints? The fiction should reveal the truth.

Two Degenerate Little Towns

Lovecraft's and Ligotti's fiction shares the basic premise, or what I called The Big Black Truth: life in this universe is a hideous nightmare. This idea is expressed in most of their stories through a similar plot pattern: a character comes across hints, by accident or through his pursuits, that our world is a much darker place than it seemed, which leads him (it is invariably, though not always, a "he") to the revelation of The Big Black Truth. This revelation usually affects him in one of these four ways: 1) it kills him; 2) it drives him mad; 3) it turns him into a monster; or rarely 4) he remains alive, but forever cursed by the horrible knowledge.

A comparison of the ways in which the discovery of The Big Black Truth is handled in two stories by these authors should be helpful to better understand the two basic approaches to dealing with pessimism within horror fiction. A comparison will be made between Lovecraft's relatively early tale, "The Festival" (1925), and Ligotti's early tale "The Sect of the Idiot" (1988), collected in his first collection *Songs of a Dead Dreamer* (1989). I have selected these because they share approximately same length (about 3,800 words) and a very similar basic plot: a solitary man comes to a secluded town which is described in great, atmospheric detail, where he encounters hints that the entire population participates in a strange worship involving otherworldly creatures, and eventually it draws him in as well.

Together with the basic plot outline, these stories also share several other similarities:

1. First person point of view narration, which stresses subjectivity and individuality.

2. Characterization: both protagonists are nameless, and both are solitary outsiders. "I was far from home"[63] are the first words of Lovecraft's story. Ligotti's protagonist opens his narrative with these: "The extraordinary is a province of the solitary soul."[64]

3. Powerful old town setting: in both stories the decrepit settlement is depicted with an obvious effort to build a palpable atmosphere.

4. Overall sense of doom, gloom and claustrophobia: architectural details lead to the sense of psychological entrapment.

5. Similar central image: both stories describe a line of cloaked figures, perhaps not fully human, involved in some sort of sinister worship. In "The Festival": "...the throng of cowled, cloaked figures that poured silently from every doorway and formed monstrous processions up this street and that..." (Lovecraft, p. 113). In "The Sect of the Idiot": "a

---

[63] Lovecraft, H. P. (1923). "The Festival" in: *The Call of Cthulhu*, S. T. Joshi, ed. (New York and London: Penguin, 2002), p. 109.

[64] Ligotti, Thomas (1988). "The Sect of the Idiot," in *Songs of a Dead Dreamer and Grimscribe* (London and New York: Penguin, 2015), p. 200.

hypnotized parade of beings sleepwalking to the odious manipulations of their whispering masters" (Ligotti, p. 205).

6. Ambiguous ending, though with different amounts and types of ambiguity.

The differences between these two stories, however, are equally telling, and particularly significant in relation to their effectiveness of conveying the pessimistic message about The Big Black Truth.

The greatest and most immediately obvious difference is in these two authors' understanding of realism and the way they use it. Although Lovecraft's story belongs to his first, more gothic and oneiric phase (as opposed to the second, characterized by a greater stress on realism, rationalism, and science-fiction), it is still governed by his penchant for realistically detailed environment: "Only the human scenes and characters must have human qualities. *These* must be handled with unsparing *realism* (*not* catch-penny *romanticism*)..."[65] Even when he depicts an atmospheric ambience, he provides numerous details (my italics): "In the twilight I *heard it* [the sea] pounding on the rocks, and I knew it lay just over *the hill* where the *twisting willows* writhed against the *clearing sky* and the first *stars* of evening" (Lovecraft, p. 109). He delivers both *sounds* and *images*. When his protagonist sees the fictional town of Kingsport, he goes into more specific details (my italics): "...*snowy* Kingsport with its *ancient vanes* and *steeples*, *ridgepoles* and *chimney-pots*, *wharves* and *small bridges*, *willow-trees* and *graveyards*; endless *labyrinths* of *steep, narrow, crooked streets*, and dizzy *church-crowned* central *peak* that time durst not touch; ceaseless mazes of *colonial houses* piled and scattered at *all angles and levels*..." (Lovecraft, pp. 109-10)

---

[65] H.P. Lovecraft (1929). "Letter to Farnsworth Wright," 5 July 1927, in H.P. Lovecraft. *Selected Letters, vol. II* (Sauk City: Arkham House, 1968), p. 150.

Subjective impressions are few and far between: concrete images are dominant. A moment later the narrator refers to actual street names and places and gets more specific about architectural details of the house he comes to, mentioning "the diamond window-panes," "the low stone doorstep," "high doors reached by double flights of steps with iron railings," "windows without drawn curtains" and "the archaic iron knocker" (Lovecraft, p. 111). In these examples, and throughout the story, Lovecraft uses his well-documented knowledge of old New England architecture and history in order to ground his fantasy in reality, to provide verisimilitude.

Thomas Ligotti, on the other hand, uses an approach almost directly opposite. Specific descriptive details are mostly replaced by impressions and feelings. No wonder, since the narrator in the very first paragraph refers to the old town's "allegiance to the unreal." It is a clear signal that one should not expect a verisimilitude of Lovecraftian type. Ligotti's authorial desire has always been "to set my stories in places as I saw them in my imagination rather than describing them from personal observation." The result has been that "my stories are set in my head rather than in any detailed world either real or fantastic."[66] This is directly opposite to Lovecraft's propensity to travels and travelogues which served as roots for his stories' settings, including "The Festival." "The story is based upon HPL's several trips to Marblehead, Mass., beginning in December 1922,"[67] to the extent that locations in the story are directly based on a real house and a real church in said coastal town. Unlike Lovecraft, Ligotti wants to stress the place's *unreality* without mediating it through realistic detail. Here are the phrases referring to his *nameless* town (my italics): "I discovered an *infinite stillness* on *foggy mornings, miracles of silence* on *indolent afternoons*, and the *strangely flickering tableau* of *never-ending nights*"

---

[66] Neddal Ayad. "Literature Is Entertainment or It Is Nothing: An Interview with Thomas Ligotti," in Matt Cardin, ed. *Born to Fear: Interviews with Thomas Ligotti* (Burton, MI: Subterranean Press, 2014), pp. 107–8.

[67] S. T. Joshi and David E. Schultz. *An H. P. Lovecraft Encyclopedia* (New York: Hippocampus Press, 2001), p. 92.

(Ligotti, p. 200). If there is a brief realistic description, like "There were balconies, railed porches, and jutting upper stories of shops and houses that created intermittent arcades over sidewalks" (Ligotti, p. 200), it is immediately followed by surreal hyperbole: "Colossal roofs overhung entire streets and transformed them into the corridors of a single structure containing an uncanny multitude of rooms" (Ligotti, pp. 200-201). Furthermore, these images are superimposed by subjective colorings and wild comparisons (my italics): "And these *fantastic* crowns were *echoed* below by lesser roofs that drooped above *windows like half-closed eyelids* and turned each narrow doorway into a *magician's cabinet* harboring *deceptive depths* of shadow" (Ligotti, p. 201). The key word throughout is – *impression*: "It is difficult to explain, then, how the old town also conveyed an impression of endlessness, of proliferating unseen dimensions, at the same time that it served as the very image of a claustrophobe's nightmare..." (Ligotti, p. 201).

In Lovecraft's *plot-driven story* the central event depicts *action*. Throngs of worshippers congregate in an old church, descend underneath its floor, through the measureless caverns, where in a melodramatic climax they encounter a host of fantastic, nightmarish creatures:

> ...out of the Tartarean leagues through which that oily river rolled uncanny, unheard, and unsuspected, there flopped rhythmically a horde of tame, trained, hybrid winged things that no sound eye could ever wholly grasp, or sound brain ever wholly remember. They were not altogether crows, nor moles, nor buzzards, nor ants, nor vampire bats, nor decomposed human beings; but something I cannot and must not recall. (Lovecraft, p. 116)

Even when he does not supply a full, explicit description, Lovecraft uses visual hints to create a host of images in his readers' minds. In Ligotti's *impression-driven story*, on the other hand, the central event is a *dream*, and its few specific images are overshadowed by countless impressions: "an intolerable knowledge," "some ultimate disclosure," "an array of repulsive analogies," "cumulative sensation," "the *triumph of the grotesque,*" "sensation… complicated and exact," "the vision of a world in a trance…" (Ligotti, pp. 204-205). Instead of a clear revelation based on precise imagery, his hero leaves the dream with a haze of abstractions (my italics): "Had these beings, for *some grim purpose comprehensible only to themselves*, allowed me to intrude upon their *infernal wisdom*? Or was my access to such *putrid arcana* merely the outcome of some *fluke in the universe* of atoms, a chance intersection among the *demonic elements* of which all creation is composed?" (Ligotti, p. 205) The protagonist has the impression of coming across The Big Black Truth, but its exact nature remains unclear (my italics): "On waking, it seemed that I had carried back with me *a tiny, jewel-like particle of this horrific ecstasy*, and, by some *alchemy of association*, this *darkly crystalline* substance *infused its magic* into *my image* of the old town" (Ligotti, p. 205).

It is obvious from these examples that Lovecraft's approach to the horror story can be labeled *fantasy-realistic*, while Ligotti's could be called *fantasy-impressionistic*. The first accepts the reality of the so-called objective world, but slowly undermines it with intrusions of fantasy; the second discards the so-called objective world altogether and places the entire story within his character's subjectivity.

Another significant difference between these two stories can be seen in their conclusions. "The Festival" ends with the protagonist waking up in a hospital and realizing that the old town of the night before is replaced by the world of prosaic "normality": "Everything was wrong, with the broad windows showing a sea of roofs in which only about one in five was ancient, and the sound of trolleys and motors in the streets below" (Lovecraft, p. 117). When the hero is faced with a disenchanted world of new architecture and new technology, he is clearly disappointed. However, he is relieved when, in an additional twist, he finds a confirmation that his nightmarish experience was true, after all. The evidence is found in the dreaded book, the *Necronomicon*, quoted in the very last paragraph. The exhilarating effect and satisfaction to the readers that the story provides in its climax are at least twofold.

1) In the most general sense, every reader of a horror story expects and desires for the supernatural to be affirmed by the story's end; otherwise, they would be frustrated, e.g., as by the Radcliffean "explained supernatural" or by the tired cliché twist of "it was all a dream." Thus, Lovecraft's double twist ending, in which the first one seemingly negates the fantastic experience, while the second confirms its reality, provides pleasure and satisfaction because it delivers upon the readers' expectations based on genre conventions. Horror's horizon of expectations is affirmed (the horror is real!), therefore reader is happy.

2) In a more specific sense, Lovecraft's ending also affords pleasure and satisfaction due to a notion shared by him and his likeminded readers, namely that anything is better than a world without magic and spirit. Even if, as *Necronomicon* reveals, "out of corruption horrid life springs," and "things have learnt to walk that ought to crawl," these ideas are still more consoling than the alternative supported by reason and science, which claims that corruption is all and death merely turns us into revolting matter. In "The Festival's" happy ending, the threat of the mundane is quickly undermined and prevalence of fantasy is confirmed. There *is* a sort of magic, after all, it implies, even if some would call it "black"! The dream *is* victorious over reality; and when reality is bad, even a nightmare is preferable.

Pessimistic ending? Not really. Even hopeful, consoling in a way.

Pessimism, according to Stoneman and Packer, would require "insinuating that the world is essentially unintelligible." Lovecraft does not do that. Contrary to that claim, very few horror stories, by any author, would imply that the world is essentially unintelligible; a vast majority is much closer in spirit to Hamlet's famous statement, that "There are more things in Heaven and Earth, Horatio, than are dreamt of in your philosophy." Typical the horror story usually embodies the idea that the world is a stranger and darker place than we usually considered. But this idea does not imply fundamentally undermining Heaven and Earth; it usually means that our understanding of Heaven and Earth requires an amendment or two, like a new discovery, a new fact, or a new way of seeing, but after those are introduced, a clearer image would appear, and quite intelligible. The ending of "The Festival" does not imply that the world is unintelligible. It does, indeed, call into question the nature of reality and disturbs the readers' worldview with what the plot reveals (existence of fantastic forces and creatures), but the ultimate effect is not to disarm the reader. The plot provides "a pleasing terror" that M. R. James stressed as the horror story's aim, and any pleasure is uplifting in itself (as opposed to the frustration that an "unintelligible" ending would produce).

One traditional way in which the horror story makes its dark world intelligible is through stock characters, such as wise men, doctors, antiquarians, mediums, occultists, magicians, priests... Lovecraft's fiction abounds in such characters: whether barely coherent rustics or most educated professors, they represent Knowledge. They *know* more about the true nature of the world; they bring about understanding of its apparently "unintelligible" aspect. They do not "un-anchor" the readers' belief in the adequacy of rational thought: their function is precisely to anchor it. They prove that "the unnamable" can be named... by those who Know.

Another source of knowledge in a horror story can be a book like Lovecraft's *Necronomicon*. It contains The Big Black Truth about the real history of the world and forces which govern it, but as the ending of "The Festival" shows, such a revelation (terrible in itself) offers a type of satisfaction particular to horror genre. A big part of the satisfaction evoked by the cognitive aspects of the horror story comes from realization: there *is* knowledge in the world, though hidden and obscure; there *are* people who know more than the common men; there *are* sources of true knowledge (books, documents, diaries, letters, reports); there *are* practices (mystical and occult invocations, rituals, divinations) to reach another world. By any of those means, Knowledge can be reached. *Those* are the common messages of horror stories: not that the world is fundamentally unknowable, but that Knowledge exists and can be attained.

Whatever the horror story's central mystery is made of, it is always more understandable at the story's end than it was at the beginning, at least in the

Lovecraftian, realistic-fantasy type. A plot-driven the horror story *requires* a resolution, even if it is partial, open-ended. At least some of the mystery (the monster's origin, motivation, weakness) is learned and the knowledge is put into practice by the end; its unthinkable nature is at least partly conceptualized. And if one can think it, one can contain it. That is quite an optimistic idea.

In contrast to Lovecraft's stories, those by Ligotti do not have an underlying, interconnecting "mythos." There is no *Necronomicon* to pop-up at his story's ending to offer explanation, nor colorful monsters and tentacles to provide the pleasure and relief of horror action. The only deity that Ligotti has ever appropriated from Lovecraft, in his own way, is the "blind idiot god" Azathoth. In "The Sect of the Idiot" it is explicitly invoked only in the motto, but it is present, through variations of the concept, as an amorphous, utterly insane, and inscrutable cosmic malignity, in "Dream of a Mannikin," "Masquerade of a Dead Sword," "Nethescurial," "The Tsalal," "The Shadow, the Darkness," and others. The world of his stories is not essentially unintelligible; rather, there is Nothing in it to be intelligible. All-pervading nothingness reigns. "There is nothing to do, and there is nowhere to go, there is nothing to be and there is no one to know."[68] Lovecraft's stories are almost always built around detection, their plots dependent on "piecing together dissociated knowledge," his protagonists amateur-detectives looking for witnesses, clues, and proofs; Ligotti's stories, quite opposed to this principle, are agnostic. This author doesn't believe in Knowledge and certainly not in Truth as an objective entity existing outside of the solipsistic interiority of his obsessive characters.

A special distinction needs to be made between these authors' approach to characterization and point of view because it also affects the "rhetorical effectivity" of their pessimistic message. Lovecraft always maintained that human characters did not interest him; instead, he preferred to deal with phenomena and atmosphere of adventurous expectancy or cosmic horror. His protagonists are colorless everymen, functioning as mere *witnesses* of the

---

[68] Thomas Ligotti. *I Have a Special Plan for This World* (London: Durtro, 2000), p. 11.

phenomena and *amateur detectives* trying to figure those out; their personal history, psychology and motivation are secondary, at best. They are mostly students, scholars, professors, scientists – all representatives of intellect, i.e., Reason. And it is through Reason that The Big Black Truth is approached. The horror which Lovecraft's characters discover, visceral as it may be, ultimately is a cognitive one: the real horror lies in what they learn.

As witnesses, these characters are coded as reliable. Their findings, in the end, are not questionable *to the reader*. His protagonists may be considered unreliable, even insane, by the authorities – but within the text, the reader is given a privileged position and from this standpoint they are not to be understood as unreliable even when they literally lose their mind. If they go crazy, or at least hysterical in the story's climax, the reader is made to understand it as the result of their encounter with The Big Black Truth, whose objectivity is affirmed. At the end of "The Festival" the reader is not expected to doubt the protagonist's sanity nor truth of his deductions, and certainly not the veracity of the *Necronomicon*.

Lovecraft's ending opens up frightful global vistas; Ligotti's ending encloses us in a suffocating solipsistic claustrophobia, because we realize that we have never left the insides of his narrator's brain – nor can we ever do it. "The Sect of the Idiot" ends with *paranoia*: "They know what I write and why I am writing it. Perhaps they are even guiding my pen by means of a hand that is an extension of their own" (Ligotti, p. 210). It ends with what may be construed as an idée fixe, an *insane delusion* about the lack of integrity of his own body: "And if I ever wished to see what lay beneath those dark robes, I will soon be able to satisfy this curiosity with only a glance in my mirror" (Ligotti, p. 210). It ends with *mystification*: "I must return to the old town, for now my home can be nowhere else. But my manner of passage to that place cannot be the same…" (Ligotti, p. 210). And, ultimately, it ends with a *mystery* beyond logical conception: "…and when I enter again that world of dreams it will be by way of a threshold which no human being has ever crossed . . . nor ever shall" (Ligotti, p. 210).

The dichotomy between the subjective and objective, which was still valid to Lovecraft's poetics, is exploded in Ligotti's "The Sect of the Idiot." His character is not depicted in any great amount of realistic detail. Still, he is not a colorless witness overshadowed by phenomena: his personality is integral to the doom that befalls him. Ligotti's protagonists are, by large, extremely subjective obsessives. They do not even pretend to be disinterested observers. Just like the protagonist of "The Last Feast of the Harlequin," Ligotti's first publishable story, they are deeply invested in their obsessions, both intellectually and emotionally. The same is exhibited by the hero of "The Sect of the Idiot." From the very beginning the reader is made to feel that this person *belongs* in this degenerate little town: "an old town whose allegiance to the unreal inspired my soul with a holy madness long before my body had come to dwell in that incomparable place" (Ligotti, p. 200). The allegiance between this town, the unreal and the narrator's soul is established in the first paragraph, with a clear premonition that both his body and soul are about to dwell in that place. There is no estrangement, no dichotomy or ambivalence towards the place which can be seen in the scene of Lovecraft's protagonist's arrival into the town of his elders.

The second paragraph of Ligotti's story almost literally spells out that his protagonist is *coming home:* "I was settled in a high room overlooking the ideal of my dreams through diamond panes. How many times had I already lingered in mind before these windows and roamed in reverie the streets I now gazed upon below" (Ligotti, p. 200). The town he arrives to represents the ideal of his dreams, a place from his mind that he has already roamed in reveries before, and at last arrives to it for real. If there is such a thing as "real."

As in the beginning, so in the rest of the story: Ligotti stresses the deeply subjective quality of the described experience through the use of highly poetic language and puts the stress on impressions, not on realistic descriptions. The cumulative effect is – strong subjectivity, an unreliable narrator, and ambiguity created by the resolution. "The Sect of the Idiot" ends with the main character's unreliable report about his hand's transformation as he stands before the mirror: "For only one of those hands was mine. The other belonged to them" (Ligotti, p. 209). It is followed by his decision to go back to the old town and join its inhabitants: "I must return to the old town, for now my home can be nowhere else" (Ligotti, p. 210). This ending is reminiscent of the one in "The Shadow over Innsmouth," but unlike Lovecraft's, this one is not meant to be a twist: it was clearly announced in the very opening. The end is not a surprise, it is a confirmation.

In Ligotti's works the story structure is often circular rather than linear, as seen in "The Sect of the Idiot," where the closing paragraph directly returns us to the opening one. The linear progression of "The Festival" is nowhere to be found. Lovecraft's *fantastic-realistic* tale develops in a logical, linear succession of descriptions, events, and discoveries, building from a slow introduction towards a rousing climax and a double twist. Lovecraftian model of narration is clearly a modernized variation of Poe's: a linear, streamlined plot, with realistic characters, settings, and events (except the fantastic), which leads towards a striking, memorable conclusion (a twist or at least a powerful sting in its tail). Opposed to that, a typical Ligottian story, like "The Sect of the Idiot," is *fantastic-impressionistic:* more reminiscent of a slow dream out of which one can wake up at any random moment, than of a logically constructed goal-oriented plot-driven story which moves inexorably forward like a fast train. Having this in mind, we should ask ourselves: How is Ligotti's structure more rhetorically effective to convey pessimism? Obviously, Lovecraft's structure is based on the belief in progress, development, and finding out something new. Ligotti's doesn't exhibit that. Quite the opposite, even the very structure of his story embodies the idea, also present on the plot level, that there can be no progress, no development, and there is nothing new to be found out – nothing that was not already known from the beginning, nothing that is outside the narrator's "I."

Unlike in Lovecraft's stories, The Big Black Truth in Ligotti's is conveyed both through the form and content. The protagonist of "The Sect of the Idiot" has very little use for reason: he does not read about The Big Black Truth in a revelatory, *Necronomicon*-like book; ultimately, he does not so much attain knowledge as he remembers it, or confirms it, through a dream and a series of impressions. Significantly, the Truth that he unveils cannot be expressed through the language of reason in the manner that Lovecraft can at the end of "The Festival." Instead, it is suggested through ambivalent, poetic language which leaves things open to interpretation. His protagonist, in the end, may have been "really" physically transformed, or he may be losing his mind. There is no way for the reader to know because there is no privileged position, no outside source to confirm or deny his impression. And impression is all that the reader is left with.

These two stories show that basically the same plot could be told in two quite different manners: as already said above, Lovecraft's is fantastic-realistic, Ligotti's fantastic-impressionistic. Now it should be clearer how these differences affect the power and effectiveness of conveying The Big Black Truth and especially how realism (or lack thereof) is related to it. Hints toward a bigger clarity may be buried in the following questions.

What is more pessimistic, that there is a cruel, inhuman, Demon-God – or that there is no God whatsoever? What is more pessimistic, that there is an inscrutable, inhuman, monstrous force or spirit permeating the world – or that the world is devoid of spirit, reduced to dull matter? What is more pessimistic, that human life is part of a bigger, though sinister plan and process – or that it is random and without reason and purpose?

Furthermore, is a pessimistic message more effective when conveyed through recognizable *prose* structure rooted in genre conventions or through a hazy, dreamlike shade of a plot more akin to impressionistic *poetry?* Is a pessimistic message more effective if it addresses reason and logic or if it speaks to emotion and intuition?

After the above comparisons between "The Festival" and "The Sect of the Idiot," these questions are almost rhetorical. It should be obvious that the first half of each alludes to Lovecraftian "pessimism," while the second half of each is closer to Ligottian. Lovecraft's horror is ultimately materialistic and rooted in reason, just like his narrator: we trust his voice even when he quotes from a book about things conceived in graves which should be dead but aren't. Ligotti's horror is impressionistic and agnostic: we cannot know what is going on precisely because we do not have a sufficient distance from his narrator. And that would seem to be a more efficient way of implanting The Big Black Truth into the readers' souls, rather than minds (as in Lovecraft). It festers there like an intuitive black seed of *je ne sais quoi*, not like a reason-based conclusion which can be reasoned-away (as in Lovecraft).

To sum up: Lovecraft conveys The Big Black Truth through concrete, realistically depicted imagery and action, via clear and linear narrative leading to a climax and a twist, following recognizable patterns of realistic storytelling which are governed by logic and reason. It firmly follows the dominant narrative pattern of Anglo-American literary tradition, whether genre or non-genre: a realistically portrayed, logically motivated sequence of actions which culminate in some sort of climax. Does this narrative structure afford pessimism the most suitable model of "rhetorical effectivity"? Certainly not, because we have already shown the positive, consoling effect of a story like "The Festival." It remains to be seen whether Ligotti's approach to storytelling possesses a greater "rhetorical effectivity" regarding pessimism spreading. But before that, we should clarify some more the role of form in placing such content.

One of the key results of the pessimistic Trojan horse hidden within a horror story, according to Stoneman and Packer, should be to undermine the belief in "the adequacy of rational thought to organize and structure the sensible world of appearance" and to insinuate that the world is essentially unintelligible. Do these two stories achieve that and with equal success?

In Lovecraft we have shown evidence of a much greater belief in the power of reason to achieve knowledge than is evident in Ligotti. Horror is certainly the soul of his *plot;* but what about his *form and structure?* Closely investigated, Lovecraft's pessimistic message is divided: while on one hand (cognitive level: *what* the story says) he delivers The Big Black Truth, on the other (form and structure: *how* it says it) he offers a paradoxical but effective consolation. And this is precisely the key aspect of the horror story's rhetoric and effect that Stoneman and Packer neglect to address. The analysis of Lovecraft's "The Festival" showed that a story with apparently pessimistic connotations on the plot level can have a positive, pleasing, optimistic effect due to certain aspects of genre conventions and story structures. The aspect of the horror story's *form* needs to be addressed further because it can significantly dilute the pessimism present in its own *plot.*

Consolations of the structure

There are at least two major reasons that a horror story's structure can undermine the full effect of pessimism of its content: 1) in general, every linear, plot-based, action-filled narration is *goal-oriented* and therefore optimistic *per se*, because it leads *somewhere*, it has a *point;* and 2) more specifically, every horror story is based on "the complex discovery plot" (see below), whose structure provides its audience a specific pleasure.

Stoneman and Packer quote Barthes when they admit that rhetoric can be conceived of as "unavoidably oriented towards the *accomplishment of some end,* that it is inescapably *goal-oriented* and *therefore optimistic.* Common rhetorical strategies, for instance – what Aristotle termed *topoi* – presuppose the possibility, if not likelihood, of discursively mediated *resolution.*"[69] They cannot deny that "the bias for optimism is as evident as it is unshakable: rhetoric is a practicable, sense-making machine with which to impose order on a fundamentally disordered nature, to forge relationships between consciousness and a world of experience calling for meaning."[70] This would imply that the rhetoric of fiction, i.e., any logically structured, linear, goal-oriented (climax-heading) narrative, inevitably imposes order on chaos, and brings more understanding, more knowledge, more meaning at the end than there

---

[69] Stoneman and Packer, 2017, ibid. p. 26; *emphases mine.*
[70] ibid, p. 27.

was in the beginning, and is therefore fundamentally optimistic. And yet, these authors seem to believe that this only applies to the discourse of science and philosophy, while, according to them, the rhetoric of fiction is fundamentally different because it does not claim anything, it just is. It *embodies* what philosophy *argues:* "weird fiction manifests or enacts pessimism, aesthetically, through the clever deployment of a range of stylistic devices and rhetorical maneuvers."[71] And yet, as the analysis of stylistic devices and rhetorical maneuvers in Lovecraft's "The Festival" has shown, a) the rhetoric of fiction is not fundamentally different from the rhetoric of non-fiction: it does include claims, both explicit and implicit; and b) the very structure of a horror story is almost inevitably conceived so that it *enacts more optimism* than pessimism (this applies to the dominant model: the plot-driven realistic-fantastic).

Philosopher Noel Carroll defined the pleasure of "art-horror" as based on the mystery-solving principle centered on what he called "*complex discovery plot.*" This plot structure has four essential movements or functions. They are: onset, discovery, confirmation, and confrontation. "The first function in the complex discovery plot is *onset.* Here the monster's presence is established for the audience...The audience, along with the characters, follows the accumulation of the evidence of monstrous, foul doings with an interest in learning what is behind all this carnage."[72] This stage is followed by *discovery.* "That is, after the monster arrives, an individual or a group learns of its existence."[73] "The confirmation function involves the discoverers of or the believers in the existence of the monster convincing some other group of the existence of the creature and of the proportions of the mortal danger at hand."[74] And finally, it all leads to *confrontation.* "Humanity marches out to meet its monster and the confrontation generally takes the form of a debacle. Often, there is more than

---

[71] ibid, p. 27.

[72] Noel Carroll. *The Philosophy of Horror* (New York & London: Routledge, 1990), p. 99.

[73] ibid, p. 100.

[74] ibid, p. 101.

one confrontation. These may assume the shape of an escalation in intensity or complexity or both. Furthermore, the confrontation movement may also adopt a problem/solution format."[75] Obviously, much of this structure is based on reasoning, looking for clues and proofs, theories, and explanations. Even if the plot may describe a dark world dominated by evil (pessimism), the structure itself is based on reasoning and understanding, gaining knowledge, reaching a solution (optimism).

And although Carroll does not take his reasoning to its logical conclusion, following his principles one could claim that horror fiction's monster, at the end of the tale, is basically reasoned-out or explained away. Or, to paraphrase the ending of *King Kong* (1933), it was not beauty, it was reason that killed the beast. Once the mystifying monster, which at the outset appears to contradict our world, is grasped by our conceptual framework, it is as good as dead. And it is quite irrelevant whether (on the level of plot) a coda shows the monster as still alive or if the audience by the end has not learned *everything* there was to know about the monster: in all cases a better part of its horror has already been dispelled by the time audience reached the confrontation phase. At that point we *know* the monster. We have *found out* its basic properties, motivation, powers, and defects. If it returns in the sequel, we will know how to cope with it. We will be better prepared.

For example, by the end of "The Call of Cthulhu" the reader may not know *everything* about the titular octopus-headed giant, but is provided sufficient scattered hints, through its fragmented narrative, to enable deduction of a much better idea about the monster's origin, nature and functioning principles than were available at the beginning. The fantastic entity is eventually brought to light just long enough to be glimpsed, before it is returned to its lair under the waves, very similarly to the creatures in "The Festival's" climax. "The Call of Cthulhu" is a perfect embodiment of archetypal horror structure: the plot is made up of a series of seemingly disconnected details, in different

---

[75] ibid, p. 103.

accounts, reports, news, testimonies, and all of them are, by the end, interconnected by the protagonist's (and reader's) reason. It is his piecing together of dissociated knowledge which enables a better understanding of the frightening phenomenon and, by extension, the world and universe at large.

The Big Black Truth thus revealed is not favorable to mankind: it does open up terrifying vistas of reality, and of our frightful position therein, but, despite the initial warning, after the story's climax the reader does not go mad from the revelation. Instead, he is purified by the cathartic almost-apocalypse and feels content because the process of making sense of the horror, of seeing the pattern amidst apparent randomness – is *pleasurable in itself.* The story's climax has dark implications on the plot level which appeal to our cognitive faculties (reason), but at the same time, it also produces exhilaration, consolation, and relief due to its story structure, which appeals to our emotional faculties, just like any other mystery-plot based narration which reaches a satisfying resolution.

Thus, we could say that the pleasure of horror, and its basic effect, seems to be based on the principle of *inoculation:* a small, harmless dose of "blackness" is introduced into our systems through the art of fiction, via a particular kind of goal-oriented storytelling, so that our conceptual systems can become acquainted with it sufficiently to render it more harmless and bearable if/when encountered again, and in larger doses, in fiction or in life. However, here is the twist – after our analysis of "The Festival" it becomes clear that the same could be said about the pessimist message implied in the horror story's *plot:* its small, harmless dose is introduced only to be eventually destroyed by the story *form's* inherently optimistic mechanism. Thus, rather than a "pessimistic Trojan horse," the horror story appears to be one of the most efficient devices for diluting pessimism into acceptable doses, rendered safe by the predominantly life-affirming, optimistic principle intrinsic to its structure.

Canadian film critic Robin Wood has convincingly shown how the dominant culture, via Hollywood cinema, introduces problematic ideological contents into its pop-products only to render them harmless through various narrative and stylistic strategies, so that, after such treatment, they are divested of their revolutionary potential to the extent that they become acceptable to the masses. The masses are then free to either embrace those harmless elements, rendered into safe, ersatz versions of their former selves, or to ignore them, because they have been rendered immaterial and irrelevant. What if the horror story, unwittingly, does something similar with pessimism? In terms of content, horror is potentially linked with subversive and non-conformist ideas (as shown by Wood, among many others), but how about its form? Does its form undermine, or at least significantly alter the ideas implied by its content? What if, instead of spreading the grim, defeatist thoughts and creating hordes of black-clad pessimists finally convinced that evil reigns supreme in this world of suffering and death, the horror story actually accepts small bits of blackness into its mechanism only to digest them, dilute them, and excrete them as palatable, optimistic, life-affirming pieces of entertainment for the hordes of harmless outsiders with hearts of gold, their black clothes, horror T-shirts, tattoos, and piercings notwithstanding?

If we "interpret the geography of horror as a figurative spatialization or literalization of the notion that what horrifies is that which lies *outside* cultural categories and is, perforce, unknown,"[76] then the horror story's resolution brings the intruding monster *into* the cultural categories. The Other is *grasped*. The Big Black Truth is understood. And this is the true source of the pleasure of horror: grasping the ungraspable, naming the unnamable. Organizing apparent chaos. Taking our Good with some Evil – only to eventually embrace the Good even harder, firmer. Receiving a small dose of the pessimism vaccine to be more resistant to the temptations of The Big Black Truth out there, in the so-called real world.

In a recent interview, horror author Clive Barker talked about real-life horrors and how the genre fiction that he is writing helps him cope with the temptation of pessimism:

---

[76] Carroll, 1990, ibid, p. 35.

> I summarize experience in a different way and in the last, let's say eight months or whatever, it so happens the world has presented me with almost endless subject matter for dark stories. This has been a very dark time in our planet's history, and whether we're talking about Ukraine, whether we're talking about Putin, whether we're talking US politics, whether we're talking about global warming, it's hard to keep your eyes open and look without feeling anxiety. Now, the way I deal with anxiety is by telling stories. Stories are structures which contain my unease by putting a pattern onto that unease. Yes? It doesn't necessarily mean that by stamping a design upon things that I'm fearful of I make the fear go away, it doesn't work that way, but what it does do is give me the illusion of control.[77]

Barker's strategy seems to be shared by most horror authors: when the world tempts one to be pessimistic, the way to deal with the perception of predominant chaos and evil is to tell stories. Even if those belong to horror genre, they still provide *structure and meaning* to the meaningless outside; they put a *pattern* onto the unease and make it endurable by providing the illusion of control. Barker may have unwittingly created the perfect and most concise definition of the horror story: *it is a structure which contains unease by putting a pattern onto that unease.* Conceptualization of the evil-embodying monster inevitably diminishes its pessimistic connotations. Many horror writers, directors (e.g., John Carpenter and David Cronenberg) and other artists have repeatedly claimed in interviews that the fear behind all their horrors was fear of the loss of control. If writing or directing horror can provide the illusion of regained control, then it is a major cure for pessimism for the artists. But also for their audience.

---

[77] Phil & Sarah Stokes, "Fear, Love, Story… and Time; The Thirty-Seventh Revelatory Interview," *The Official Clive Barker Website* (29 and 31 March, 1, 23 and 26 April and 31 May 2022) < https://www.clivebarker.info/intsrevel37.html >

Can Horror Even Be Pessimistic?

Is there, then, any hope for pessimism in the horror story? Is there any undiluted blackness to be found at the end of this seemingly endless "horror" tunnel which insidiously, between its black lines, promotes the maxim "to live, laugh and love"? Or is this cheerful, life-affirming, consoling aspect of horror, as revealed through examples from "The Festival" and everything else above (including Barker), all that we are left with? Perhaps stories by Thomas Ligotti, based on a different poetics, offer a possibility for embodying The Big Black Truth in its full, undiminished glory?

One way of contrasting Lovecraftian and Ligottian horror is the distinction proposed by Matt Cardin:

> Lovecraft, it seems to me, was emotionally and intellectually focused on the horror of "*cosmic outsideness*," of vast outer spaces and the mind-shattering powers and principles that may hold sway there, and that may occasionally impinge upon human reality and reveal its pathetic fragility... Ligotti, by contrast, seems focused more upon the horror of deep *insideness,* of the dark, twisted, transcendent truths and mysteries that reside within consciousness itself and find their outward expression in scenes and situations of warped perceptions and diseased metaphysics.[78] (Cardin 2022: 37)

This distinction is inevitably simplified: much of Lovecraft's horror also comes decidedly from *inside*, from his protagonists' genetic and psychological makeup predestined by the family and race. Still, in general terms, it is a reasonably accurate way to distinguish two variants of pessimism: both are black and frightening, but Lovecraft's is often outbound, agoraphobic, wide, global, scientific-reasonable, materialistic, philosophical, whereas Ligotti's is more

---

[78] Matt Cardin. *What the Daemon Said: Essays on Horror Fiction, Film, and Philosophy* (New York: Hippocampus Press, 2022), p. 37.

inbound, claustrophobic, cramped, individual, intuitive-emotional, ethereal, mystical.

Both express The Big Black Truth of existence, but the bitter pill is sugar-coated in Lovecraft by the form of streamlined narratives which all (following Poe) lead to powerful climaxes and by the content which largely addresses reader's reasoning, which makes it all the more palatable and ultimately satisfying (for reasons sketched in Carroll's "complex discovery plot"), even consoling. However, the bitter pill in Ligotti has very little to no sugar on it, since his form is not so much plot/climax-based, it is not action-driven, and it is mostly lacking the entertainment value aspect (including the mystery-solving, reason-applying satisfaction of the "complex discovery plot"). Instead of the Lovecraftian "payoff" in the end, his stories' conclusions often refuse to "pay" the readers, leaving them frustrated with endings which are too open, too ambiguous, and non-cathartic. Since Ligotti 's stories are not plot-driven, but dream-logic-driven, their actual plots are easily dissolved into fragments which are then mixed-up with those from his other stories. His brand of horror is impression driven. His stories are not so much genre-narratives as they are dream-narratives, barely translatable into the reasonable, waking world's language; they are mostly aimed, like poetry, towards the readers' intuition and emotion. (This does not imply that Ligotti's stories lack structure, but only that their structure is not linear, but circular instead.)

Although he clearly shares Lovecraft's bleak vision about the cosmos and humankind's position in it, Ligotti strips it of almost all genre paraphernalia – certainly of the most lurid excesses of fantastic iconography (ancient temples, vast aeon-old cities, decrepit churches, monsters, rotting corpses, ghouls). Imagery in Ligotti's stories is low key, a minimalist poetics of hazy mist and shadowy darkness within desolate urban environments (old factories, cinemas, schools). If Lovecraft's stories are in wild pulp Technicolor, Ligotti's are in ascetic sepia. This reduces the latter's entertainment value and mass appeal but makes their blackness purer. Just as "The Sect of the Idiot" shows, the horror is less overt, more indirect, insidiously so. Ligotti's effect of horror is produced by relative absence of action on any grand scale: his plots delineate *intimate, personal apocalypses*, not – as Lovecraft's – global threats to The World As We Know It.

The distinction between these two types of presenting pessimistic message in horror does not imply value judgment, in the sense that one is superior to the other. Both approaches to sugarcoating the bitter pill have a reasonable degree of paradoxical effect of consolation. Lovecraftian horror may be the most anti-anthropocentric prose out there, when viewed on the level of themes and plot; and yet, its structure appeals to the defining quality of *homo sapiens* – Reason. And what reason tells us, after the end of a Lovecraft's story, is to cling even harder to our humanity, to appreciate this small island of ignorance that we call "our world," and to be happy that we cannot see the creatures "from beyond," swarming around us incessantly; we should be thankful that we cannot hear the avatars of Azathoth piping idiotically at the center of "our" cosmos.

There is another way that Lovecraft's prose can be consoling, and Ligotti testifies to this kind of effect it had on him:

> As soon as a receptive mind discovers the works of someone such as Lovecraft, it discovers that there are other ways of looking at the world besides the one in which it has been conditioned. You may discover what kind of nightmarish jailhouse you are doomed to inhabit or you may simply find an echo of things that already depressed and terrified you about being alive. The horror and nothingness of human existence—the cozy façade behind which was only a spinning abyss. The absolute hopelessness and misery of everything. After publishing his first book in French, which in English appeared as *A Short History of Decay* (1949), Cioran learned from that volume's enthusiastic reception that his manner of philosophical negation had a paradoxically vital and energizing quality. Lovecraft, along with other authors of his kind, may have the same effect and rather than encouraging people to give up he may instead give them a reason to carry on. Sometimes that reason is to follow

his way—to communicate, in the form of horror stories, the outrage and panic at being alive in the world.[79]

Ligotti developed this idea – that an apparent negation had a paradoxically vital and energizing quality – in his essay "The Consolations of Horror": "This, then, is the ultimate, that is only, consolation: simply that someone shares some of your own feelings and has made of these a work of art which you have the insight, sensitivity, and - like it or not - peculiar set of experiences to appreciate."[80] When asked recently if he had changed his mind regarding the basic point of this essay, originally written in 1982, he confirmed:

> There can be a consolation in reading horror literature, and even in writing it. However, anything can be taken away from you; everything is in danger of being lost. You may find it again, but you may also lose it again. Everything is contingent on the whims of our biology and our emotional vagaries. There is something called "musical anhedonia," a condition wherein someone who once felt a great love for music and deeply responded to it who one day, for no discernable reason, loses that love and that response, which was never in the music but in himself.[81]

Whether the bitter pill of The Big Black Truth is somewhat sugarcoated (in Lovecraft) or presented almost "as is" (in Ligotti), it does not make much of an aesthetic difference. Ligotti's pill may be harder to swallow, closer to hermetic poetry than to genre prose, which means that its philosophy is purer, i.e., less compromised. Ligotti's poetics may offer a more suitable model of rhetorical effectivity in terms of embodying the pessimistic rhetoric, because it is not based on "complex discovery plot" structure; however, the fact that it is not

---

[79] Cardin, 2022, ibid, pp. 23-4.

[80] Thomas Ligotti. (1982). "The Consolations of Horror" in *Nightmare Factory* (New York: Carrol & Graf, 1996), p. xxi.

[81] Thomas Ligotti, personal correspondence, e-mail to the author, dated Sept. 1, 2022.

immediately accessible makes it unfit for mass appeal, which therefore makes it inefficient in terms of pessimistic proselytizing on a grand scale. On the other hand, Lovecraft's pill, more palatable (due to recognizable genre tropes, familiar iconography, conventionalized narrative structure under the guise of pulpy entertainment), makes him popular on a much grander scale, and thus he reaches vaster numbers of audience and implants in them, Trojan-horse-like, the bitter pill of The Big Black Truth to slowly fester from inside. The question remains open as to how effective, i.e., undiluted his particular pill is, or how often and how effective it is in blossoming inside his fans.

We can embrace Carroll's model of art-horror structure as at least a partial answer to the problem of paradoxical pleasure derived from unpleasant emotions. Or we can go back to a much older answer regarding the positive effect of evoking negative feelings by art: Aristotle's idea about purification of the audience's feelings through catharsis. Both, in their direct or indirect way, imply that a story filled with horrors can provide a particular sort of pleasure, or satisfaction; otherwise, it would not have such a wide, universal, and long-lasting appeal. To this we can add that the pleasure in a horror story can be cognitive ("now I know more about monsters/myself"), emotional/spiritual ("now I feel purified of my negative emotions"), psychological ("now I have pleasurably employed my faculties, such as reason and logical thinking") or even philosophical ("now my suspicions about the evil in this world are confirmed"). In all these cases, including the last one, which seems closest to pessimism, the result is a satisfying, pleasurable conclusion which one will want to repeatedly go back to.

If part of horror's appeal has to do with the pessimistic aspect of its message, its ultimate effect is not a dark revelation which leads to hopelessness, melancholy, and despair. Even the Ligottian kind of horror does not create that effect. Quite the opposite, it generates a sense of belonging: if the horror tale confirms one's worst suspicions about mankind and the universe (or, horror of horrors: about oneself!), the extraordinary is no longer a province of the solitary soul. Even in its bleakest form it can result in the sense of fraternity, the sense of belonging to a "sect" of "idiots," those of us who have rent the veils of illusion, seen The Big Black Truth, and lived to talk about it. And now we keep coming back to it, over and over again – in order to "dance to the bizarre music of our own misery."[82] In order to enjoy it. Because now our home can be nowhere else.

---

[82] Ligotti, 1996, ibid, p. xxi.

BIBLIOGRAPHY

Ayad, Neddal. 2014. "Literature Is Entertainment or It Is Nothing: An Interview with Thomas Ligotti." In Matt Cardin, ed. *Born to Fear: Interviews with Thomas Ligotti*. Burton, MI: Subterranean Press.

Stokes, Phil & Sarah. 2022. "Fear, Love, Story… and Time: The Thirty-Seventh Revelatory Interview." <https://www.clivebarker.info/intsrevel37.html>

Baumgartner, Brad. 2021. *Weird Mysticism, Philosophical Horror and the Mystical Text*. Bethlehem: Lehigh University Press.

Beach, Matthew. 2019. "Lovecraft's Consolation." *Lovecraft Annual*, No. 13. New York: Hippocampus Press.

Blake, Terence. 2017. "Lovecraft Noetic Dreamer: From Horrorism to Cosmicism."<https://www.academia.edu/35050840/LOVECRAFT_NOETIC_DREAMER_from_horrorism_to_cosmicism>

Cardin, Matt. 2022. *What the Daemon Said: Essays on Horror Fiction, Film, and Philosophy*. New York: Hippocampus Press.

Carroll, Noel. 1990. *The Philosophy of Horror*. New York & London: Routledge.

Ford, Carl. 1988. "Notes on the Writing of Horror: An Interview with Thomas Ligotti." *Dagon* No. 22/23 (September–December)

James, M. R. 2011 (1929). "Some Remarks on Ghost Stories" in: M. R. James, *Collected Ghost Stories*. Oxford: Oxford University Press.

Joshi, S. T. 1990. *The Weird Tale*. Austin: University of Texas Press.

Joshi, S. T. and David E. Schultz. 2001. *An H. P. Lovecraft Encyclopedia*. New York: Hippocampus Press.

King, Stephen. 1983. *Danse Macabre*. New York: Berkley Books.

Ligotti, Thomas. 1996 (1982). "The Consolations of Horror" in *Nightmare Factory*. New York: Carrol & Graf.

Ligotti, Thomas. 2000. *I Have a Special Plan for This World*. London: Durtro.

Ligotti, Thomas. 2010. *The Conspiracy against the Human Race*. New York: Hippocampus Press.

Ligotti, Thomas. 2015 (1988). "The Sect of the Idiot," in *Songs of a Dead Dreamer and Grimscribe*. London and New York: Penguin.

Lovecraft, H. P. 1929. "Letter to R. Michael, 20 July 1929." <http://www.yankee-classic.com/miskatonic/dliterature/authors/lovecraft/bio/autobio.htm>

Lovecraft, H. P. 1968 (1929). "Letter to Farnsworth Wright," 5 July 1927, in H.P. Lovecraft. *Selected Letters, vol. II.* Sauk City: Arkham House.

Lovecraft, H. P. 1971 (1929). "Letter to James F. Morton," 30 Oct. 1929, in H.P. Lovecraft. *Selected Letters, vol. III.* Sauk City: Arkham House.

Lovecraft, H. P. 1976 (1935). "Letter to Helen V. Sully," 23 Sept. 1935, in H.P. Lovecraft. *Selected Letters, vol. V.* Sauk City: Arkham House.

Lovecraft, H. P. 2002 (1923). "The Festival" in: *The Call of Cthulhu*, S. T. Joshi, ed. New York and London: Penguin.

Lovecraft, H. P. 2002 (1921). "Facts Concerning the Late Arthur Jermyn and His Family" in: *The Call of Cthulhu*, S. T. Joshi, ed. New York and London: Penguin.

Lovecraft, H. P. 2002 (1926). "The Call of Cthulhu" in: *The Call of Cthulhu*, S. T. Joshi, ed. New York and London: Penguin.

Lovecraft, H. P. 2019 (1935). "Letter to Helen V. Sully," 15 Aug. 1935, in H.P. Lovecraft. *Letters to Wilfred B. Talman and Helen V. and Genevieve Sully.* Ed. David E. Schultz and S. T. Joshi. New York: Hippocampus Press.

Machen, Arthur. 1923. *Hieroglyphics.* New York: Knopf.

Ognjanović, Dejan. 2021. "The Three Paradigms of Horror." *Vastarien*, Vol. 4, no. 2.

Poe, Edgar Allan. 1981 (1842). "The Masque of the Red Death" in: Peithman, Stephen, ed. *The Annotated Tales of Edgar Allan Poe.* New York: Doubleday & Company, Inc.

Radcliffe, Ann. 2007 (1826). "On the Supernatural in Poetry" in: Clive Bloom, ed. *Gothic Horror: A Guide for Students and Readers (Second edition).* Basingstoke and New York: Palgrave Macmillan.

Shelley, Mary. 1996 (1831). "Introduction to *Frankenstein*, Third Edition," in: *Frankenstein* (A Norton Critical Edition), J. Paul Hunter, ed. New York and London: W.W. Norton & Company.

Stokes, Phil & Sarah. 2022. "Fear, Love, Story... and Time; The Thirty-Seventh Revelatory Interview," *The Official Clive Barker Website* (29 and 31 March, 1, 23 and 26 April and 31 May 2022) < https://www.clivebarker.info/intsrevel37.html >

Stoneman, Ethan and Joseph Packer. 2017. "No, Everything Is Not All Right: Supernatural Horror As Pessimistic Argument." *Horror studies*, Vol. 8, no 1.

Walpole, Horace. 1994 (1765). "Preface to the Second Edition" in: *Four Gothic Novels*. Oxford and New York: Oxford University Press.

Merriam Webster Online Dictionary. (https://www.merriam-webster.com) <https://www.merriam-webster.com/dictionary/pessimism>

CONTRIBUTORS

Paula D. Ashe is a writer of dark fiction. Her debut short fiction collection, *We Are Here to Hurt Each Other*, was released in February of 2022 from Nictitating Books, and was nominated for a Bram Stoker Award.

Paul L. Bates studied liberal arts and painting at Kenyon College, architectural design at RISD; was a member of MENSA, is retired from a career in construction management. He began *social-distancing* and *sheltering-in-place* well before Covid-19 was a repugnant glimmer in a Petri dish. Recent short fiction publication credits include Vastarien: A Literary Journal, *Dim Shores Presents Vol. 1*, and *The Lost Librarian's Grave*. He has over 65 publication credits during the past three decades, including the slip-stream novels *Imprint* and *Dreamer*; shorter work appearing in literary magazines *Lynx Eye* and *Literal Latte*; Canadian Pro SF magazine *Parsec*; anthologies *For When the Veil Drops, Darker than Noir, Arcane, Beyond the Last Star, Transversions* and *Twisted Boulevard*.

Christa Carmen lives in Rhode Island and is the Bram Stoker Award-nominated author of the short story collection *Something Borrowed, Something Blood-Soaked*. Her debut novel, *The Daughters of Block Island*, will be released this fall from Thomas & Mercer. Additional work can be found in *Vastarien, Nightmare, Orphans of Bliss, Year's Best Hardcore Horror,* and the Stoker-nominated anthologies, *Not All Monsters* and *The Streaming of Hill House.*

Shenoa Carroll-Bradd writes fantasy and horror from her home in sunny southern California. Her short fiction has appeared in more than three dozen anthologies and magazines, including several pieces performed on podcasts such as Tales to Terrify.

Laura Cranehill a writer based in Portland Oregon, where she lives with her partner and three sons. Her work has been published in *Abyss & Apex*, *Strange Horizons*, and *The Future Fire.*

Jacob Derin is a second-year law student at UC Davis School of Law. His short story, "Bloodless Vivisection," was published by the UC Davis literary journal *Open Ceilings* in 2020. This is Derin's first professional publication, hopefully the first of many.

Pamela Durgin writes horror, dark fiction, and weird fiction. She lives in San Francisco with my husband and 3 cats. "I-90" is her first publication.

Ukata Edwardson s a Queer nonbinary writer of color from Nigeria, a finalist for the Anzaldua Poetry Prize (2022), the second-place winner of the SprinNG Poetry Contest (2021), longlisted for the Frontier OPEN (2022), shortlisted for the IHRAF Creators of Justice Prize (2021), honorably mentioned in the Starlit Awards (2021), and the Dan Veach Poetry Prize (2021). They have works featured and forthcoming in *POETRY*, *Channel, Lolwe, FO-LIO, Consequence, DREICH, Solarpunk, Aster Lit, Afritondo*, and elsewhere.

Brian Evenson is the author of a dozen books, most recently the story collection *The Glassy, Burning Floor of Hell* (2021). His penultimate collection, *Song for the Unraveling of the World* (2019), won the Shirley Jackson Award and the World Fantasy Award and was a finalist for the Ray Bradbury Prize. Other recent books include *A Collapse of Horses* (2016) and *The Warren* (2016). His novel *Last Days* won the ALA-RUSA award for Best Horror Novel of 2009. His novel *The Open Curtain* was a finalist for an Edgar Award and an International Horror Guild (IHG) Award. His 2003 collection *The Wavering Knife* won the IHG Award. He is the recipient of three O. Henry Prizes, an NEA fellowship, and a Guggenheim Award. His work has been translated into more than a dozen languages. He lives in Los Angeles and teaches at CalArts.

Corey Farrenkopf's lives on Cape Cod with his wife, Gabrielle, and works as a librarian. His short stories have been published in *Three-Lobed Burning Eye, SmokeLong Quarterly, Uncharted, Catapult, The Southwest Review, Reckoning, Flash Fiction Online, Bourbon Penn*, and elsewhere.

Patrick Hurley has fiction published in *Deep Magic, Paizo's Pathfinder, Flame Tree Press,* and *Abyss & Apex.* He attended the 2017 Taos Toolbox Writer's Workshop taught by Nancy Kress and Walter Jon Williams and is a member of SFWA.

Born under the sun sign of Leo, **Serena Jayne** is naturally a cat person. Her fiction has appeared in *The Arcanist, Crow & Cross Keys, Daily Science Fiction, Unnerving Magazine, Vastarien: A Literary Journal*, and other publications. Her short story collection, *Necessary Evils*, was published by Unnerving Books.

Andrew Koury is a weird fiction writer in Cincinnati, Ohio. He focuses on queer, unsettling fiction.

Carl Lavoie likes Hirschvogel's landscapes, stories by Ron Weighell, and his Polish muse, Zytnia. He lives in Southwestern Ontario.

Simon Lee-Price hails from Liverpool and lives and writes in the UK. His fiction and creative non-fiction works have appeared in *Prole, Prose and Poetry*; *Sein und Werden*; *Interpreter's House*; *The Caribbean Writer*, and in numerous horror and speculative fiction anthologies. In his day job he is an academic, with current research interests in decolonization, autotheory, and the politics and philosophy or horror.

Romana Lockwood is a lady, and ladies do not reveal their age. Her many incarnations have included nurse in a devastating war, typist, war correspondent, television news anchor, housewife, waitress, and columnist. Her column "In My Eyes," which ran from 19_ to 20_ was, in the eyes of many, a serious contender for the Pulitzer Prize, or at the very least the Horace Greeley or the Breindel awards. Her first marriage was to Ernest James Hayden, a shoe salesman, who passed in 19_ from a failure of the heart, the variety that physicians refer to as "massive." Of her second marriage she does not speak. She rejects in toto the Abrahamic religions. She takes daily walks, her coffee black, her cats calico, and her tea sweet.

S.P. Miskowski has received two National Endowment for the Arts Fellowships. Four of her books (*Knock Knock*, *Delphine Dodd*, *Muscadines*, and *The Best of Both Worlds*) have been nominated for a Shirley Jackson Award. Her second novel, the grunge-era ghostly noir *I Wish I Was Like You*, was named This Is Horror Novel of the Year and was a finalist for a Bram Stoker Award. Her stories have been published in *Nightmare Magazine*, *Supernatural Tales*, *Black Static*, *Identity Theory*, *Strange Aeons*, *Other Voices*, and *Eyedolon Magazine*, and in numerous anthologies including *The Best Horror of the Year Volume Ten*, *Haunted Nights*, *The Madness of Dr. Caligari*, and *Darker Companions: Celebrating 50 Years of Ramsey Campbell*.

Karolina Mochniej is a visual artist from Poland whose artwork draws on the occult, the feminine, and the esoteric motives.

Christi Nogle is the author of the Bram Stoker Award® winning and Shirley Jackson Award nominated novel, *Beulah* (Cemetery Gates Media, 2022), and co-editor with Willow Dawn Becker of the Bram Stoker Award® nominated anthology *Mother: Tales of Love and Terror* (Weird Little Worlds, 2022). Christi's debut short story collection *The Best of Our Past, the Worst of Our Future* is out now from Flame Tree Press. Her collections *Promise* and *One Eye Opened in That Other Place* are coming from Flame Tree Press in 2023 and 2024. Her short stories have appeared in many publications, including *PseudoPod, Vastarien, Mooncalves*, and *Horror Library*.

Dejan Ognjanović was born in 1973 and lives in Niš, Serbia. Got his PhD in Literature ("Historical Poetics of Horror Genre in Anglo-American

Literature") at the University of Belgrade. He writes book and film reviews and articles for *Rue Morgue* magazine since 2010 (including the booklet *The Weird World of H.P. Lovecraft*, 2017). In Serbia he has published three horror novels, a story collection, three studies on horror cinema and two collections of essays and contributed to *100 European Horror Films, 101 Horror Movies You Must See Before You Die*, and to academic collections *Speaking of Monsters* (Palgrave, 2012) and *Digital Horror* (IB Tauris, 2015). At Orfelin Publishing (Serbia) he edits the series of books "Poetics of Horror" (32 titles since 2015). He was shortlisted for Bram Stoker award in 2022, for his *Vastarien* essay "The Three Paradigms of Horror" and was recipient of the Rondo Hatton Classic Horror Award in 2023. for his *Rue Morgue* essay "Hex of the Century".

Karley Pardue earned an MFA from the University of Nevada, Reno. Her writing explores complex relationships, liminal spaces, and gendered terrors. For now, she lives in Reno with her lovably miscreant cat. Her work has been published in *The Meadow* and featured in the Nevada Arts Council's *Nevadan to Nevadan: What I Need to Tell You*.

Jesse Peper began his artistic journey in the early 1990's. His latest works are surrealistic watercolors and mixed-media paintings that traverse psychological, mythical, and fantastic realms through his idiosyncratic use of line, color, and symbolic content.

Nadia Shammas is a Palestinian-American writer from Brooklyn now living in Toronto, Canada. Her previous sci-fi horror piece, "THE CENTER OF THE UNIVERSE," which was published in *Strange Horizon*'s Palestine

Special Issue in 2021, went on to make the BSFA longlist, the Locus Award Recommended Reading List, and was nominated for an Ignyte Award for best short story. She is also known for her work in comics, like the eldritch graphic novel (co-created with Marie Enger), *Where Black Stars Rise*, published by Tor Nightfire.

Richard Snowden-Leak (he/they) is a PhD candidate and writer from Liverpool whose work tends toward the (New) Weird and the absurd. His thesis explores the mental health benefits of New Weird fiction, and the importance of the communities that form online surrounding these challenging horrors of what Thomas Ligotti called "Confrontational escapism." He has fiction published and forthcoming in *CHM*, and essays forthcoming in other horror analysis journals—all of which have arrived to the page from the dreams that keep him up at night. They hope someday they might get a full night's sleep.

Dr. Raymond Thoss is a Licensed Psychologist and has spent his career working primarily with child trauma victims and their families. He has worked on state level trauma initiatives in addition to both SAMSHA and W.H.O. national and international child trauma initiatives conducting research, training providers, and providing direct care. He also worked closely with first responders and front-line providers on secondary trauma initiatives and has been on site for critical incident response (e.g., national disaster zones) multiple times in his career. He has been on faculty at multiple Tier 1 universities and was most recently faculty at an Ivy League medical school providing direct care and teaching trauma informed care. He is proud to have the honor of having his little volume of dialogue, *Trauma and Discovery: Rebellion Against the Conspiracy Against the Human Race*, forthcoming from Grimscribe Press. He gives these credentials not out of hubris, but so that when his readers realize he is insane, they will also know that he speaks with precision about his topic. He has lived in many different places in the continental United States but has yet to find his terminus. Regardless of where he is, he continues to fight the Monsters in the dark. This is the Mission he has dedicated his life to. He will never stop.

Brian Thummler is an old man who does as he pleases, but mostly found crawling through the wooded ravines of western Pennsylvania looking for the hideous and the gruesome.

Baph Tripp is a Canadian living in Australia (unless dead at the time you are reading this). Tripp's fiction has been published in *Black Static* and his noisemaking as x.a.o.s has been praised in the industrial music press. He continually extracts oxygen from the air and replaces it with the asphyxiant, carbon dioxide.

Marissa van Uden is a speculative-fiction editor from New Zealand who currently lives next to a beaver pond in the woods of rural Vermont. My short stories have appeared in *Dark Matter Magazine* and the *Los Suelos Anthology*.

Tim Waggoner Tim Waggoner's first novel came out in 2001, and since then he's published over fifty novels and seven collections of short stories. He writes original dark fantasy and horror, as well as media tie-ins. He's written tie-in fiction based on Supernatural, *Grimm, The X-Files, Alien, Doctor Who, A Nightmare on Elm Street*, and *Transformers*, among others, and he's written novelizations for films such as *Halloween Kills, Resident Evil: The Final Chapter* and *Kingsman: The Golden Circle*. His articles on writing have appeared in *Writer's Digest, The Writer, The Writer's Chronicle*. He's the author of the acclaimed horror-writing guide *Writing in the Dark*, which won the Bram Stoker Award in 2021. He won another Bram Stoker Award in 2021 in the category of short nonfiction for his article "Speaking of Horror," and in 2017 he received the Bram Stoker Award in Long Fiction for his novella *The Winter Box*. In addition, he's been a multiple finalist for the Shirley Jackson Award and the Scribe Award, and a one-time finalist for the Splatterpunk Award. His fiction has received numerous Honorable Mentions in volumes of Best Horror of the Year, and he's had several stories selected for inclusion in volumes of *Year's Best Hardcore Horror*. His work has been translated into Russian, Portuguese, Japanese, Spanish, French, Italian, German, Hungarian, and Turkish. In addition to writing, he's also a full-time tenured professor who teaches creative writing and composition at Sinclair College in Dayton, Ohio.

GRIMSCRIBE PRESS